THE EXPANSION OF NEW ENGLAND

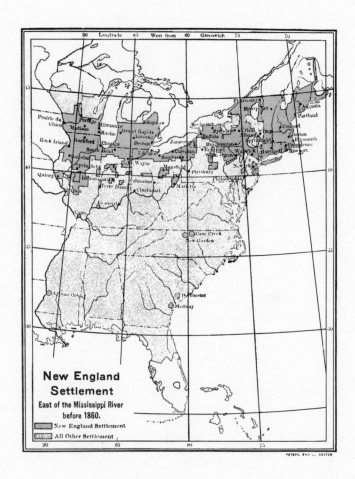

New England
Settlement

East of the Mississippi River
before 1860.

New England Settlement

All Other Settlement

THE EXPANSION OF NEW ENGLAND

THE SPREAD OF NEW ENGLAND SETTLEMENT AND INSTITUTIONS TO THE MISSISSIPPI RIVER 1620–1865

BY

LOIS KIMBALL MATHEWS

NEW YORK

RUSSELL & RUSSELL · INC

1962

In Memoriam

G. R. M.

PREFACE

THE present study is an attempt to untangle, from the complex skein of our national history, the one strand of the New England element. In attempting to set forth clearly and convincingly one phase of our development, it may seem that a loss of proportion and of perspective has resulted. The study makes no pretensions to being either complete or exhaustive; but it is sent out with the hope that it may at least suggest some new points of view.

The initial impulse to the work, and much of its spirit, are due to Professor Frederick J. Turner, of the University of Wisconsin. The actual beginnings of the study were made at Leland Stanford Junior University during 1903–04, in a seminar conducted by Professor Max Farrand, now of Yale University. The next stage of development was reached under the guidance of Professor Edward Channing, resulting in the presentation of the study in thesis form in partial fulfillment of the requirements for the degree of Doctor of Philosophy at Radcliffe College. Since that time it has been expanded and almost entirely reconstructed, to be published in its present form. The author has in preparation another study designed to supplement this one, having as its theme New England settlement beyond the Mississippi River, and in the South since 1865.

It would be impossible for the author to acknowledge

all the suggestions and aid of which she has availed herself in this study ; but she wishes to express her especial
indebtedness to those above mentioned with whom so
much of the work was done, and to Professor Lucy M.
Salmon, to Mr. Payson J. Treat, and to Professor J.
Leverett Moore.

L. K. M.

VASSAR COLLEGE, POUGHKEEPSIE, NEW YORK.
February, 1909.

CONTENTS

LIST OF MAPS

THE EXPANSION OF NEW ENGLAND

THE EXPANSION OF NEW ENGLAND

CHAPTER I

INTRODUCTION

THE history of the spread of settlement in the United States is the story of an ever-retreating wilderness, an ever-advancing frontier. From the first straggling villages stretched in a thin, wavering line along the Atlantic Coast, their inhabitants the frontiersmen of the England they had left behind, bands of pioneers, recruited by successive generations, have penetrated slowly and steadily into the wilderness. It is this feature of American history that is unique,—that from 1607 until about a decade and a half ago there had always been a frontier in the United States, a "far west" where areas of cheap land were large and plenty, where there were few or no inhabitants. The far west has receded before the homeseeker since the time when hardy Englishmen began their towns on the James River and on Massachusetts Bay,—then the far west to their comrades in England,—until now the term is applied only to the territory beyond the Rocky Mountains. With the retreat of this receding region, the frontier has moved on also, the one marking the outer confines of the other. It was with the vanishing of the frontier in 1892, when practically all the government land had been marked off into farms or cattle ranges, and every county in the United

States had a few inhabitants, that the first period of our history really closed. That period has been subdivided and studied in its political and constitutional aspects; but until recently what seems to be its real character, its unique quality, has been ignored.[1] Yet this character has often furnished the key to some whole period. The frontier and the builder of it—these have been potent factors in the growth and the development of the United States; for the pioneer has been influenced by the institutions and the character of his old home in England or upon the coast, and has in turn brought to bear upon those older regions influences which originated in his Western home. The conservatism of the established community and the radicalism of the frontier have acted and reacted upon each other, producing finally the compromise between the two which makes the individuality of the United States.

The causes of frontier-making have been many and varied. The first settlers came from England with mingled motives, of which the most potent were probably the religious difficulties which became acute under Stuart rule.[2] Certain it is that the desire to worship God in his own way led many a Puritan to Massachusetts Bay in the days of James I and his son Charles. It is significant, too, that emigration to America fell off when

[1] Professor Frederick J. Turner, of the University of Wisconsin, has done more than any other person to call attention to the significance of the frontier in our history. To his suggestive articles in the *Atlantic Monthly*, the *American Historical Review*, and elsewhere, I desire to acknowledge my indebtedness at every stage of my work.

[2] See G. L. Beer, *The Origin of the British Colonial Systems, 1578–1660* (New York, 1908). Chapters i and ii give a discussion of the causes for emigration from England.

Puritanism triumphed under Cromwell. So closely, however, were religious and political questions associated in the minds of the opponents to royalty, that devotion to democratic ideals and to a form of government where middle-class interests were uppermost was curiously intermingled in the minds of our ancestors with their ideas of democracy in church as well as in state. At all events, the first settlers in New England were radicals in religion and in politics, — and they emigrated, as many a radical among their descendants has done.

Economic difficulties also forced many a pioneer to America. In the seventeenth century, when times were still " hard " in Europe, as a result of the monetary and economic disturbances brought about by the great influx of gold and silver from the New World, many a younger son betook himself to a region where his fallen fortunes might be retrieved. The shifting of industry in England under Elizabeth and James had made many a peer envious of the newer aristocracy which owed its title to the wealth acquired through trade and commerce, and had contributed not a little to a desire on the part of the younger men to try their fortunes across the sea. As knowledge of the New World increased, its opportunities seemed more varied and more alluring. Chances for agriculture were great where limitless tracts of land lay unappropriated, and ownership in land was most highly regarded not only as a road to wealth, but as the basis of social and political position. Opportunities for trade and commerce also offered possibilities for making money;—the fur-trade was long a rich field for an energetic young Englishman, and mines of gold and silver have always loomed large among the probable resources of a new country.

Besides these tangible causes for emigration, there were the more subtle but no less real ones of restlessness and discontent with the life of settled communities. The *Wanderlust* in the Anglo-Saxon blood had been potent in urging Englishmen to a part in the Crusades and later to voyages of exploration and discovery. Now it assumed the form it had taken in earlier centuries, and impelled not only individuals, but families, and groups of families, to emigration over seas. Love of adventure, curiosity concerning unknown lands, dreams of prosperity impossible under their present condition, — all these have played a part in recruiting the ranks of pioneers to the New World.

The motives which impelled the second generation of frontiersmen, sons of the settlers upon the coast, to lead the march to the interior, have been very like those of their fathers. Here again the desire for economic, religious, and political freedom has played its part, for the tendency of those portions of the country first peopled has been to grow conservative, and even to crystallize, as England had seemed to have done when the first emigrants left her shores. As the towns on the coast grew slower to change character and institutions, the more radical spirits began to chafe, and to turn to newer sections where they might be unhampered by either tradition or habit. They have not, however, been wholly divested of either, and have turned as their fathers had done to the civilization of their birthplace for precedents, compromising, conceding, and readjusting because of new conditions and new elements, and thus shaping institutions which were neither wholly new nor entirely old. Again and again, with each succeeding generation, has the process been repeated, with England as the background, the older colonies as the "middle distance," and the newest of our states as the foreground. The story of the frontier is not merely a study of settlements; it is also a study of institutions transplanted and transformed, the old ones influencing the new ones, the new ones reacting upon the old, making the latter broader and more flexible. In this way the spirit of radicalism so conspicuous among the pioneer's motives has been immeasurably helpful to the country as a whole.

But along with the pioneer's radicalism and sometimes excessive individualism have gone other motives, such as the desire for greater material prosperity, which, as has been said, had urged on many of the first emigrants from England. The great stretches of fertile lands, cheap and plenty, have lured many a settler to the West. The extensive tracts of timber land have offered opportunities for wealth, as have also the mines; and the well-nigh limitless cattle ranges, together with the salt marshes, are mentioned again and again by pioneers as a great inducement to emigration. Nor is the desire for prosperity solely a selfish one; it is usually bound up with the hope that the children may have advantages denied to the fathers and mothers, and be spared the hardships of frontier life. This desire is again an impelling force in each succeeding generation, urging on the unsuccessful together with the ambitious and the venturesome.

With these causes and motives, what shall be said of the character of the frontier? In the first place, there is the tendency to radicalism in all matters. The conservative element always tends to remain in settled portions of the country, where conditions are fairly determinate, and where results may be estimated roughly at least. Dissatisfaction in a conservative does not readily become so acute as to impel removal to an isolated, unknown region, to begin life anew in unfamiliar surroundings. It has been upon the whole the radical who has moved, the conservative who has stayed. Moreover, the pioneers have usually been men and women not beyond the prime of life, and most frequently they have been young, with the faults and virtues of youth,—frankness, impulsiveness, courage, impatience over restraint, hope well-nigh unlimited. All these qualities have been needed if the hardships of frontier life were to be overcome, and all of them have been exemplified again and again in the march of settlement across the continent.

Certain other characteristics stand out clearly. Independence of thought and of action along religious, moral, and economic lines has always been a significant feature of frontier life. While the Congregational Church was still dominant in New England, descendants of the Puritans were living peacefully in Wisconsin towns, where at least seven denominations had churches, and in lieu of an organization of their own, sometimes allied themselves with Methodists or Baptists or Presbyterians. Without any judiciary at their command, the early settlers often took such crimes as horse-stealing into their own hands, and lynched the thief with little

formality. In the field of economics, colonial ideas of
the relation existing between England and her subjects
across the Atlantic seemed to the British Parliament as
crude and unscientific as the Western agitation for free
silver in 1896 seemed to New England conservatism.
Such independence has frequently been the outcome
of another trait, — excessive individualism. Inability to
adapt one's self and one's ideas to the prevailing order
of things in any community has made many a "chronic
pioneer," who has emigrated at short intervals from one
settlement to another, until old age has overtaken him.
One finds such men to-day in the least thickly populated
portions of the West, — men who found California
stifling in 1855, and perhaps settled down reluctantly in
northern Montana in 1890. Western Canada is at this
moment illustrating the same point. With the accumulation of wealth, this individualism often gives way to
a self-complacency born of a pride concerning hardships
overcome, — the pride of the "self-made man." Such
an attitude of mind is easily comprehended by any one
who has watched a Western city develop from a few log
cabins to a commercial centre numbering its inhabitants
by hundreds of thousands, all within a half-century. It
is this complacency which has bred the provincialism
common in new communities.

On the other hand, side by side with this excessive
individualism exists a strong social sense, which is one
of the most attractive characteristics of pioneer life.
Such a sense is illustrated in the house and barn rais-
ings of any frontier community, where all the settlers
for miles around come to give their help without pay,

but with the tacit understanding that such assistance
will be repaid in kind if necessity demand it. Quilting-
bees, log-rollings, and corn-huskings, where the whole
country-side assembled, have marked the social life of
all frontier communities. The survival of such a spirit
can still be found at harvest time in Iowa or Minnesota,
where the neighborhood comes together first at one farm,
then at another, to assist in threshing.

All these characteristics tend to disappear with settled
economic and social conditions, and radicalism gives way
to conservatism, provincialism breaks down before education and travel, and the new community tends to grow
more and more like the old. Yet there are differences
which are never leveled down, which yield a wholesome
opposition most necessary to progress. From the beginning, elements from all the various parts of the country
have mingled, and the result has been to produce types
which are reminiscent of their origin, though they do
not exactly reproduce it. Most of the colonial pioneers
were offshoots of a common English stock, from the
same social class in Devonshire or Somersetshire or Yorkshire or some other English county, but new environment and changed conditions altered them in their trans-
Atlantic homes, till the different local divisions took on
different characteristics, and the Virginian was easily
distinguished from the man of Massachusetts, and the
Pennsylvanian from either. Within New England itself,
the Vermont type was unlike that of eastern Massachusetts. Pushing in beyond the confines of New England,
in New York and the Northwest, these sons of Massachusetts and her neighbors were thrown with pioneers

from the Middle States and from the South, and the population became further differentiated from that of any of the older states, while the institutions reflected earlier ones found in all. Yet with care one can untangle certain strands in the skein, and the object of this study is to ascertain roughly what part New England has played as a frontier-maker; — how she has founded towns and institutions not only within her own borders, but far beyond the Hudson and the Alleghanies.

Accident cannot explain the homogeneous character of the institutions of the New England States; for despite differences in the character of the people, the institutions they have wrought bear a striking similarity one to another. The reason is not difficult to understand when one has traced the pioneers from Connecticut and Massachusetts who builded together to make New Hampshire, and who united with frontiersmen from New York to frame Vermont's constitution. Why should western Massachusetts bear a closer resemblance to Connecticut in its attitude toward political questions than it does to Boston and the other commercial coast towns? The reason is not hard to find when one has, for instance, traced the settlers of Berkshire County in Massachusetts to their first homes in Norwich, or Hartford, or Wethersfield in Connecticut. Going farther afield, one works back from the distinctly New England forces which went to the building of Newark in New Jersey, or of Southampton on Long Island, to these same northeastern colonies which furnished the first freemen to both. And far away upon the shore of Mobile Bay, or at Natchez, or at Whitman College on the Pacific slope, when there

is found a Comstock, or a Carman, or a Denton, one
needs only to go back to Connecticut, or to Massachusetts, or to their neighbors, to discover the birthplace
of the bearer of the name. Is it by chance that the
Michigan town-meeting bears a striking resemblance to
that of Massachusetts? Is it a superficial catchword that
denominates Western Reserve University a "younger
Yale"? Why should a town in the Willamette valley
of Washington have white houses with green blinds set
gable-end to the street around a public square? Is it by
accident that there should be found in southern California an intangible but distinct New England individualism and hospitality grown less reserved under a tropical
sun? If we find New England civilization, changed yet
recognizable, from the Atlantic coast to the Pacific,
there must be found an explanation of it in a study of
the spread of settlement and institution outward from
the first straggling villages about Massachusetts Bay, —
in a history of the march of the pioneer from Plymouth
to the Columbia River.

CHAPTER II

THE BEGINNINGS OF AN AMERICAN FRONTIER

THE earliest settlement in New England embodied many of the features which characterized later enterprises of the same sort. In the first place, the very name of the settlement New Plymouth was reminiscent of that English port from which the Mayflower had set sail for the New World. One has but to place the maps of England and New England side by side to find many such illustrations of the effort on the part of early settlers to perpetuate in a new country the local names of their former homes. Moreover, Plymouth in New England was founded by transplanting part of a church — deacon and members — from Leyden (which had been but a temporary home) to America. So closely were church and state allied in the minds of these emigrants in search of religious independence, that membership in the one was identical with membership in the other. Before they landed to begin their town, the settlers drew up, in the cabin of the Mayflower, a compact which all the men signed, whereby a "civil body politic" was formed, under whose crude constitution laws to regulate local concerns might be made. At the same time, however, loyalty to the king and dependence upon him in larger concerns were clearly set forth. Deacon John Carver was chosen governor by popular vote of the "freemen" (as the signers of the compact were called), and with Car-

ver was associated one assistant. As has been said, church
and state were closely united, and the town government
managed not only the business, for example, of admitting new freemen, but such matters as regular church
attendance as well. About the church centred much of
the life of Plymouth, and the records of parish affairs are
in outline, at least, a history of the town itself. From
the first days of the settlement care was taken that the
education of children should not be neglected. Where
the sermon occupied so large a portion of the service
and was the medium through which theology was taught
to old and young, an educated people was a necessity.
Moreover, one outcome of the Protestant revolt all over
Europe had been to force dissenters to defend the individualistic tendencies of their creed, and be prepared to
argue out to their conclusion independent views upon
religion. Thus education became a first consideration,
and Governor Bradford noted in 1624 that, although
families taught their own children and there was as yet
no common school, it was not because the need of education was not realized.

Though accident had brought the emigrants of 1620
to the shores of Massachusetts, the deserted cornfields
and abundance of running water which they found undoubtedly had weight in determining where the site for
the infant settlement should be. Huddled close to the
sea the little town grew up, with its cluster of houses
and its church, while round about it, running back toward the interior, lay the farming lands. The plan to
hold these tracts in common was given up shortly; in
1624 to each freeman was assigned one acre as a per-

manent holding, and three years later twenty acres were allotted to each. By this time a number of new names appear on the records, for thirty-five emigrants had arrived in the Fortune in 1621, and about sixty in the Anne in 1623. Originally supporting themselves by agriculture and fishing, the pioneers soon found trading with the Indians a profitable addition to these employments, and in 1627 determined to erect a fur-trading station on the Kennebec River in what is now the state of Maine. Plymouth attempted few such enterprises, however, and the expansion of the settlement continued to be restricted to a comparatively small and compact district about the original town. This process of expansion may be well illustrated in the case of Scituate, where some emigrants, newly arrived from Kent, in England, made their home in 1630. These newcomers voted in Plymouth, and there they went to church. They complained six years later, when the number of freemen was sixteen, that they were too crowded, and that their lands were "stony and hard to be subdued." Even the salt-marshes and good pasture-lands which had first attracted home-seekers seemed to them inadequate, and they petitioned to be allowed either a larger grant of land, or permission to remove to Marshfield. The former plan was adopted, and shortly Scituate was incorporated as a separate town, with its own independent church. The settlers in Marshfield and in Duxbury found the Plymouth church inconveniently far away, and in 1632 formed separate organizations. A little later they, like Scituate, were incorporated separately, though all three were members of Plymouth Colony.

While this sort of expansion was taking place, other small towns, independent of Plymouth in their origin, had obtained a foothold up and down the shore. Hull, Weymouth, Braintree, Quincy, Salem, Lynn,[1] and Marblehead had all been founded in 1629, their inhabitants engaged in farming and fishing. The sites of these towns were selected because of good water or reasonably fertile soil, but so small were they for several years, that the establishment of churches came only after their success was assured. The same condition is illustrated in the early New Hampshire towns, — Strawberry Bank (the Portsmouth of a later time), Oyster River (Durham), and Dover, all of which were in 1623 villages scattered along the shores, with a few fishermen and farmers in each.

Still farther to the east there were planted before 1630 the trading-post of Plymouth Colony on the Kennebec, Cape Porpoise, Piscataqua, Damariscotta, and a trading-post at Pemaquid, around which grew up gradually a settlement that after the granting of a patent in 1630 became a flourishing town. Sagadahoc made a feeble beginning in 1623, while Sheepscot grew in seven years to a population of fifty families. Across the river from the New Hampshire towns of Dover and Strawberry Bank lay the villages of South Berwick and York; Saco and Portland came into existence, and farther on St. George was planted.

The New England coast in 1629 was, then, dotted

---

[1] It is interesting to note the location of the English towns represented in some of these homes. From the eastern counties of Norfolk and Essex come Lynn and Braintree. Weymouth is in Dorsetshire, Hull in Yorkshire.

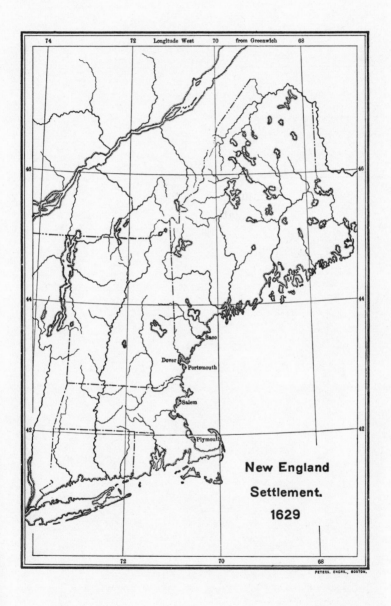

Saco

Dover Portsmouth

Salem

Plymouth

New England

Settlement.

1629

Rev. Mr. Hooker, went also as an organized church. They, like the Windsor pioneers, about one hundred strong, driving their one hundred and sixty head of cattle before them, made their way overland for a fortnight, from Massachusetts Bay to Hartford.[1]

Although they were still under the jurisdiction of Massachusetts (for it was only on that condition that they were allowed to go), the idea of local self-government was too firmly implanted for these Connecticut pioneers to give up the idea of courts of their own. Two men were elected from each of the towns for the transaction of ordinary business, but for extraordinary occasions, such as deciding upon peace and war, and making Indian treaties, they were joined by three others from each town, thus forming so-called committees.[2] For two years the freemen had but little voice in making the laws, save as they acted through their representatives. As in Massachusetts, church and state were closely united, the members of the one being the freemen of the other.

out their pastor, the Rev. Mr. Phillips ; and, having no settled minister at first, fell into unhappy contentions and animosities. These continued for a number of years, and divided the inhabitants of the town, as well as the brethren of the church. They were the means of scattering the inhabitants, and of the formation of new settlements and churches in other places." *Ibid.*, i, 120.

[1] One often wonders what became of the lands vacated by emigrants to newer towns. The lands which the Hartford settlers had left vacant by their removal were purchased by the congregation of Mr. Thomas Shepard, Mr. Hooker's successor in Cambridge, who had come with his people from England in 1634. Trumbull, *Connecticut*, i, 65.

[2] Note the difference between this arrangement and that of Plymouth, where the freemen allowed only advisory powers to their representatives till the towns became four or five in number.

Dutch; and added that " the minds of his people were
strongly inclined to plant themselves there." After a
long and heated debate, leave was given to the malcontents to depart, and emigration began, first to Wethersfield, then to Windsor, and finally to Hartford, the
pioneers calling the towns (until 1637) Watertown,
Dorchester, and Newtowne from their homes on Massachusetts Bay. The pioneers of Windsor, by purchasing
their right of settlement from the old Plymouth Company in England and from the Indians, acquired the
clear title, which was one of the dearest possessions of
the New England farmer of that day, as it is of his
descendants. One hundred in number, they made the
overland journey of fourteen days; through swamp and
forest, following Indian trails, they moved as an organized church, taking their two reluctant ministers with
them.[1] The second company, bound for Wethersfield,
went in all probability by water from Boston, perhaps
arriving before their companions who were bound for
Windsor.[2] The third colony, under the leadership of the

[1] See Dr. H. R. Stiles, *Ancient Windsor* (ed. of 1859), 17, where he says
that many of the Dorchester people were engaged in the fur business, and
that the furs which Hall and Oldham had brought to Boston in 1633 made
the discontented much more eager because of the opportunities the fur-
trade offered.

Stiles is sure these first settlers went along the north border of Pomfret on their way from Boston to the Connecticut. See *Ancient Windsor*,
footnote on p. 26. Also Bowen, *Woodstock*, 13. Also Benjamin Trumbull,
History of Connecticut (ed. of 1818), i, 64–66, who says that the ministers
had to move because their whole church and congregation had left for
Connecticut.

[2] Stiles, *Ancient Windsor*, 28. Also Trumbull, *Connecticut*, i, 59, 60.
Trumbull accounts for the future litigious character of the Wethersfield
people thus : " The brethren of the church at Wethersfield removed with-

That the General Court recognized the hardships likely to be the lot of these frontiersmen, as well as the desirability of such an outpost, seems probable from the fact that three years' exemption from taxes was a feature of the grant, as came to be the case oftentimes in all the colonies.

The break in the frontier line having once been made, pioneering in the wilderness became general. The Plymouth Colony had in 1633 erected a trading-post on the Connecticut River, through the efforts of William Holmes, a representative of the "Plymouth Trading Company." John Oldham, of the same Company, had made expeditions up and down the river from the trading-post, and had brought back glowing reports of the rich intervale lands in the Connecticut valley. When certain of the inhabitants of the coast towns, chafing under what seemed to them the narrowness of the Winthrop-Cotton administration of Massachusetts Bay, determined to migrate for a second time, it was very natural that the vicinity of the Plymouth trading-post should be chosen as their goal. A few adventurous men had gone in 1634 as a vanguard, making their way by water, and had built huts upon the site of Wethersfield, in which they managed to live through the winter. The Rev. Thomas Hooker, pastor of the Newtowne (Cambridge) church, argued that permission to remove be given his congregation, on the ground that their scanty lands were too cramped for the number of cattle they kept, and also prevented their friends in England from joining them. He urged the fertility of the soil upon the Connecticut as a great inducement for removal, alleging also that new settlements would effectually shut out the

sion to 1635. Brookline (called Muddy River) was taken up as an outland for Boston and Cambridge, since the tract abounded in good soil, well-grown timber, and large tracts of marsh land and meadow.[1] Here the cattle were pastured during the summer, the farmers bringing them into the older towns after harvest, and making no permanent settlement until the end of the decade. Upon the whole, then, the first fifteen years of New England settlement show hamlets built up along the coast, with the gradual extension of farming-lands into the interior, which lands later became the sites for new villages.

Each of the older towns had its own church, and about this church centred the social and religious life of the community. Church members only were allowed to be freemen and take part in legislation, so closely was church allied with state in the minds of the Puritans. Each town, moreover, had its own " common," and the grouping of the houses to face this plot of ground, with the farming-lands completely surrounding the group, was already a marked characteristic of the New England settlement.

The planting of Concord illustrates a new phase of expansion from the coast toward the interior. As has been said, the new settlements up to 1635 had been pushed back toward the interior only as extensions of coast towns. In that year, however, the General Court of the Massachusetts Bay Colony having made a definite grant of a tract six miles square to twelve or fifteen grantees, these men and their families founded the town of Concord, the first inland settlement in New England.

[1] Rev. John Pierce, " Brookline," in *Mass. Hist. Soc. Coll.*, 2d ser., ii, 141.

that year dates the rapid growth and prosperity of the
Massachusetts settlements, which, beginning as had the
Plymouth Colony, with little hamlets huddled close to
the sea, soon found their farming-lands too small for
the needs of an increasing population which made agriculture the chief means of livelihood. To meet the
demand for larger fields and pastures, settlement was
begun in Newtowne (the Cambridge of our day) in 1631.
When a company arrived in 1635 from Hingham in
England, bringing their minister with them, the newcomers made their home a new Hingham, attracted by the
heavy timber with which the district was well supplied.
In the same year families moved to Ipswich and Gloucester, thus adding to the number of towns north of
Boston. Ipswich offered advantages in facilities for
farming, fishing, and pasturage, and filled up so rapidly
that four years later the town was considered too thickly
populated, and families from Ipswich, together with newcomers from England, — forty families in all, — migrated as a church, taking their minister with them, to
Newbury. Gloucester, on the other hand, had only here
and there a bit of arable land, and had once before been
abandoned by the few fishermen who had tried to make
homes there. It is indicative of the rapid growth of the
settlements up and down the coast that so undesirable
a site should now be chosen; it is also significant that
out of eighty-two persons named as proprietors of the
soil between 1633 and 1650, two thirds ultimately
migrated to newer towns to try their luck under more
favorable conditions.

One other illustration will show the mode of expan-

here and there with little fishing and farming villages; [1]
the only settlement of any size was Plymouth, with its
outlying farms and little towns split off from the older
one. But in that year began the great migration from
England to America due to the acute discontent engen-
dered by the policy, political and ecclesiastical, of the
second Stuart king. The vanguard consisted of three
hundred and eighty emigrants, who arrived in Salem
and Lynn under the leadership of John Endicott, the
whole enterprise based upon the charter of the Massachusetts Bay Company. This company had organized
as a trading corporation under a patent of Charles I,
which bears a striking resemblance to the mercantile
charters of that day, such as the one granted to the
East India Company. By the terms of the Massachusetts
Bay Company's charter, the members of that "body
corporate and politique" were to elect annually a governor, a deputy-governor, and eighteen assistants, who
were to meet at least once a month in a court to regulate colonial affairs, and with all the freemen were to
meet four times a year in a general court to admit freemen and make laws for the regulation of civil and
religious matters. Once a year this General Court elected
officers for the next year. It was in accordance with
such terms that the Endicott Company arrived. The
next year no less than one thousand people came to the
shores of Massachusetts, and began the towns of Boston,
Roxbury, Watertown, Medford, and Dorchester, besides
contributing new settlers to Lynn and Salem. From

---

[1] See map opposite this page. All the settlements made to 1629 are
plotted on the map, although their names are not inserted.

The same year that the Massachusetts people moved to Connecticut saw the beginnings of a military post at Saybrook under the guidance of John Winthrop, Jr., son of the Governor of the Bay Colony; thus towns to the number of four were scattered along the river before 1636, when the reports of John Oldham, who seems to have been of an adventurous spirit, and had traveled farther up the Connecticut than any other white man, induced a company to remove to what is now Springfield.

SETTLEMENTS ON THE CONNECTI-
CUT RIVER, 1637.

With one of the most prominent men of the colony, William Pynchon, as their chief man of affairs, a number of families from Roxbury, Massachusetts, took leave of their friends on the coast, to begin a new home far out in the wilderness.[1] The rich intervale land offered great opportunities for raising farm products, the Connecticut River afforded transportation facilities, and the towns farther down the river were near enough to furnish some protection in case of Indian attacks. To Pynchon himself the beaver-trade was an alluring prospect, and from the first he engaged in it to

[1] When John Cable left Springfield, in 1641, he sold his house and lands to the town for the sum of £40, to be paid in three installments, — in money if possible, if not in money, then in goods, to be agreed upon by Cable and the towns-people. The next year the town sold this property to one Thomas Cooper for £25. See *First Century of Springfield*, i, 153–155.

his great profit. A significant feature of the founding
of Springfield was the signing of a compact by the settlers, after the manner of the Plymouth pioneers. By
the first resolution they expressed their intention of
providing themselves with a minister as soon as possible; by the second, they limited the number of families
who should be admitted to the town to forty, with the
privilege of enlarging it to fifty if they chose.[1]

South of Plymouth Colony, a settlement was begun
in Rhode Island in 1634 at Cumberland, and two years
later Roger Williams, with a company of friends from
Salem, began his town of Providence. Finding himself
out of harmony with the " close corporation " of Massachusetts Bay, he purchased lands of the Indians, and,
with other disaffected persons, established a new home,
where religious and civil peace might be maintained
without interference from their neighbors on the north.
New emigrations from the two Massachusetts colonies
added to the population, until in 1638, two years after
the planting of the new settlement, thirteen heads of
families shared in the first division of land.[2] Thus Rhode
Island seemed an asylum for malcontents in other parts

[1] Each settler was to have a house-lot on the west side of the main
street, eight rods wide from the street to the river ; the same width in
meadow in front of his house ; a wood-lot of the same width; and, where
practicable, an intervale lot on the west side of the river, as nearly as possible opposite his house. The first comers were, however, young unmarried
men, less than twenty of those who came in the first five years bringing
families with them. See *First Century of Springfield*, i, 19. The first town
government was not representative, for all the freemen discussed matters
in town meeting ; only in 1644 was authority delegated to a board of selectmen. See *ibid.*, 23.

[2] W. R. Staples, *Annals of Providence*, 17–40.

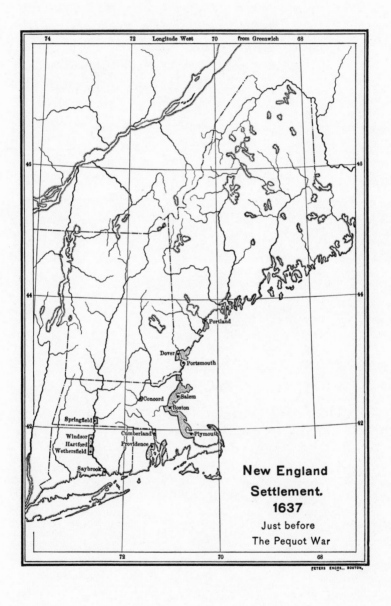

46   46

44   44

Portland

Dover
Portsmouth

Concord   Salem
           Boston

Springfield

42   Plymouth   42

Windsor   Cumberland
Hartford   Providence
Wethersfield

Saybrook

New England
Settlement.
1637
Just before
The Pequot War

of New England, as all New England seemed to be for the disaffected in England itself.

Although the Indians had never been very desirable neighbors, hostilities did not break out until 1637. At that time the frontier line extended in ragged fashion from the Kennebec River to the mouth of the Connecticut.[1] Inland, there were five outposts on the Connecticut River.[2] Springfield lay farthest north, while Concord marked the farthest extension to the northwest, and Taunton (in the Plymouth Colony) with the Rhode Island towns was comparatively isolated in the south. The Indians had resented what was to them the intrusion of the white settlers, and by petty annoyances visited upon immigrants moving overland or by sea had prepared the way for the outbreak of 1637. Had the Narragansetts joined the Pequots, the infant towns would in all probability have been wiped out of existence; but Roger Williams managed to hold his Indian neighbors in check, and upon the Connecticut settlers fell the brunt of the strife. Massachusetts and Plymouth responded to the call of their Connecticut neighbors for help, and a little intercolonial army fell upon the unprepared Pequots, administering such chastisement as not only exterminated the Pequots themselves, but

[1] See map opposite.

[2] The population of the four Connecticut towns is thus estimated by Trumbull: " There were, at the close of this year [1636], about two hundred and fifty men in the three towns [Wethersfield, Hartford, and Windsor] on the river, and there were twenty men in the garrison, at the entrance of it. . . . The whole consisted, probably, of about eight hundred persons, or of a hundred and sixty or seventy families." See *Connecticut*, i, 68.

freed the towns from further danger from Indian tribes
for forty years. Those forty years gave such opportunity
for growth in the number and strength of the towns,
and for their extension inland, that, although they
might suffer greatly from a war, no extermination of
the white settlers was ever again imminent, as it had
been in 1637.

Besides affording peace and quiet for the towns, the
Pequot War did even greater service in bringing to the
knowledge of the Connecticut pioneers the fertile lands
to the east and west of their own towns. As a direct
result of the march of the army, the sites of New
Haven and Fairfield were discovered, and the settlement
of that part of the country followed immediately. A few
settlers began New Haven in 1637; in 1638 came the
Davenport and Eaton Company, which, after a preliminary agreement with the Indians by which the
latter were to have the use of the land between New
Haven and Saybrook, purchased in December a tract
ten by thirteen miles.[1] This was by far the wealthiest
company that came in early days to New England.
The original settlers of 1636 were mostly from London,
and were for the greater part merchants, hence they
chose a place which would afford a convenient centre
for trading.[2] Several characteristics of the early New

---

[1] Trumbull, *Connecticut*, 96–98, 99. New Haven was called Quinnipiack
until 1640. The first purchase included East Haven, Woodbridge, Cheshire, Hamden, North Haven, Branford, and Wallingford, besides what
is now New Haven.

[2] By 1643 there were in the colony 122 planters, 414 persons in all.
Barber, *Hist. Coll. of Conn.*, 134–137, also *New Haven Col. Rec.*, 1638–49,
90 ff.

England settlers stand out in a study of the Davenport
Company, in their attitude both towards England and
towards the older Puritan towns on Massachusetts Bay.
Charlestown and Newbury both made large offers to the
Company as an inducement to live in their midst, but
the newcomers were bent upon forming no entangling
ties. They gave out that they were afraid of a general
governor's being appointed for all New England, and
that they wished to be " more out of the way."[1] It seems
quite clear that the leading spirits were determined to
found a wholly new government, which should be
modeled in both civil and ecclesiastical matters entirely
upon their own ideas.

Mr. Whitfield's company, which in 1639 settled Guilford, came mostly from Surrey and Kent in England,
and chose land as nearly like that of their former
homes as they could find. Country-bred, and farmers
by occupation, with scarcely a mechanic among them,
the arable lands about Guilford attracted their notice,
and purchases were made for all the inhabitants. Every
planter of the original forty, after paying his propor-
tional part of the general expense incurred by laying
out and settling the plantation, drew a lot of land in
proportion to the amount he had expended, and to the
number in his family. A church was gathered at once,
and the town's history began.[2]

[1] Trumbull, *Connecticut*, i, 96.
[2] B. C. Steiner, *Guilford*, 26–35. Also Trumbull, *Connecticut*, i, 107,
108. Steiner thinks the church was gathered in 1643 ; Trumbull says it
was begun with the town, with seven leading men as its first members.
Henry White thinks the New Haven, Guilford, and Milford people had
organized in England as they intended to settle in Connecticut. He says:

In 1639 the first town was planted upon the Housatonic, — Milford. Here a company of four men was sent ahead to explore and make purchases for the planters who were to take possession. The settlers came from the counties of Essex and York in England, with a few seasoned frontiersmen from Wethersfield. There were probably two hundred arrivals in the first year.[1] The spirit of unrest which had led already to the settling of just such towns as Milford drew twelve of its original settlers within a few years to either Southampton or Easthampton, Long Island; Newport, Rhode Island; Fairfield, Guilford, and Branford. Within a few years all these towns had settlers from Milford among their inhabitants. Another town where different elements mingled was Stratford, which was purchased and settled in 1639. It numbered among its pioneers one family from England, several from Roxbury, two from Concord, some from Boston, others from Wethersfield, and one from Milford. Such a settlement can hardly be called an offshoot of any one town; it is significant that it afforded a home to families which for one reason or an-

"Three of these plantations, New Haven, Milford and Guilford, were undoubtedly the result of a . . . united emigration and of a contiguous settlement. The agricultural portion of these emigrants came mostly from the three English counties of Yorkshire, Hertfordshire and Kent. It is not an improbable conjecture that before they left England they were arranged by these affinities into three companies — the Yorkshire men, for the most part, uniting with the London merchants and tradesmen who settled New Haven — the Hertfordshire men forming the bulk of the company which settled Milford — and the Kentishmen going in a body to Guilford." "The New Haven Colony," in *Papers of the N. H. Hist. Soc.*, i, 2.

[1] Of the fifty-four freemen, forty-four were church members, and ten were not. Barber, *Hist. Coll. of Conn.*, 230, 231.

other had found their earlier settlements unsatisfactory, and thought to better their condition by moving out to the edge of civilization.

After 1640 the Connecticut settlers formed smaller villages with great rapidity. Hartford people moved across the river, and lived where formerly they had had only fields. The excellent soil of Norwalk had drawn twenty families there between the time of the first purchase and the year 1651.[1] Wethersfield, which had contributed settlers to Stratford, saw an exodus of about twenty families to Stamford because of a church quarrel, one of several in that town which led to new settlements.[2] New Haven, foreseeing expansion in the near future, had in 1638 purchased the site of the future Branford; the dissensions of the Wethersfield church led to its repurchase in 1644 and its settlement the same year by families from Wethersfield and from Southampton, Long Island. So strongly individualistic were these pioneers that they were constantly complaining of the burdensome yoke of the New Haven jurisdiction under which they lived, and longed to be absolutely independent.

John Winthrop, the typical frontiersman who had begun Saybrook and a plantation on Fisher's Island, was back of the project of settling New London, and thus opening up what was known as the " Pequot Country." Several persons came in 1646, but although the planters were actually in possession of lots, no grants

[1] The purchase was made in 1640. Barber, *Hist. Coll. of Conn.*, 389.

[2] Henry White, "The New Haven Colony," in *Papers of the N. H. Hist. Soc.*, i, 4. Twenty-eight men went to Stamford in 1641 with their families ; in 1642 there were fifty-nine pioneers there. See Huntington, *Stamford*, 18–26.

were recorded until 1647. In the next year the settlement numbered more than forty families; soon after,
three more came from Wethersfield and seven from
Gloucester, Massachusetts, the latter bringing their minister with them.[1]

While new towns had been springing up along the
rivers and coast of Connecticut, expansion had been
going on rapidly in Massachusetts in much the same
manner. Church quarrels proved an important factor in
planting new settlements; — for example, the nine families who went to Sandwich on Cape Cod from Lynn,[2]
and the minister with his congregation from Scituate
who began the town of Barnstable.[3] When a few families had begun homes, they were usually joined by
others who came from various of the older settlements.
Moreover, steady immigration from England continued,
the newcomers having unallotted lands given them, as
was the case with the company of sixty who came from
Yorkshire in England, almost all of them weavers, and
were given the tract where Rowley now stands. Other
immigrants settled Sudbury, and still others, who came
from Salisbury in England, kept one tradition of their

[1] These are not all the towns settled by this time; they are merely instances of the nature of such settlement. Every town planted before 1660
is, however, included in the map of settlement for that year.

[2] Lynn settlers also began the town of Yarmouth and the village which
became South Reading.

[3] *Mass. Hist. Soc. Coll.*, 1st ser., iii, 15. It would seem that church quarrels were a most fruitful source of new towns in Massachusetts as in
Connecticut. Eastham owed its beginnings to a church difficulty in Plymouth, by which forty-nine persons removed to begin new homes. They
scattered over the territory which is now included in Wellfleet, Orleans,
and Eastham, the three towns dating from 1644 under the name of Eastham. See *Mass. Hist. Soc. Coll.*, 1st ser., viii, 165.

old home in naming their new abode Salisbury. It is noted of each of these towns that they had a church and a minister within two years or less.

The crowding of the coast towns also tended to push back the frontier. Cambridge, Charlestown, and Woburn all asked for new grants and received them.[1] But so marked had become the tendency for the pioneers to scatter their farmhouses that as early as 1635 the General Court of Massachusetts Bay Colony issued an order forbidding the building of any dwelling-houses more than half a mile from the "meeting-house," to insure greater safety.

So rarely was a site chosen by pure accident, as Plymouth had been, that the founding of Edgartown, on Martha's Vineyard, seems worthy of note. Some immi-

---

[1] Cutter, "Woburn," in *Middlesex County* (D. H. Hurd, ed.), i, 343–345. The grant of Woburn is so exactly a type of all Massachusetts town grants of that period that it ought to be described at length. Its bounds were fixed by the General Court, four miles square, the grant being made to seven men upon condition that within two years houses be erected and the settlement of the town under way. These seven men were to grant lands to any persons who wished to make homes upon their tract, and to admit these settlers to all common privileges of meadow and upland, according to the number of cattle and of persons in the family who could make proper use of the land; but the tracts were not to be so large as to preclude other later comers from finding farm-lands. These seven men laid out the streets of the town and distributed the lands, giving those who lived nearest the church a smaller quantity about their houses and more at a distance; the poorest having a meadow lot of six or seven acres, and an upland lot of about twenty-five. No more than sixty families were to be admitted without leave. Lands still belonging to the town because unassigned were (after the English custom) held in common by all the citizens. Thus there was obtainable for every freeman severalty in land through his home-lot, and the sense of community of interest through the common lands. See Johnson, "Wonder-working Providence," in *Mass. Hist. Soc. Coll.*, 1st ser., vii, 38 ff.

grants bound for Virginia were driven by storms to this
harbor, and because they were nearly out of provisions,
there they decided to remain. They soon formed a
church, and in 1642 were living comfortably — twelve
families in all — in their new homes, maintaining themselves by fishing and farming.

That the search for good land was a most potent cause
for emigration is well illustrated in the history of Lancaster, called "Nashaway" in the early records, and
"Prescott" in 1652. The productive soil and proximity
to the Nashua River made the tract most desirable, even
though Sudbury marsh lay like a barrier between it and
the older towns. From its beginning as a trading-post,
"Nashaway" was never wholly deserted. A new feature of pioneering appears here in 1643–44, when the
Nashaway Company, made up chiefly of Boston and
Watertown men, was formed for the purpose of convert-
ing the marshes into a mill power. This system of proprietors who might or might not be permanent residents
of their grant is one which became common; to these
proprietors the General Court made the grant, which
was merely a preëmption right, not to take effect until
the Indian title had been extinguished. These proprietors sold tracts to settlers, or admitted desirable persons
to the town upon certain conditions. The plan was probably not a speculative one at first, for land was to be had
almost for the asking, and no one needed to buy at second hand from proprietors when one might get a grant
at first hand from the colony. It was only when land
was in greater demand because the most profitable portions had been taken that speculation began.

Although the tendency to expansion was great in most quarters, it was sometimes difficult to induce settlers to go out to frontier towns. Salisbury had parted with a few families between 1645 and 1648 to begin the town of Amesbury, the new settlers continuing for twenty years to support and attend the Salisbury church. In 1655 eighteen men signed an agreement as to town government; yet the population grew so slowly that in 1659 offers of gifts of land to the oldest sons of families who would remove to Amesbury were used as inducements to new settlers to fill up the town. In 1666, when the town was organized, it contained only thirty-six freemen. The history of Framingham is similar. One family moved there from Sudbury in 1645 or 1646; a second in 1647; but in 1662 it was still spoken of as a "tract of waste land" and a "wilderness." The fact that it was on the old Connecticut path from Cambridge to Hartford was not a great enough inducement to help build it up; and only in 1675 was it possible to support a church for its inhabitants, who had up to that time gone to Sudbury or to Marlborough every Sunday.

New Hampshire grew very slowly. Settlers from England had made their homes in Rye in 1635. In 1638 thirty-six men, under the leadership of Rev. John Wheelwright, withdrew from the Boston church and founded Exeter, while other adherents of Mrs. Hutchinson and of Wheelwright, who came mostly from Lynn, settled Hampton the same year.[1] Other settlers came to

[1] For Exeter, see Bell, in Hammond, *Town Papers*, xi, 639. Also Dr. Samuel Tenney, in *Mass. Hist. Soc. Coll.*, 1st ser., iv, 87. For Hampton, then called Winnicumet, see Palfrey, *Hist. of New England*, i, 515, 516 (ed. of 1882). In 1639 there were sixty families here.

the latter town from Newbury, and the town was from
the first a cattle-raising centre of considerable importance. The only government established was municipal,
for the inhabitants regarded themselves still as subject
to the jurisdiction of Massachusetts. The Isles of Shoals
proved too attractive a fishing-ground for their isolation
to keep settlers away. Before 1641 the inhabitants of
Hog Island had erected a meeting-house, and Gosport
was a flourishing little village. In 1661 there were forty
families on the eight islands, the majority of whom
lived in Gosport.

It was necessary for all these towns to be more closely
united than they had been, and in 1641 they were organized into four governments, — Portsmouth, Dover,
Exeter, and Kittery (in Maine), — and were joined to
Ipswich and Salem for purposes of jurisdiction. In 1643
the three first named and Hampton were added to Salisbury and Haverhill, to form the new county of Norfolk,
Massachusetts, each retaining its own organization for
local purposes.[1]

The history of Maine settlements is scarcely more
than a rehearsal of names and dates, for the records of
the earlier settlements are most meagre, and one gathers
only that a few fishermen and traders led a precarious
existence in tiny villages along the coast. A few settlers
from Exeter, New Hampshire, began the town of Wells
in 1643, under the leadership of the Rev. John Wheelwright, who had found Exeter as uncongenial as Boston
and Lynn had been, and had quarreled over some religious matters with a portion of his New Hampshire pa-

[1] Belknap, *Hist. of New Hampshire* (ed. of 1784), i, 54–56, 100.

rishioners. The inhabitants of Wells formed themselves into a regular proprietary organization, with thirty-five proprietors, and were in a few years made a town of York County by the General Court of Massachusetts.[1] But the villages in Maine continued small, and their records are quite uneventful.

Rhode Island, too, grew but slowly. Portsmouth was settled in 1638 by Anne Hutchinson and her adherents; within a few months they had quarreled among themselves, and some, under the leadership of William Coddington, withdrew to Newport. These two settlements with Providence and Warwick[2] were united in 1644 under a charter obtained through the efforts of Roger Williams. But Coddington, with a faction of his own, managed to obtain a separate charter for Newport and Portsmouth in 1651, and a feud arose which lasted nearly ten years, and ended by the union of all under the old charter of 1644. From the beginning of her history Rhode Island represented excessive individualism and fanaticism, and the story of her early history is one of lack of harmony, and of civil and religious contention.

Before 1660, then, five of the present New England states had towns planted within their limits, and the two most populous ones, Connecticut and Massachusetts, had sent bands of pioneers up and down the coast, and far inland, to begin new settlements in the wilderness. But expansion did not cease at the borders of New Eng-

---

[1] Williamson, *Maine*, i, 293, 351.

[2] *Rhode Island Hist. Soc. Coll.*, i, 11. North Kingstown was settled in 1658, when a few families from Boston and Portsmouth moved there.

land ; in 1640 the first English settlement was made on
Long Island, at Gravesend, by emigrants from Massachusetts. Five years later their town records were
begun, and by 1656 the population was perhaps two
hundred.[1] In the same year that Gravesend was settled,
forty families from Lynn moved to Southampton, erecting
their church the following year. They alleged that they
removed because they were " so straitened at home,"
but the church quarrels which had led three parties from
the same town to Cape Cod since 1637 make one suspicious that the alleged reason was not the real one. In
1657 sixty-one houses were occupied in the settlement.
Other towns were founded by former inhabitants of
Massachusetts and Connecticut, until in 1660 eleven
distinct villages had been settled, scattered from one
end of the island to the other, either along the coast, or
on smaller bits of land, like Shelter Island.

Each of the English towns on Long Island was at
first independent, all questions being determined by
majority vote in town-meeting. The people of Southampton entered into a social contract, which they signed
previous to their settlement, agreeing to be bound by
the will of the majority, and to support the magis-
trates in the administration of the laws so made. The
people of Southold and Easthampton did the same;
but the latter and those of Southampton sent to Connecticut for a copy of the laws in force there, and either
used them exactly, or made others similar to them. By
1662 all the Long Island towns had united with either
New Haven or Connecticut. One must note, also, a set-

[1] Thompson, *Long Island*, ii, 168–169, 175, 177.

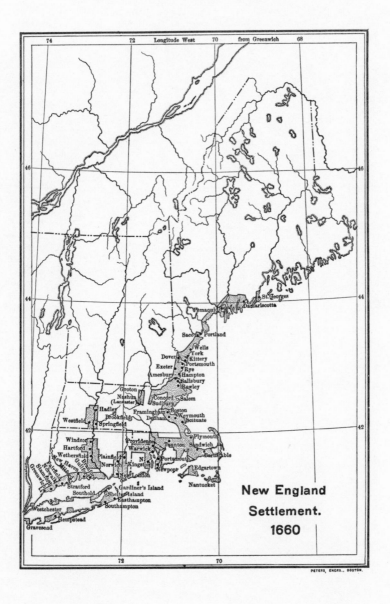

PETERS, ENGRS., BOSTON.

tlement in Westchester, Westchester County, New York, by a company of thirty-six men "from New England," who secured their grant from the Dutch, and whose town was at first called Eastdorp by their neighbors.

In 1660 the frontier line extended along the coast, not far inland, from the Penobscot to Manhattan Island.[1] It was not continuous, as a glance at the map will show, and it tended to follow the larger rivers, for its only extension inland was caused by the attraction of rich lands along the banks, and by the transportation facilities so necessary to any settlement. The fear of Indians kept settlers from pushing far into the interior, and the same danger made the pioneers plant new towns next to old ones, except in rare cases. Having once established themselves in an outpost, the pioneers were subject to some restrictions as to removal. The General Court of Massachusetts issued an order on August 12, 1645, that since Concord, Sudbury, and Dedham were inland towns but thinly peopled and consequently exposed to great danger, no man living in any of the three, be he married or single, should move to another town without permission of a magistrate or selectman, until "it shall please God to settle peace again, or some other way of safety to the above named townes, whereupon this Cort, or the council of the comon weale, shall set the inhabitants of the said towne at their former liberty." When the march inland did not follow the rivers, it proceeded by some well-known Indian trail such as the Pequot path, or the old Connecticut

[1] See map opposite.

path, or the trail to Lancaster and to Springfield.[1] Beyond the mainland there were outposts on the Isles of Shoals, New Shoreham, Nantucket, and Martha's Vineyard, besides those upon Long Island and its coast islands.

By 1660 the New England colonies had taken definite form, and 'presented the various features which were to mark them off as distinctly different organizations from those farther to the west and south. Certain traits were common to all; in other ways each was quite distinct from any other.

All of the colonies had this feature in common, that they were settled directly because of the desire for religious freedom. It was but natural, therefore, that their community life should grow up around their church; and this we find to be the case. In almost every town there was a meeting-house with a minister; around this church were grouped the homes of the settlers, rude cabins at first, gradually replaced by more substantial houses.[2] The pioneers had, as has been shown in many cases, come directly from England as organized churches — minister, deacons, and members — to plant new homes

[1] The New York, New Haven and Hartford Railroad follows closely the old Pequot path from Boston to Providence, following the Sound to New York. The old Connecticut path is almost exactly the line of the railroad from Providence to Hartford through Putnam and Willimantic ; while the Boston and Albany is practically everywhere the old Indian trail from Boston to Springfield through Brookfield.

[2] These town houses were commonly set gable-end to the street. Out on the frontier, the log cabin was the unvarying sign of a new settlement, as it was much later in the West; but in the coast towns there were to be found the really comfortable houses of people who were building permanent homes for themselves and their children.

across the ocean. Rev. Thomas Hooker's followers, for example, true to their tradition, moved as an organized church when they left Massachusetts for a second frontier home in Connecticut. Their places were immediately taken by Rev. Thomas Shepard and his congregation, who took over the lands and the church which the Hooker emigration had left for later comers. The spirit which had animated the first Puritans, the determination to found a Bible commonwealth, had animated their descendants; and those who made new homes too far from any existing parish to attend its meetings on Sunday either took their minister with them, or sent back for one as soon as enough families to support a minister had built houses on the new tract. To induce ministers to move out to the frontier, it was a very common thing for the proprietors of a new town to set apart one of the original lots for the first minister, and often another for the "support of the ministry," besides building the church (and frequently a parsonage as well) by a common assessment.

In both Connecticut and Massachusetts Bay the close union of church and state was a marked feature of the constitutional development. In the latter only church members enjoyed the franchise; in New Haven the same rule obtained. In Plymouth and Connecticut, while there was no law on the subject, the franchise was in practice really about as limited as in Massachusetts Bay. The freemen in the town-meeting made regulations for both civil and religious affairs; the General Court, made up of representatives of the towns, admitted freemen, granted lands to settlers, appointed committees

to lay out new plantations, and made church laws as
well. The whole idea was that of a close union of tem-
poral and spiritual affairs, and by that practice the life
of the colonies was regulated. In 1639 the Connecticut
General Court drew up a written constitution, which
really formulated Massachusetts governmental practice
as it existed at that time, including the town system
which Massachusetts Bay had developed in accordance
with her needs. By this means the practice in the two
colonies came to be very similar; but Connecticut, more
conservative than her neighbor, retained the system
unchanged long after Massachusetts had superimposed
a county system for judicial purposes. There were,
however, in the two colonies the town-meeting, a pri-
mary assembly of all the freemen; and the representative
General Court for the larger concerns of all the towns.
The New Hampshire settlements, as well as some of
those in Maine, were under the jurisdiction of Massachusetts Bay, each one retaining, however, its own
organization for local concerns. Rhode Island, as has
been shown, possessed two charters, each being used
for a portion of the colony, while the towns maintained
their local organization also. The Long Island towns,
as we have seen, while preserving the New England
tradition of town-meetings, united with one of the two
Connecticut colonies, and sent representatives to act for
them in the General Court.

Besides their substantial agreement in the character of
their governmental and religious institutions, we find
the New England colonies, largely because of the demands of their religious creeds, favoring schools and the

education of children from the first. Plymouth had for a long time only family teaching; in the laws of 1658 advice was given to each town to consider the matter of getting a schoolmaster. In 1677 the General Court ordered that in each town of fifty families or upwards a grammar school be supported, any deficit in the rate to be made up from the profits of the Cape fishing. The Massachusetts Bay General Court passed an act in 1649 compelling every town of fifty householders to appoint a teacher for all their children ; and further requiring a grammar school for every town of one hundred families or more. Connecticut and New Haven adopted the same system, as did Plymouth at a later time. In higher education Massachusetts led the way, when in 1636 Harvard College was founded as a missionary enterprise. Thus from the first the foundations of education for all children were laid, and traditions established, which were to distinguish the Puritans' descendants for all time.

BIBLIOGRAPHICAL NOTES

Out of a wealth of material for the study of New England history, a few books have been conspicuously helpful in the preparation of this work. Of the more general works, Palfrey's *Compendious History of New England* (4 vols.) is indispensable as far as it goes (to 1765), but has to be corrected in some places because of later investigations in local history. John Winthrop's *History of New England*, from 1630 to 1649 (Savage edition), is of course invaluable. William B. Weeden's *Economic and Social History of New England, 1620 to 1789* (2 vols.), contains an enormous mass of valuable material, which is, however, badly organized. A work which was never carried through into the second volume, but is a very good and convenient compilation for the settlement of Maine, Vermont, and New Hampshire, with an exceptionally good map, is Coolidge and Mansfield's

History and Description of New England (Boston, 1859) ; here every town in the three states has its short history, taken sometimes from other works, as are certain whole paragraphs on Vermont towns copied *verbatim* from Thompson's *Vermont.* John Warner Barber's *Historical Collections of Massachusetts,* and *Connecticut Historical Collections* take up the history of every town in these two states, and are fairly accurate. The books must, like Coolidge and Mansfield's work, be corroborated as far as possible by other testimony. Rhode Island is the only one of the New England States which has no such convenient compilation. For early New England institutions, and the general historical background, the latest and best work is in Professor Edward Channing's *History of the United States,* vol. i, which bears the subtitle *The Planting of a Nation in the New World,* and vol. ii, *A Century of Colonial History* (1660–1760).

As for more specialized works : for Massachusetts, there are such contemporary works as William Bradford's *History of Plymouth Plantation* (Deane Edition), Thomas Prince's *Annals,* Alexander Young's *Chronicles of the First Planters of the Colony of Massachusetts Bay* (1623 to 1636), and Captain Edward Johnson's *Wonder-working Providence* (W. F. Poole's ed., 1867). The *Collections of the Massachusetts Historical Society* contain a mass of material, with such contemporary accounts as Josselyn's *Accounts of Two Voyages to New England.* There are also the admirable collections of colonial records (for the colonies of New Plymouth and Massachusetts Bay), supplemented by the laws known as *The Acts and Resolves, Public and Private, of the Province of Massachusetts* (15 vols., covering the period from 1692 to 1780), which need no comment. There is a good deal of material on settlement in Thomas Hutchinson's *History of Massachusetts,* 1628 to 1774 (3 vols.), and in J. S. Barry's *History of Massachusetts* (3 vols.). The county histories, especially those compiled by D. H. Hurd and S. L. Deyo, necessarily vary in value, since the articles are by different persons, many of them untrained for the work, and the books are popular in character. For many small towns, however, these compilations contain all the material at present available, and thus they serve their purpose. Local histories, such as Sylvester Judd's *History of Hadley* and J. G. Holland's *History of Western Massachusetts* (2 vols., 1855), are excellent, and, as tested by other material, prove accurate ; many other local works are worthless save for such portions as the biographies of citizens. Works commemorative of special occasions, such as Timothy M. Cooley's " Historical Discourse," in *The Granville Jubilee,* delivered in Granville, Massachusetts, in 1845, are very suggestive for the emigration of inhabitants from New England towns. Centennial celebrations of the founding of churches can usually be relied upon to produce useful statistics in the same way.[1] For a study of population, evidence has to be gathered from poll tax lists, lists of church members, etc., save in the case of such a later compilation as Jesse Chickering's *Statistical View of the Population of Massachusetts from 1765 to 1840* (Boston, 1846), which is especially suggestive on the decades from 1820 to 1840.

For Connecticut, the *Public Records of the Colony of Connecticut* (15 vols., Hartford, 1850 to 1890) and the *Records of the Colony and Plantation of New Haven* (2 vols., Hartford, 1857–58) are full of records of settlement and institutions. The *Connecticut Historical Society Collections* (11 vols., Hartford, 1860–1907) are indispensable, as are the *Papers* (7 vols., New Haven, 1865–1908) issued by the New Haven Colony Historical Society. Benjamin Trumbull's *Complete History of Connecticut, Civil and Ecclesiastical* (2 vols., covering the period 1620–1764) is useful and accurate. There are many excellent local histories, among which are Dr. C. W. Bowen's *Woodstock*, Miss F. M. Caulkins's *History of New London* and her *History of Norwich*, Rev. A. B. Chapin's *Glastenbury for Two Hundred Years*, and Dr. H. R. Stiles's *History of Ancient Windsor, Connecticut* (new edition of 1891, 2 vols., is best). There are others quite as good as these. The *Record of the Celebration of the Two Hundredth Anniversary of the Founding of Yale College* (1902), and Franklin B. Dexter's *Sketch of Yale University* (1897) show the widespread influence of the Connecticut institution, especially in the West. Dr. B. C. Steiner's *History of Education in Connecticut* gives a little information on early schools.

The *Collections of the Rhode Island Historical Society* (10 vols., Providence, 1827–1902) are not so good as the similar collections for Massachusetts and Connecticut. There are sometimes articles useful for such purposes as this study affords in the *Publications* (8 vols.) and the *Proceedings* (in a number of pamphlets, 1872–92, 1900–02) of the Rhode Island Historical Society. Samuel G. Arnold's *History of the State of Rhode Island and Providence Plantations* (2 vols., New York, 1859–60) is still the best history of Rhode Island. Dr. G. W. Greene's *Short History of Rhode Island* contains some material not in Arnold's work. In local history, W. R. Staples's *Annals of the Town of Providence* (Providence, 1843) is valuable.

Maine local history can be found, as has been noted above, in Coolidge and Mansfield ; in the *Collections of the Maine Historical Society* (1st series, 10 vols., 1831–91 ; 2d series, 11 vols., 1865–1908; and a 3d series, 2 vols.,

[1] The references above are those found most useful for the text of this study. Many more works have been utilized in the preparation of the maps. For example, forty-two local histories were used for the Massachusetts maps, besides the twenty or more used for the text.

1904–06) ; in the *Collections of and Proceedings of the Maine Historical Society* (2d series, 10 vols., 1890–99) ; in James Sullivan's *History of the District of Maine* (Boston, 1795) ; and in W. D. Williamson's *History of the State of Maine,* 1602 to 1820 (2 vols., 1832). Governor Sullivan tries to untangle the skein of overlapping grants as a lawyer would ; Williamson's work is very like Trumbull's *Connecticut,* and contains much material not available elsewhere. William Willis's *History of Portland,* from 1632 to 1864 (2d ed., 1865) is a good piece of work, as is James W. North's *History of Augusta,* but there has been all too little work done on local history in Maine.

The standard general history of New Hampshire is Jeremy Belknap's *History of New Hampshire* (3 vols.), which can be supplemented by that of George Barstow (in 1 vol.). There are various sets of documents : *Provincial and State Papers,* in many volumes, edited by Dr. Nathaniel Bouton, Isaac W. Hammond, and Albert S. Batcheller, — 29 volumes in all. Since, in many New Hampshire towns, settlement took place long before incorporation, the collections of charters in the set given above are not of value in many cases for such a study as the present one. The local histories are few in number, and are mostly concerned with towns settled at a later date.

For Long Island in this period, the *Historical Collections of the State of New York,* by John W. Barber and Henry Howe, is a valuable book, to be supplemented by Martha Bockée Flint's *Early Long Island* (New York, 1896); H. G. Spafford's *Gazetteer of the State of New York ;* the old standard work of B. F. Thompson, *The History of Long Island* (2d ed., 2 vols., New York, 1843) ; also Silas Wood's *Sketch of the First Settlement of the Several Towns on Long Island* (3d ed.), Brooklyn, 1828. Besides these there are the admirable *Records of the Town of East Hampton, Long Island, Suffolk County, New York* (4 vols.), covering the period from 1639 to 1849. The *Collections of the New York Historical Society,* 1st series (5 vols.), also contain a little material. Daniel Denton's *Brief Description of New York,* printed in London in 1670, but reprinted in 1902, is valuable as the work of a contemporary writer. Of local histories, the best are George R. Howell's *Early History of Southampton, Long Island,* and the Rev. Epher Whitaker's *History of Southold, Long Island.*

For Westchester County, there is a good work in two volumes by Robert Bolton, Jr., *History of the County of Westchester.*

CHAPTER III

THE INFLUENCE OF INDIAN WARFARE UPON THE FRONTIER

1660–1713

THE history of the frontier from 1660 to 1713 was largely determined by the frequent Indian wars during this period. The rush of population to the margin of danger would have been enough in itself to account for such an outbreak as that instigated by King Philip; but when with this normal expansion was combined the added impetus of those colonial wars which made up one feature of the European struggles of the same period, it was little wonder that the Indians took advantage of their position as coveted allies to pay off old scores. In order to understand the situation, it is necessary to glance for a moment at the relations existing between England and her colonies in the years immediately succeeding the accession of Charles II.

The English Restoration of 1660 inaugurated an era of conservatism in church and state. The troubled years of the Long Parliament and the Protectorate had caused many an Englishman, were he Royalist or Puritan, to look back with regret upon the time when a king held the reins over him. Yet when Charles II and his advisers inaugurated a policy strongly suggestive of that adopted by Charles I in the early years of his reign, it was but natural that many should resent such reaction-

ary measures, and that emigration should set in toward
the colonies, whose development had been going on
steadily during the troublous times of Cromwell. The
fact that the colonies had been left so largely to their own
devices for a number of years was conducive to the quiet
growth of the democratic institutions which had been
evolved out of an innate love of liberty, and had been
fostered and developed by the exigencies of life in the
wilderness, far from the restraining hand of the Englishmen who governed the mother country. To these colonies, then, came many Puritans who feared a régime of
absolutism and a return to the principles of Archbishop
Laud, along with other emigrants who were moved by
the economic and social causes which had been operative
throughout the century. The acts of Parliament bearing
upon commerce, which had been passed under Cromwell
and reënacted and enlarged in their scope after the
Restoration, were aimed at Dutch shipping at the same
time that they fostered English industries. In the
impetus these acts gave to the English carrying-trade
the colonies were to share. Thus greater opportunities
opened up before the prospective emigrant, and the
population of the Atlantic seaboard increased accord-
ingly. Whatever grievances the Indians had with regard
to the limitation of their hunting-grounds were but
aggravated by the expansion necessitated by the arrival
of the newcomers.

The *laissez-faire* policy of Cromwell and his advisers
had not, however, resulted in any weakening of the
relation between the mother country and her colonies;
but the bonds which were to hold them together seemed

to need strengthening. Soon after the accession of Charles, new charters were issued to several colonies, but the conditions already in existence were not materially altered. To Connecticut was granted the document which the inhabitants of that colony regarded as the safeguard of their liberties until the early part of the nineteenth century. It was secured largely through the efforts of a colonist who stood high in favor with certain English noblemen, — John Winthrop, Jr., the founder of Saybrook, of the Fisher's Island settlement, and of New London.[1] Its terms provided for a governor, deputy-governor, and twelve assistants, to be elected annually by the General Court and the Assembly. The former body was to consist of not more than two representatives from each town (elected by the freemen), and the latter to be made up of the governor, deputy-governor, and at least six assistants. Twice a year these organizations were to meet to admit freemen, elect officers, and in general to make laws regulating the affairs of the colony, subject only to the condition that they should not be repugnant to the laws of England. Thus representative government was given the Connecticut people with an extraordinary degree of latitude; the town-meeting was left as it had grown up, and the development of liberty was assured to the colonists. In this charter, New Haven was joined to the other Connecticut towns; but it was some time before the settlers were brought under its jurisdiction.

So promptly did Rhode Island proclaim the accession of Charles II, that her petition for a charter was favor-

[1] See pp. 21 and 27.

ably regarded at once. A delay in issuing the document was caused by the indeterminate boundaries of Massachusetts, Connecticut, Rhode Island, and John Winthrop's grants, so that it was not until 1663 that the charter was granted. By its terms, the Rhode Island towns of Providence, Newport, Portsmouth, Warwick, and Coventry were united under the title of the "Rhode Island and Providence Plantations," to be governed by a governor, deputy-governor, and ten assistants, elected annually by the representatives of the various towns. The representatives in Rhode Island were not to be the same in number for each town, but were apportioned roughly according to population, — six for Newport, four for Providence, Portsmouth, and Warwick, and two for every other town settled then or later. The organization of the General Court and of the Assembly was like that in Connecticut, and they were to make laws as in the latter colony, subject to the condition that these laws be not repugnant to those of England. In Rhode Island, then, as in Connecticut and Massachusetts, representative government was established, while the town-meeting of all the freemen developed beside it.

About the same time that these charters were issued, England concluded a war with Holland. By the terms of the peace, carried out by Colonel Nicolls in August, 1664, the Dutch colony of New Netherland came into the possession of the English, — a fact of the utmost importance for the future history of America. In the first place, the fear of Dutch encroachments upon New England — a menace since 1633, at least — was thus ended; in the second place, the coast from Virginia to

Maine became wholly English by the removal of what
was then the only rival claimant to the soil; and in the
third place, the first foreign element was introduced
into the English population of the colonies. To the last-
named condition may be ascribed the adaptations such as
those made presently in the laws for the newly acquired
colony, which alone could make the assimilation of that
element possible. Moreover, the Dutch had their own
institutions, and some readjustment was obviously necessary if antagonisms were to be avoided. The acquisition
of New Netherland thus introduced problems of assimilation and adaptation which had not presented themselves in homogeneous communities like New England,
but which were, nevertheless, prophetic of similar questions to be solved at later times. The first code of laws
for the conquered territory was proclaimed in 1665, and
bore the title of " The Duke of York's Laws." These
statutes bear a striking resemblance in many ways to
those in force in Massachusetts; the English towns and
the English settlers in the Dutch towns probably aiding
in shaping them to accord with what was then colonial
practice for New England. Town-meetings had from
the first furnished the machinery for governing the
Long Island towns, and they were provided for in the
Duke's Laws, in order to elect a constable and eight
overseers for the administration of local concerns, but
with more power than was given the New England
selectmen, who were merely executive officers. Over several towns was superimposed, for judicial purposes, the
riding, which later became the county, whose chief officer was the sheriff. In 1703 each town elected a county

supervisor, who with his fellow supervisors formed a county board, representing all the towns, and standing between the town and the General Court of the colony. Here, then, is a mixed system of town and county government somewhat different from the New England form, yet closely allied to it in its fundamental features. The Duke's Laws provided one feature, however, which differed materially from Massachusetts or Connecticut practices; they vested much more power in the hands of a governor and council than was given in the neighboring colonies, leaving the people little voice in affairs which concerned anything beyond the riding.

Another consequence of the acquisition of New Netherland was the grant made by the Duke of York to his intimate friends, Lord Berkeley and Sir George Carteret, of the land lying between the Delaware and the Hudson. The name New Jersey, given to the tract, was in compliment to Carteret, who had held the Island of Jersey during the troublous days of the Civil War. There were "squatters" already on the soil, and for these and prospective settlers the proprietors drew up a plan of government not unlike that in the New England colonies under the charter just issued, save that the right to annul laws lay with the proprietors, and the oath of allegiance to the king was to be supplemented by one to the proprietors.

From 1660 until 1675, what with immigration from England and the natural expansion of the colonies, settlement went on rapidly, and the frontier was pushed farther out into the wilderness. As the area of occupied soil grew larger, the size of the Indians' hunting-

grounds diminished, and therein lay perhaps the most
potent cause of the conflict between the two races. In
order to show how great havoc could be wrought it is
necessary to show conditions in the years preceding the
outbreak of hostilities in 1675.

In Massachusetts, families moved from the older
towns into the outlying districts, which were still near
enough to be included in the older parishes; — such
was the emigration to Merrimac (for two centuries a
part of Amesbury), and to East Bridgewater (a parish of
Bridgewater). Other settlements were made about Plymouth and on Cape Cod; a church quarrel in Barnstable
furnished the pioneers of Falmouth, fourteen of whom
are mentioned in the allotment of lands in 1661. Not
only were the unoccupied tracts near the coast taken
up, but the more remote districts to the west and north
of the colony also. It was a bold man who wished to
remove to Brookfield in those days, but so fertile was
the soil that although their nearest neighbors were miles
away in Springfield, Lancaster, and Sudbury, six or
seven families were in the settlement in 1667.[1] Mendon,
too, was an outpost; begun in 1660 by people from
Braintree and Weymouth, it was incorporated seven
years later, and in 1675 had a population of thirty-
eight families. Dunstable, on the northern border, then
included Tyngsborough, and extended a little way into
New Hampshire, — a distinctly frontier outpost. In the
Connecticut valley, Samuel Frary, of Medfield, led the
way for the Hinsdale and Plympton families, who fol-

[1] Most of these were from Ipswich. In 1675 there were twenty families
here. W. T. Davis, "Brookfield," in *History of Worcester County*, i, 511–514.

lowed to plant Deerfield ; other Dedham pioneers went after this vanguard, attracted, as Frary had been, by the excellent soil of the region. To John Pynchon and his associates was granted the tract named Northfield, which drew settlers from Northampton, Hadley, and Hatfield. Various grants were made in Worcester from 1657 to 1664, but the tract was too isolated, and the danger from Indians too great to make it attractive to settlers. The General Court finally sent out a committee to look over the ground and report upon its suitability as a site for a town; they brought back word that there was enough good land for thirty families, or for sixty if other grants were annexed. Settlement followed, and before 1675 thirty houselots had been laid out, houses built for some thirty families, and the farms were under cultivation. These are but a few of the many settlements made in the first fifteen years following the Restoration.

North of Massachusetts there was almost no growth. In Maine but one new town was begun, — Brunswick, whose first settler arrived in 1675. New Hampshire grew but little, the only attempts at new towns being in the vicinity of Dunstable, and above Northfield, as continuations of those settlements.

Rhode Island, determined to win her case as to the western boundary, had in 1669 stationed thirty families in the territory now occupied by Westerly, Hopkinton, Charlestown, and Richmond. Two families began the town of Woonsocket in 1666, and Barrington (till 1717 part of Swansey) was settled in 1667. East Greenwich owed its beginning to the boundary dispute, for families were encouraged to go there by offers of ninety acres to fifty men, on condition that they build homes on the land within a year, and open a road from the bay into their country. The grants were made in 1667, and settlement followed the same year both in East and West Greenwich; but the latter settlement, because of its poor land and lack of communication with Narragansett Bay, was of very slow growth.

In Connecticut the tendency to expansion took the form of filling in about the old towns; — for example, the Windsor people moved over into East Windsor about 1662. Ten years later twenty-seven men are named as a "list of persons on the East side of Great River," who were appointed to work the highways. The lands of the first settlers almost all ran three miles back from the river; their houses were usually erected on the upland, but as their number increased they were compelled to move back into the woodlands. Haddam was purchased from the Indians in 1662, and twenty-eight young men from Hartford, Wethersfield, and Windsor began new homes for themselves on both sides of the river. Doubtless many of these were sons of the pioneers of those towns, who had inherited the instinct of frontiersmen, and determined to begin life on farms of their own where land was cheap and plentiful. In 1668 the town was large enough to be incorporated. In the north and west expansion took place, as when Hartford, Windsor, and Guilford sent out twelve planters who began Killingworth in 1663.[1] Wallingford, "New Haven Vil-

---

[1] Barber, *Hist. Coll. of Conn.*, 529. The town was named Kenilworth; the present name of the town is a corruption from it. *Ibid.*, 530.

lage," had been purchased by the Davenport-Eaton Company in 1638; for thirty-two years the tract was unoccupied, but the year after its settlement it had a town-meeting, when there were about one hundred inhabitants, and in 1674 it settled its own minister, though regular services had been held on Sunday since the first days of the arrival of inhabitants.[1] Half of the congregation of Stratford, about fifteen families, taking their minister with them, settled Woodbury in 1673 after a church quarrel, — the old and fruitful source of Connecticut towns. These towns serve as types of the great expansion within the borders of Connecticut.

Off the Connecticut coast lay Long Island, to which New Englanders had emigrated from time to time, until in 1670 it was inhabited from one end to the other. In the western portion lay four or five towns whose population was wholly Dutch; the rest of the island, containing twelve towns and scattered farmhouses, was entirely English.[2] Expansion in that direction was no longer possible, and the extension of the frontier must obviously take place elsewhere.

Connecticut, far from being the "land of steady habits," had always been productive of the new towns which were plain illustrations of the unrest of her inhabitants. Not restrained by the limits of the colony, large emigrations took place after 1660 to another district, — New Jersey. About the time that the grant to Berkeley and Carteret was made, a few pioneers from

[1] Davis, *Wallingford*, 70–108. There is an interesting compact drawn up at the time of the settlement of the town; *ibid.*, 77, 78.

[2] Denton, *New York* (ed. of 1902), 41.

Connecticut began the town of Shrewsbury, to which came shortly other families from Rhode Island and from New York (as the New Netherland acquisition soon came to be called). A typical Connecticut removal was the defection of a portion of the New Haven colony to New Jersey in 1666. Some of the New Haven people had opposed strenuously any acknowledgment of the Restoration, and feeling had run high between the ultra-republicans and the more conservative party which could see but one safe course, namely, to follow the lead of England in her attitude towards King Charles. In 1661 some of the more democratic families opened negotiations with Governor Stuyvesant of New Netherland, with a view to removal from New Haven. Nothing came of this attempt, but four years later the problem was solved by the arrival in East Jersey of its new governor, Philip Carteret. Immediately upon his arrival the governor sent agents into New England to publish the terms which the proprietors offered to settlers and to invite them to these lands. The offer was a liberal one, and in the following year a committee from the Connecticut towns of Guilford, Branford, and Milford was sent ahead to look over the country, learn more exactly the terms of the offer, and ascertain how friendly the Indians were apt to be. The members returned with a favorable report, and were straightway sent back with power to buy a township, select a site, and make all arrangements for immediate settlement. Thirty families set out by boat from New Haven, and established themselves in what is now Newark, in separate neighborhoods, according to

the towns from which they had come.[1] Immediately
after their arrival delegates were appointed to draw up
a form of government, by the terms of which no one
could become a freeman, or vote, or hold office who
was not a member of the Congregational Church. True
to their traditions, the church in Newark was a Connecticut church moved in its entirety, — pastor, deacons,
records, and major part of the congregation. The first
school was established in 1676. The College of New
Jersey, now known as Princeton University, was begun
in Newark, over half a century later, and thus the
foundations of higher education in New Jersey were
laid by the descendants of the Connecticut pioneers
who had laid the foundations of the town and had given
it the character it was to maintain. Governor Belcher
testified to the tenacity with which Newark people
insisted upon their rights at the time of the Revolution;
— an interesting comment upon the transmission of
political theories from generation to generation.[2]

Connecticut did not furnish all the pioneers to New
Jersey. Settlers from the Massachusetts towns of Haverhill, Newbury, Yarmouth, and Barnstable removed to
Woodbridge in 1666–67, and in a few years controlled
about thirty thousand acres through the homes and
farms of the six hundred people living there. A small
company from Piscataqua in New Hampshire came
about the same time to found Piscataway. Elizabeth
was settled by a mixed population, in contrast with the

[1] This arrangement was soon broken up by the sense of mutual danger,
and the settlement was made more compact.

[2] Barber and Howe, *Hist. Coll. of N. Y.*, 173–176. Some of this
Newark colony settled in Bloomfield. *Ibid.*, 156.

homogeneous character of such a settlement as Newark.
The pioneers of Elizabeth were drawn from England,
Scotland, New England, and Long Island. A typical
first settler was John Strickland, who had come from
England with Winthrop's company and settled in
Watertown. He was one of the members of the church
in that place who moved to Wethersfield. Soon after
he took up his abode in Fairfield, from which town he
went with the founders of Hampstead, Long Island,
and began a fourth pioneer's home. In 1661 he was
living in Huntington, Long Island, but was induced
to move to Jamaica, a little farther away. In 1666 he
made what was probably his last move, — to Elizabeth,[1]
where most of the settlers had come as had Strickland
from Long Island, the majority of them from Southampton.[2]

New Jersey was settled rather thickly from the first,
for several reasons. Its proximity to New York assured

[1] Hatfield, *Elizabeth*, 59, 60.

[2] They were men from twenty-five to forty years of age, with wives
and children. The whole settlement was planted quite in accord with
Denton's description of the mode of settlement prevalent in New Netherland in 1670. Denton says that towns were usually begun by the banding
together of about enough families to make a town, who went (with the
governor's consent) to look at a tract of land which appeared desirable.
Upon their return, they were accustomed to petition the governor for a
grant of the land selected, and upon being admitted into the colony, the
patent was accorded to the original company and their associates. These
persons thereupon made a settlement, and admitted inhabitants until the
town was full, when land was allotted "suitable to every man's occasions," the rest being held in common till the time seemed ripe for a
second division. The pasture land was, however, never divided, but "lies
in common to the whole Town." See Denton, *Brief Description of New
York* (ed. of 1902), 57, 58.

the pioneers a steady market for their surplus products
as well as for the fruits of their Indian trade, besides
enabling them with little difficulty to obtain in return
what they needed; the Indians, far from being a menace to the settlers, were generally friendly, and there
was from the first a lively traffic in furs, skins, and game.
These facts, combined with the advantages of good soil
and climate, and the generous policy of the proprietors,
contributed not a little to the prosperity of the colony.
In 1668 was drawn up the first New Jersey code of laws;
and it is, as one would expect, essentially a New England product. Deputies from each village met in Elizabeth, and, the Puritan element predominating, the laws
(especially those relating to criminals) are almost identical with the Massachusetts laws of the same period. The
refusal of the inhabitants, now grown accustomed to
individual ownership in land, to pay the quit-rents demanded by the proprietors led to a rebellion in 1672,
in which the settlers won their point.

In 1675 there were probably one hundred and twenty
thousand people in New England, of whom sixteen thousand could bear arms. We have seen how widely they
were scattered, and how great had been the extension of
the frontier since the Pequot War forty years before.[1] A
singularly astute and capable Indian, Philip, had since
about 1662 been more or less of an annoyance to the
Plymouth and Rhode Island settlers; but in 1674 it was
evident that a general Indian uprising, planned and instigated by Philip, was imminent. In that year he and
his warriors descended upon Swansey, in Rhode Island,

[1] See map opposite.

New England
Settlement
1675
J. E. Elliott
Marblehead, Mass.

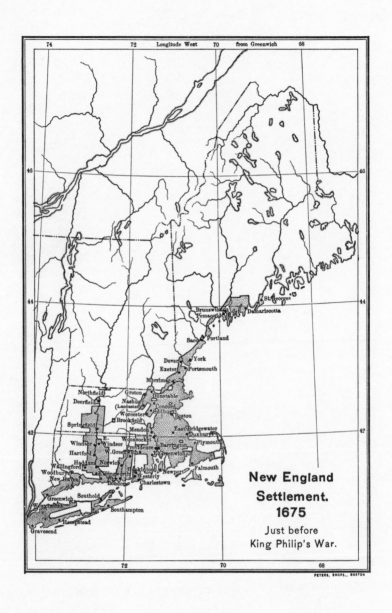

New England
Settlement.
1675

Just before
King Philip's War.

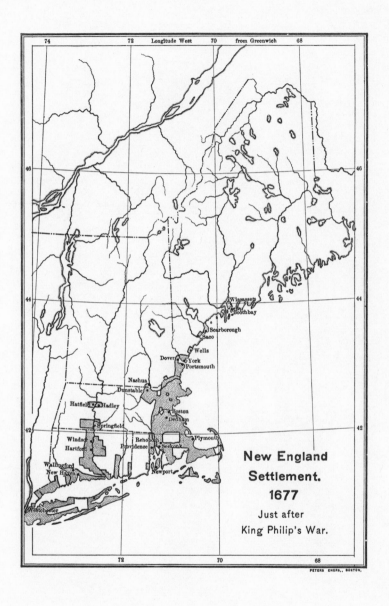

Wiscasset
Boothbay
Scarborough
Saco
Wells
Dover
York
Portsmouth
Nashua
Dunstable
Hatfield
Hadley
Boston
Dedham
Springfield
Windsor
Rehoboth
Plymouth
Hartford
Providence
Seekonk
Wallingford
New Haven
Newport
Westchester

**New England
Settlement.
1677**

Just after
King Philip's War.

and for nearly two years — until his death — all of
New England lived in terror. The struggle is of the
keenest interest to us because of its effect upon the
expansion of settlement which had at the time of the
outbreak reached the greatest extent attained up to
that time.[1] There was not a New England colony which
did not suffer, there was scarcely an outpost which was
not wholly deserted and burned, or which did not receive a severe blow from which it took long to recover.
The outposts of settlement naturally suffered most. The
district of Maine, which in 1675 contained thirteen towns
and plantations, and could muster perhaps a thousand
soldiers in case of need, was desolated. Every settler in
Kennebec County had fled by 1677, though fifty families
had lived there seven years before. Bristol had been
burned, Wiscasset harassed, Biddeford destroyed, Portland deserted and then burned, Brunswick reduced to
ashes. The whole country east of Casco Bay was a waste,
and of all the towns and plantations enumerated five years
before, only about six remained in 1680. The allies of
Philip had dealt the country east of New Hampshire a
blow from which it did not recover in half a century.

New Hampshire suffered hardly at all. Even Nashua,
the extreme frontier, had one hardy fighter, Jonathan
Tyng, who stayed when all his neighbors here and over
the line in Massachusetts had fled, so that the town was
never wholly deserted.

Massachusetts suffered greatly. From Seekonk and
Rehoboth in the southern part, to Northfield and Dunstable in the north and west, sixteen towns were either

[1] See map opposite.

destroyed or deserted.[1] Others, like Springfield, were partially burned; and even so populous a town as Dedham was threatened to such a degree that several terrified families fled to Boston.

In Rhode Island four towns were either destroyed or abandoned, — Warwick, Coventry, Westerly, and Charlestown. Connecticut suffered comparatively little; the Wallingford people fortified their homes, anticipating an attack, and the Woodbury settlers fled to Stratford, where they remained a year. Simsbury was destroyed, the inhabitants taking refuge at Windsor; Waterbury was abandoned from 1675 to 1677, Granby, Woodbury, and Southbury for a year or two.

The blow was in itself a severe one, and it would have been long before the frontier again regained its former limit, especially upon the northern boundaries, had this been the only struggle. Scarcely had the memory of King Philip's War faded, however, when the colonies were drawn into the first of that series of con-

---

[1] The towns were Worcester, Mendon, Berlin, Deerfield, Northfield, Groton, Lancaster, Stow, Brookfield, New Bedford, Medfield, Marlborough, Middleborough, Milford, Ayer, and Maynard.

At the time there were about forty families in Groton, twenty in Brookfield, and thirty-eight in Mendon. W. T. Davis, "Brookfield," in *History of Worcester County*, i, 514 ; G. B. Williams, "Mendon," *ibid.*, 376 ; S. A. Green, "Groton," in *History of Middlesex County*, ii, 509. "The number of settlers in Northampton was, according to the records, about one hundred, and allowing three to the family of each settler, which would seem to be a reasonably estimated average, that town contained four hundred inhabitants. Hatfield and Hadley probably contained from two hundred to four hundred more, while Westfield, Deerfield, and Northfield contained an aggregate, perhaps of two hundred. Fifteen hundred would doubtless be an extravagant estimate of the valley at the date stated, and the majority of these were dependents." See Holland, *Western Massachusetts*, i, 72.

flicts between England and France for supremacy in the
New World which have sometimes been called their
second hundred years' war. The struggle which began
as the War of the Palatinate in Europe was extended
to the colonies as King William's War. Here the French
and English contended for the aid of the Indians, and
the horrors of savage warfare were added to the other
hardships of the conflict. When the Peace of Ryswick
was signed in 1697 the possessions of the two countries
remained as they had been at the opening of hostilities
in 1689, but the frontier-line had been again thrust
back by reason of burned and abandoned towns. The
second of these European contests began in 1700 as the
War of the Spanish Succession, known in the colonies
as Queen Anne's War. Here, again, the Indians played
a large part in the devastation of frontier villages, and
plundered and laid waste large areas of thinly populated
territory. The Peace of Utrecht in 1713–14 terminated
hostilities, and was of the greatest importance to the
development of the colonies, especially in the north, for
New England was now surrounded by friends, not foes;
since England had, with the aid of the colonial army,
wrested Nova Scotia from France, and had wrung an
acknowledgment of sovereignty from the Iroquois Indians,
— the fiercest tribes which threatened the pioneers who
had explored the lands west of the Hudson River. An un-
precedented opportunity was thus opened for expansion to
the west, and the outpouring of population in that direction followed immediately. A study of the details of settlement will show clearly how expansion was seriously hin-
dered by these successive conflicts from 1675 to 1713.

So widespread had been the devastation during the years of warfare that various precautionary measures are to be found in the records of the several colonies. For instance, in 1677 orders for laying out the town of East Greenwich, Rhode Island, were issued, on condition that each of the forty-eight freemen to whom grants were made should settle upon his houselot within a year, and build a house "fit and suitable for habitation." Neglect of this order was to mean forfeiture of the share. In the district of Maine, a large portion of which Massachusetts had purchased in 1677 for £1250, renewal of settlement was regulated by the General Court of Massachusetts, which enumerated certain towns as being open to reoccupation, but in these no less than twenty or thirty families were to go together. They were, moreover, to build near the shore, upon lots of three or four acres to a family, the village to be a compact one, with the farmlands lying about it. In this way it was hoped that the destruction of the frontier might be avoided.[1]

[1] Connecticut made similar attempts to protect outlying settlements. An order of the General Court in 1704 thus enumerates the frontier towns : Simsbury, Waterbury, Woodbury, Danbury, Colchester, Windham, Mansfield, and Plainfield. It also enjoins the settlers in those places not to break up the towns or desert them without permission from the court, on penalty of forfeiting title to their estates. See *Conn. Col. Rec.*, iv, 463.

One or two more instances show both these points : in 1708–09, twenty-five families from Norwalk, attracted by the limestone soil, purchased the tract thirteen by three miles upon which Ridgefield is located. In 1712 a petition was drawn up for a church ; the next year a minister preached from time to time, and one was formally settled in 1714. See D. W. Teller, *Ridgefield*, 3–14, 92.

In 1708 the General Court granted Newtown to thirty-six petitioners, and appointed a committee of four (one each from Stratford, Fairfield,

But even such precautions were of no avail in restoring a feeling of confidence which might lead settlers to the lands lying north and east of Massachusetts Bay. In Maine, not a single town was planted in those forty years, and there were actually fewer people and fewer towns in Maine at the end of the period than there had been in 1660.[1] New Hampshire was, as has been said, but little affected by the ravages of Indian warfare from 1674 to 1676. But no one wanted to venture his life in a new plantation, so that, although the old towns filled up, new ones were not begun. A truce with the Indians in 1694 led to the granting of a charter to twenty petitioners from Hampton who wished to settle at Kingston. Many were obliged to return to their old homes within two years, though after the war they resumed their enterprise; it was 1725, however, before the first minister was settled. Greenland, settled in the latter years of the seventeenth century from Portsmouth and as a part of it, petitioned in 1705 for a minister and schoolmaster of its own, and begged to be exempted from the support of the Portsmouth church and school, since it had a population of three hundred and twenty inhabitants. In 1708 it was estimated that there were not a thousand men in the colony. Hudson was settled in 1710, but there was no further expansion of New Hampshire till 1716.

In Massachusetts the towns which had been destroyed or depopulated during King Philip's War were rebuilt almost immediately afterward. Lancaster lay desolate

Woodbury, and Danbury) to allot the land to these thirty-six, who must settle their land within four years and live there for four years. In 1711 the land was divided among the proprietors, and the town incorporated.

[1] See map opposite page 70.

till 1679; two years later seventeen or eighteen families had returned and petitioned successfully for exemption from " county rates " because of their hardships. Some towns, like Framingham, grew very rapidly. Stow, which had no town-meeting for five years, was filled up by returning families who brought with them others from Concord, so that not only was the town incorporated, but it supported its own minister. Dunstable people returned immediately after the close of the war, and completed their church within two years. In 1711 there were seven garrisoned houses, two of which were within the present limits of Tyngsborough; to these garrison-houses were assigned nineteen soldiers, and thirteen families claimed their protection. But presently the community split into two, because each desired the control of its own civil affairs "for greater convenience of public worship "; and over the location of the meeting-house the town separated into the two villages of Dunstable and Tyngsborough. Of new towns, some were settled in Plymouth County from the older towns in the old colony, — Halifax, Hanson, Wareham, and Lakeville. Settlers moved from Eastham to Truro, settling that town and Provincetown about 1700, though land had been purchased several years before. But the growth in the southern part of Massachusetts was chiefly because of increased population in the old towns. In Worcester County, the records of the town of Worcester are like those of the Maine towns, — a series of dates of settlement and abandonment, till only one family remained in 1701, the reason for its final desertion being that the General Court had stricken it from the list of frontier-

towns which were not to be abandoned. Its permanent
settlement dated from 1713. Oxford, a new Worcester
County town, whose proprietors included the governor
and deputy-governor of Massachusetts, was settled in
1686 by thirty French Protestant refugees, one of the
many companies driven out of France by the revocation
of the Edict of Nantes. To these emigrants were granted
about twelve thousand acres. Upon the breaking up of
the settlement by Indians in 1696 the settlers went to
Boston, and the land reverted to the proprietors; these
granted it to new settlers in 1713, on condition that at least
thirty families settle the tract at once. The condition was
fulfilled, and the town incorporated the same year.[1]

Rhode Island, after King Philip's War, built up the
towns which had been destroyed, but aside from natural
increase in the older towns and some immigration, it
had no expansion. A company of forty-five French Protestant families began a plantation called Frenchtown in
1686, and built a church and twenty-six houses; but
their neighbors made life such a burden to them that
the refugees were dispersed. Four of the five towns later
received from Massachusetts were settled at this time, —
Little Compton, Warren, Tiverton, and Bristol, the last-
named settled by Boston merchants who named it for

---

[1] *Mass. Hist. Soc. Coll.*, 3d ser., ii, 29–32. Hopkinton is slightly different from the others. It was settled on a tract which was purchased for
the purpose of perpetuating the legacy of Edward Hopkins to Harvard
College. To the settlers of 1710–12, the president and trustees of the
college leased it. These pioneers came singly from Sudbury, Framingham,
Sherborn, Concord, Needham, and Marlborough ; the eighteen families
who joined them in 1719 came from Scotland and Ireland. See *Mass.
Hist. Soc. Coll.*, 1st ser., iv, 15, 16, and Clement Meserve, " Hopkinton,"
in *History of Middlesex County*, iii, 800.

Bristol in England, with the hope that its fine harbor might cause it to rival its namesake. Scituate (Rhode Island), which had grown but slowly, and had no very good reputation for law and order, received a better class of settlers in 1710 from Scituate, Massachusetts, whereupon it took the name of the latter place, and was incorporated in 1731. Since the seventeenth century most new towns in Rhode Island have had their origin in the subdivision of old towns then in existence. In 1715 there were, perhaps, nine thousand people in the colony; nine towns sent delegates to the colonial assembly.[1]

Connecticut expanded more rapidly than any other New England colony during the period 1676 to 1713. The towns which had suffered during the war were quickly rebuilt, and the development of Woodbury is typical of others. In 1675 its people fled to Stratford, some returning the next year, though others were afraid to take up their old home for several years; in 1682 its population was four or five hundred.

The first new town planted after the war was Meriden, which drew its pioneers from Wallingford, and was for a long time a parish of that town. To the east, Preston and Groton were settled about 1680; to the north, Enfield the next year. Danbury, Mansfield, and Windham were founded before 1687. Plainfield numbered persons from many towns among its first inhabitants; — from Massachusetts, Woburn, Stow, Chelmsford, Haverhill, Ipswich, and Concord; from Connecticut, Stonington, New

---

[1] Palfrey, *New England*, iv, 466 (ed. 1882). The towns were Newport, Providence, Portsmouth, Warwick, Westerly, Kingston, New Shoreham, Jamestown, and Greenwich.

London, and the vicinity of the latter town. The settlement was retarded because of the impossibility of getting a clear title to the lands. In 1704 it was still a frontier-town; the next year it had a church for the first time. At the same time that Plainfield was settled (1690) settlers from Hartford, Newtown, Woburn, Dorchester, Barnstable, and Medfield began the town of Canterbury, the two towns claiming thirty families in 1699, when Plainfield was incorporated, including Canterbury. Four years later Canterbury was incorporated as a separate town, but evidently Plainfield had far outstripped it in numbers.

Woodstock owed its existence to settlers from Roxbury, Massachusetts, who found their town "too small for its inhabitants," and in 1686 moved—thirty families strong—over the old Connecticut path to New Roxbury. Oxford and Mendon were their nearest neighbors; but their isolation seems not to have troubled them. It was in all probability their pastor, John Eliot, who told them of the beauty and fertility of the "Nipmuck" country in which they settled. In 1690 they renamed their town Woodstock, held a town-meeting, and settled a minister. But the town grew slowly, for immigration was not rapid to a place where private proprietorship was the rule.[1]

Lisbon grew but slowly, retarded, as was Plainfield, because of the difficulty of getting a clear title. Purchases were made here by men from Ipswich, Massachu-

---

[1] E. D. Larned, *Windham County*, 18–44. Also C. W. Bowen, *Woodstock*, 20, 23, 24. Pomfret was settled the same year as Woodstock, by farmers also from Roxbury, but only a few came until after 1695, for fear of the Indians. Barber, *Hist. Coll. of Conn.*, 437.

setts, in 1694–95, and settlements were begun at once; yet in 1718 there were only sixteen persons on the roll of accepted inhabitants.[1] Northampton families joined others from Windsor, Saybrook, and Long Island to begin Hebron in 1704, before the township was granted. The town's growth was delayed for two reasons, — the Indians were troublesome, and the proprietors, non-resident themselves, claimed extensive tracts upon which they would neither settle themselves nor allow others to do so. The General Court was compelled to appoint several committees to encourage and assist the planters, and were so far successful that about 1713 "they were enabled to erect a meeting-house, and settle a minister among them."[2]

This period saw settlers leaving New England for other colonies, — for Bedford in Westchester County, New York, for example.[3] A settlement had been made in the town of Westchester many years before, so that the district was not unknown. Settlers also went in large numbers to East Jersey,[4] where they not only

---

[1] F. M. Caulkins, *History of Norwich*, 257–259. The river towns at this time sent settlers to Colchester, but complaint was made that the settlement was being delayed by Saybrook men, who claimed large grants of land there. See *Conn. Col. Rec.*, iv, 298.

Hartford and Northampton furnished the pioneers of Coventry chiefly, though others came from "a great variety of places." See Trumbull, *Connecticut*, i, 443, 444.

The first settlers of Durham were from Guilford, two arriving in 1703, and others shortly after; yet in 1707 there were but fifteen families. The next year the town filled up with newcomers from Northampton, Stratford, Milford, and other towns. See *ibid.*, 400.

[2] Trumbull, *Connecticut*, i, 430, 431.

[3] See map opposite.

[4] New Jersey had been divided in 1674 into East and West Jersey.

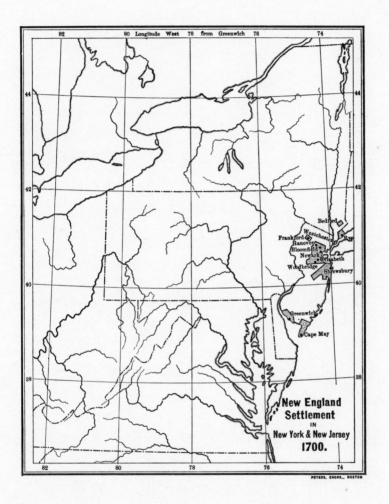

82 80 Longitude West 78 from Greenwich 76 74

44

42

40

38

Bedford
Westchester
Frankford Rye
Hanover
Bloomfield
Newark
Elizabeth
Woodbridge Shrewsbury

Greenwich
Cape May

**New England
Settlement**
IN
**New York & New Jersey
1700.**

82 80 78 76 74

filled up the towns already established, but began new ones. About 1682 Quakers from Rhode Island and Long Island settled in Springfield; in 1697 pioneers from Fairfield, Connecticut, planted a new Fairfield and organized a Presbyterian church the same year. Besides the new towns, settlers from Long Island and New England were constantly moving to Newark, Elizabeth, and Middletown, which on account of their increasing population either continually extended their limits, or formed in their neighborhoods centres for new villages. But for about ten years (1693 to 1703) immigration was almost shut off because of uncertainties as to land tenure and land titles. An interesting phase of development was manifested in the number of religious sects represented in East Jersey, where such a variety of churches was maintained that religious intolerance could hardly exist. The people of Newark and Elizabeth were Congregationalists, and each town had its own church. There were, however, among them a few Church of England adherents, Presbyterians, Anabaptists, and Quakers. The first Episcopal service held in Elizabeth was in 1703. The Rev. John Brooke wrote in 1706 that he held service in the Dissenters' meeting-house with their permission till his church was built, and that some stayed after their own service to attend his.

As to population, Colonel Morris reported in 1700 that there were in East Jersey ten towns, with a population of about eight thousand. Most of the towns were thickly settled in one part, with outlying farms and little villages, all bearing the name of the more compact

town. He found settlers generally " of very narrow fortunes and such as could not well subsist in the places
they had left." [1]

Another enterprise which illustrates admirably the
character of New England pioneering for all time belongs to this period. On the 22d of October, 1695, the
Rev. Joseph Lord was ordained in Dorchester, Massa-

Dorchester Colony
SOUTH CAROLINA
1695-6

chusetts, by representatives
of the churches in Roxbury,
Boston, Milton, Charles-
town, and Nonantum, so
that he might go to South
Carolina. A church coven-
ant was entered into by
Mr. Lord and eight others,
among whom were num-
bered one William Norman of Carolina (it is thought
that he had come up from the South to encourage the
undertaking), three men from Concord (Massachusetts),
two from Dorchester, one from Reading, and one from
Sudbury. The object was undoubtedly a missionary one,
for the cause of removal is stated to be "a desire to
promote the extension of religion in the southern plantations." The emigrants moved as an organized church,
taking their minister with them, and retaining the Congregational form of government. They sailed in two
ships to the Ashley River, and on the 2d of February,
1696, took the sacrament of the Lord's Supper under an
oak, and began to build a settlement which they called

[1] "Memorial of Colonel Morris," in *N. J. Hist. Soc. Proc.,* iv, 118–
120.

Dorchester. They erected a meeting-house immediately, thus perpetuating another Puritan tradition.[1]

Harvard College was the only institution of higher learning in New England until the movement for a second college was begun in 1701 in New Haven, which had always fostered a hope that some day it might harbor such an institution of its own. Two graduates of Harvard College consulted as to plans, and these, with other ministers, founded the college by giving, in the succeeding years, books for that purpose.[2] After the preliminaries of securing a charter and organizing with trustees were carried through, a "collegiate school" was started at Saybrook in 1702. Soon after its removal to New Haven in 1716 it took the name of Yale College, out of gratitude to its first liberal patron, and there were laid the foundations which assured its future prosperity.[3] The president from 1716 to 1722 was a Harvard graduate, as was the Rev. Thomas Clap, who guided the college affairs from 1739 to 1766.[4] It was but natural that the first college in New England, itself a missionary enterprise, should thus help in establishing a second institution upon a similar foundation.

What with the scattering of pioneers from Maine to the missionary enterprise in South Carolina,[5] the influx

[1] *History of Dorchester, Mass.*, 261–263. See, also, *Mass. Hist. Soc. Coll.*, 3d ser., i, 55–59, for a project previous to 1663 in which New Englanders were involved, for planting a colony on the Charles River "in Florida."

[2] Dexter, *History of Yale University*, 8.

[3] *Ibid.*, 9–19.

[4] *Ibid.*, 21, 27.

[5] That there are emigrations about which scarcely any records exist is certain from an item in the family history called *The Doane Family*. One Daniel Doane of Eastham, Cape Cod, Massachusetts, with his family, and

of French refugees and emigrants from England, and
the fact that even the natural increase was not carefully
recorded, it is no wonder that figures indicating population should be well-nigh impossible to ascertain. Most
of the estimates to be found are perhaps but shrewd
guesses. Trumbull thought that Connecticut had in
1665, at the time of the union, some eight or nine thousand inhabitants, with about twenty ministers. In 1680,
the answers to the Lords of Trade and Plantations (given
by the governor and council) estimated the militia at
2507, from which Trumbull thinks the whole population
about twelve thousand, including Rye and Bedford
(now in New York). The inhabitants of Rhode Island
were 7181 at the time of the first census, in 1708;
Palfrey has estimated the male population of New
Hampshire in 1708 as under one thousand, while no
figures are available for Maine, so precarious had been
the existence of that district during the entire period.

By 1713 the settlers on the frontier had become differentiated more or less from their brethren who stayed
in such coast towns as Boston and New Haven.[1] Whereas
in the latter prosperity had made the rise of a leisure
class possible, — a class which could take on a degree

one William Twining, with his family, from the same place, joined the
Society of Friends, and about seventeen hundred removed to New Town,
Bucks County, Pennsylvania. They made the journey of seven hundred
miles overland, took up land, and affiliated with the Quakers of that section. Their descendants were either pioneers in Montgomery and Lycom-
ing counties in Pennsylvania, or moved with the Pennsylvania emigrants
to North Carolina, while still later descendants will be taken up in the history of Quaker settlements in Ohio and Indiana. See *The Doane Family*,
53–55, 78, 79, 123.

[1] See map opposite.

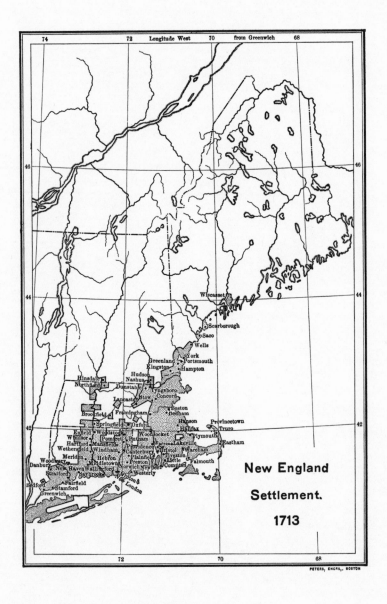

New England

Settlement.

1713

New England
Settlement
1913

of culture and refinement which bore some likeness to
that of the mother country,— out on the frontier life was
still rude and hard. The incoming English settlers who
arrived from time to time seem to have settled in the
older towns, and there their influence would be felt.
But the pioneer was most frequently the son of a pioneer, his wife the daughter of another, and together they
began a new home where land was cheap and plenty,
and money went farther than it did on the coast. An
instance of the economic development of the coast as
contrasted with the interior is the increasing diversity
of occupation in the former as over against the latter.
Under the fostering care of the Navigation Acts there
had developed a great increase of intercourse between
the Old World and the New, and such interests as those
of shipping, along with the kindred ones of trade and
commerce, had grown enormously. It was to the men of
the coast towns that these opportunities came, for they
represented the moneyed class, whereas the pioneers on
the frontier usually made a home in the wilderness with
a distinct view to bettering their unsatisfactory financial
condition. A prosperous traffic with the West Indies
had sprung up, and promised rich returns. Shipbuilding
became one of the most important industries of New
England, thus rendering the colonists still more independent of the mother country in respect to all features
of the carrying trade. While the population of the seaboard thus became on the economic side more like England, the frontier continued to be rural, engaged in
rural occupations, with cattle-raising, lumbering and
dairying as adjuncts to the chief industry, — farming.

Besides the more evident economic differences, the two regions represented more subtle distinctions. It was on the frontier that men from the various colonies mingled, and while they held in common the stern religious views and educational ideas of their ancestors, these were tempered by contact with others of somewhat different cast; so that while fundamentally the ideals of all were the same, — all were striving toward civil and religious liberty, and all were tenacious of their rights, — individualism still found its freest development out at the edge of civilization. Conditions were not unlike those which had produced the first emigrations from England, — the radical still departed for the wilderness, leaving the conservative in possession of the field. The church quarrels which continued to be a potent factor in the development of new towns had been at the root of many an exodus to New Jersey, as well as to the unoccupied regions of the older colonies. Curiously enough, however, when the malcontents found themselves in the majority instead of in the minority (as they had been before their removal), they frequently became as intolerant as their comrades had been. On the other hand, they often grew broader minded, as was the case in New Jersey, and made extraordinary adaptations and compromises. Upon the whole, however, one could expect more toleration in the newer communities than he was apt to find where conditions had become more crystallized. In spite of superficial differences, the fundamental institutions of the town-meeting, the church, the school, — all these the pioneer carried to his new home, and the region so recently a wilderness took on

more and more the character of the older colony towns.
The pioneer of Maine and of western Massachusetts and
Connecticut, who had rebuilt his log house three or
four times, and who tilled his field with a gun slung
across his shoulders, had perforce to be a man of purpose and of perseverance, with little time for anything
save the business of getting a living and rearing a family of children. Yet to his descendants he gave a heritage of traditions of democracy, religion, and education;
when they reached man's estate, they did as their father
had done, — took up a search for a new home where
land was cheaper than in the older settlement,[1] and
when that home was found, they made it their business
to see the town-meeting, the church, and the school
established as their fathers had founded them. Whether
the pioneer dwelt on the Maine rivers, in the wilds of
New Hampshire, beyond the Connecticut River, in New
Jersey, or in South Carolina, his traditions and his general character were the same. The differences were but
superficial, and he was after all a New Englander grown
more independent and probably more tolerant under his
new environment; — but not even many removes from
the Englishman of his day.

[1] Another reason is given in a letter of Isaac Addington to Fitz-John
Winthrop in *Mass. Hist. Soc. Coll.*, 6th ser., iii, 338; it is dated Boston,
July 1, 1706. "His Excellency [Governor of Massachusetts] thinks he
can tell where one hundred Massachusetts men are gone into Connecticut
Colony to save themselves from taxes and service in the present war."

BIBLIOGRAPHICAL NOTES

THE general works cited at the close of the second chapter are of value for the period 1660–1713.

For Massachusetts, many of the books mentioned earlier prove useful for this chapter. Such histories as that of Worcester County (D. H. Hurd, compiler) furnished the only available material for certain smaller towns, and the *Massachusetts Historical Society Collections* must be called into constant requisition. Henry D. Nourse's *History of Harvard, Massachusetts* (Harvard, 1894), is one of the better class of local histories.

There are a few excellent local histories for Connecticut towns planted in this period, which supplement admirably the more general works such as Trumbull's. Miss F. M. Caulkins's *History of New London* (New London, 1852) and *History of Norwich* are illustrations, as are William Cothren's *History of Ancient Woodbury, Connecticut* (3 vols.), and Miss E. D. Larned's *History of Windham County* (2 vols.). Dr. Charles H. S. Davis's *History of Wallingford* (Meriden, 1870) contains the compact under which Wallingford was settled. Dr. C. W. Bowen's *Woodstock* is the work of a scholar. Dr. Franklin B. Dexter has published in compact form the data concerning the early years of Yale College in his *Sketch of the History of Yale University* (New York, 1887).

For Rhode Island the following local histories, — C. C. Beaman, *Historical Sketch of the Town of Scituate, R. I.* (1877) ; Rev. Frederic Denison's *Westerly (Rhode Island) and its Witnesses,* 1626–1876 ; and D. H. Greene's *History of the Town of East Greenwich and Adjacent Territory* (from 1677 to 1877) proved helpful.

Barber and Howe's *Historical Collections of the State of New Jersey* (New York, 1846) is a good starting-point for the emigration to that territory. William A. Whitehead's *East Jersey under the Proprietary Governments* is still a standard work for the field it covers. Joseph Atkinson's *History of Newark,* and the Rev. Dr. E. F. Hatfield's *History of Elizabeth* (including the early history of Union County) are excellent, as is L. T. Stevens's *History of Cape May County.* Joseph F. Tuttle read a paper before the New Jersey Historical Society in May, 1869, on *Annals of Morris County,* which is published in pamphlet form. The *Proceedings* of the New Jersey Historical Society contain some interesting material. But the material for the study of New Jersey local history shows that much labor must be expended before a final piece of work can be done which shall interpret its history along the lines attempted in this study.

The *Collections of the New York Historical Society* (1st ser., 5 vols., 1811–1830) contain in volume i the "Duke's Laws." Daniel Denton's *Brief Description of New York* (London, 1670, but reprinted 1902) is a valuable, contemporary account of that colony as it was at the time the English wrested it from the Dutch.

The early charters, such as those of Connecticut, Rhode Island, the Massachusetts charter of 1692, and the New Jersey grant and first code of laws will be found in carefully compiled form in Dr. William Macdonald's *Select Charters and Other Documents Illustrative of American History, 1606–1775*. Each document is preceded by a brief account of its history, and a well-selected bibliography.

Such admirably compiled histories as that of *The Doane Family* (by A. A. Doane, Boston, 1902) prove most valuable in giving items not otherwise available as to the emigrations of a family in whom the pioneering instinct was strongly developed.

For the Dorchester (South Carolina) colony, see Edward McCrady, *History of South Carolina under the Proprietary Government. 1670–1719* (3 vols., New York, 1897), and the *History of . . . Dorchester, Massachusetts*, published by the Antiquarian and Historical Society of that town in 1859.

CHAPTER IV

FORTY YEARS OF STRIFE WITH THE WILDERNESS

1713–1754

FOR forty years almost ccaseless warfare had been waged along the New England frontier. The outposts of the colonies had seen a succession of Indian raids, and the history of many a village was one of alternate destruction and replanting. Even the hardiest pioneer shrank from the prospect of carving a new home out of the forests on the outskirts of any colony; for the future was reasonably certain to bring disaster, and he and his family might think themselves fortunate if they escaped with their lives. But the forty years had seen a constantly increasing density of population, and with the Peace of Utrecht there came an outpouring of settlers bound for the frontier, where there was no danger of being crowded by one's neighbors.

The treaty of Utrecht began a period of comparative peace which lasted for more than a quarter of a century.[1] Indian raids had been common since King Philip's War; Ryswick had been an unsatisfactory settlement, a temporary expedient. Utrecht marked the end of active hostility, though the pioneers on the edge of the wilderness were sometimes threatened by the Indian

---

[1] The series of campaigns against the Indians of northern and eastern Maine known as Lovewell's War, covering the period 1722–25, affected settlement chiefly in Maine, and consequently is not taken up in detail in this study. See Williamson, *Maine*, ii, 111–151.

bands which roved through the nearby forests. By the terms of the treaty England had come into possession of Nova Scotia, while to the northwest the Iroquois had been acknowledged to be tributary to the British nation. The period of peace following the war of 1713 was of immense importance to the colonists; it made possible the expansion of trade, commerce, and settlement; it gave opportunity for the quiet development of colonial institutions; it saw the foundations laid upon which New England, together with the rest of the colonies, built a social, political, and economic fabric which was to withstand the assaults of a later time; and it furnished the materials for the making of a new nation on this side of the Atlantic. Settlements were planted to the west and north, and were sufficiently peopled, so that when King George's War again let loose bands of Indians upon the frontier the struggle was but an episode, a time of apprenticeship for the greater conflict to follow.

After the treaty of Utrecht, then, the expansion of colonial settlements was resumed. A lesson had been learned from the years of warfare just preceding the peace, years in which isolated villages had been destroyed time and again; and the Massachusetts grants of the next few years contain provisions for larger groups of settlers on a new tract than had hitherto been the case. The conditions in Worcester County are typical of others. In the case of Rutland [1] the purchase made from

[1] The grant was made in 1715. Families were gathered from Boston, Concord, Lexington, Sudbury, Marlborough, Framingham, Lancaster, and Brookfield, with a few from Ireland. See C. R. Bartlett, "Rutland," in *History of Worcester County*, ii, 1287-1288.

the Indians in 1686 was confirmed by the General Court in 1713, on condition that within seven years sixty families should be planted there ; the condition was fulfilled, and the town was incorporated. In the Leicester grant the number of families was to be fifty, with the provision that a portion of the tract allotted be reserved for a church and a school ; otherwise the conditions were like those of Rutland; but the progress of Leicester was very slow, because of the isolation of the settlers. Even so large a number as fifty seemed defenseless when no neighbors could be called in at a crisis. Lunenburg was filled up by Scotch-Irish families, who moved in beside settlers from other New England towns.[1] Sturbridge is another Worcester County town. In 1714 a few grants of land were made here; a little later a committee was appointed to lay out the town; and in 1729 the grant was made on the terms which had become usual, — a certain number of families had to be established within a definite time. At least twelve of the grantees became settlers : many others sent their children and grandchildren. Since nearly all the proprietors and settlers were from Medfield, the town was called New Medfield until its incorporation.[2] Almost the whole of Worcester County was taken up by home-seekers ; the greater part of it had been passed by previously because of its exposed situation, and because its uneven surface was less attractive to home-seekers than the more level lands of the Con-

---

[1] E. S. Stearns, "Lunenburg," in *Hist. of Worcester County*, i, 761, 762 ; Barber, *Hist. Coll. of Mass.*, 582. Other Scotch-Irish, who came at this time, settled Palmer, Coleraine, Hopkinton, Blandford, and Pelham.
[2] L. B. Chase, "Sturbridge," in *ibid.*, i, 105–107.

necticut valley. The intervale lands to the west being well filled, newcomers stopped midway and took up the less desirable Worcester County lands.

Nor was the pressure for new lands confined to the seaboard. The soil along both sides of the Connecticut was all occupied, and yet lands lay vacant to the west, between the older towns and the Hudson River. In 1722 Joseph Parson and one hundred and seventy-six other persons of Hampshire County in Massachusetts petitioned the General Court for two townships on the Housatonic River. Into one of these, Sheffield, in accordance with the provisions laid down by the General Court, settlers poured to the number of sixty families, mostly from Westfield, in the seven years preceding the first town-meeting in 1733. South Hadley and Granby were settled from Hadley. Amherst had among its pioneers families from Hadley, Hatfield, Deerfield, and Northampton, many of whom seem to have been young, unmarried men. Poor soil had prevented the settlement of Ware, but between 1729, when the first family moved in from Brookfield and "squatted" there, and 1742, when the settlers petitioned for incorporation, thirty-three families had established themselves on the tract.[1]

Berkshire County, on the border between Massachusetts and New York, attracted pioneers from both directions, and in Egremont and Great Barrington, New Englanders and Dutch families mingled. The proprietors of

[1] Hyde, *Ware*, 12–14. To Wales went settlers from Salem, Palmer, and Grafton, in Massachusetts; from Windham, Tolland, Hampton, and Union, in Connecticut. The settlers organized a Baptist church of thirty members within six years of their arrival. See Holland, *West. Mass.*, ii, 140.

these western towns were usually Massachusetts men, but
most of the settlers came up from Connecticut, following the rich intervale lands of the Housatonic. The sev-
enty-two proprietors of New Marlborough were mainly
Marlborough (Massachusetts) men. They represent the
speculator element, for very few of them ever lived in
New Marlborough ; the settlers came from Canterbury
and Suffield, Connecticut, Northampton and Dedham in
Massachusetts.[1] Connecticut settlers founded Alford.
The proprietors of Sandisfield were Worcester County
men; the settlers were from the Connecticut towns of
Enfield and Wethersfield, and from Cape Cod towns.[2]
To Lenox went pioneers from West Hartford and Wallingford, Connecticut; while Otis settlers represented
Enfield, Granville, Suffield, Woodstock, and Hebron,
though the proprietors were from Tyringham (Massachusetts).[3] Williamstown was begun by Connecticut fa m-
ilies, mingling with others from Northampton and Hatfield ; [4] Wethersfield men founded Pittsfield.[5] One might
reasonably expect to find at the time of the Revolution
what is actually the case, — that western Massachusetts
supplied the most radical element in the new state. Not
only had the western part been settled last, and therefore was scarcely beyond the pioneering stage of its history, but its inhabitants were drawn largely from an-

[1] Barber, *Hist. Coll. of Mass.*, 83.

[2] Holland, *West. Mass.*, ii, 569–571.

[3] Holland, *ibid.*, ii, 540.

[4] Perry, *Origins of Williamstown*, 384–386 ; Holland, *West. Mass.*, ii,
609, 610.

[5] Holland, *ibid.*, i, 186 ; *ibid.*, ii, 548, 549; Barber, *Hist. Coll. of Mass.*,
87.

other colony (Connecticut), and therefore had no special reverence for the conservatism of the Massachusetts coast towns. Built up by men with sufficient initiative to move to the most exposed part of the colony, the border counties developed a most independent attitude towards England in the early part of the Revolution, and towards the conservative seaboard while the new state was forming.

A new feature entered into the movement for expansion at this time, and colored more or less the character of the whole period up to the beginning of the French and Indian War. For the first time speculation in lands became common. With the economic, social, and industrial changes incident to a century of growth and development, there had come not only the accumulation of wealth, but the necessity for its investment. The fishing and coasting trade occupied many persons ; ordinary mercantile pursuits provided occupations for more ; but the demand for lands which came with the Peace of Utrecht offered an outlet for the speculative tendencies of others, and many young men became proprietors, making a business of buying lands and selling them at a higher figure to actual settlers. Such speculations in land became an increasingly significant and important feature of the process of expansion. England was passing through a period of speculative craze which was to find its climax in the wild schemes of 1720, — such as the gigantic "bubbles" of John Law, and other less well-known "promoters" of the day. The colonies felt the wave which was sweeping over the mother country, although to a far less degree, since the number of en-

terprises to be affected was very small, and the new
country had neither capital nor capitalists enough for
the movement to be of any great importance.

The Massachusetts speculations are the most important, and are probably typical of less extensive ones in
the other colonies. The older and more prosperous
towns, like Boston and Salem, where there was not only
more experience in business life but also more capital
free for investment, showed a marked disposition to buy
wild lands in new towns, and whatever could be purchased of the commons in the old ones.[1] Mr. Jeremiah
Dummer, an English agent, apparently imbued with the
speculative mania then raging in England, tried to get
up a "bubble" in waste lands in 1720, "but had not
time for any great success."[2] The first extensive speculation came in 1727. The Massachusetts government
had been very prudent before that time in the granting
of territory, and lands had been distributed purely for
the sake of settlement. As a usual thing new grants had
adjoined old ones, making the towns reasonably compact, both as a defense against Indians, and in order
that advantages of church and schools might be common to all. Now plans were suddenly laid for large
grants of new lands along the border between Massachusetts and New Hampshire. Undoubtedly, Lieutenant-
Governor William Dummer, who was most instrumental
in getting the General Court to appoint committees and
make grants, had in mind strengthening the claim of
Massachusetts to the disputed lands of her northern

[1] Weeden, *Econ. and Soc. Hist. of New Eng.*, ii, 513.
[2] Hutchinson, *Hist. of Mass.*, ii, 221, n.

neighbor, as well as a plan which should aid in the
effort for relieving the pressure of an increasing population in the seaboard towns. Nine townships were
granted in 1727 to the heirs of the militia or soldiers
who had taken part in the Canadian expedition of 1690.
These tracts, each six miles square, ran from the Merrimac River across thirty-five miles of unoccupied land, to
the Connecticut River, in order to provide a barrier
against Indians. They formed a double line of varying
value for cultivation, some being rocky and mountainous, and hence slowly settled, while others containing
good land were quickly occupied.[1] In June, 1728, the
General Court of Massachusetts appointed a committee
(five in number) to lay out in some of the vacant lands
of the Maine district two tracts of land in townships six
miles square. These were granted to officers and soldiers
(or their heirs) who had fought in the Narragansett
War of 1675. The report of the committee having been
accepted, five other townships were laid out in 1732,
on condition that the one hundred and twenty grantees
of each township should assemble within two months
and arrange the preliminaries of settlement. Furthermore, sixty families must be settled in each township,
with an orthodox minister, within seven years. These
townships lay in a line from the Saco and Presump-
scot rivers in Maine, across into New Hampshire. The
grantees included men from about all the towns that

[1] Ashburnham (called Dorchester Canada, because most of the grantees
were Dorchester men) was settled in 1735–36 ; it was deserted from 1744
to 1750, and had a precarious existence till 1759. See E. S. Stearns,
"Ashburnham," in *Hist. of Worcester Co.*, i, 194.

were able to send soldiers in 1675 to the defense of the
colonies, and were grouped somewhat roughly by neighborhoods.[1] In 1736–38, twenty-eight townships (each
six miles square) were laid out between the Connecticut
and Merrimac rivers, in accordance with the surveys
which the General Assembly of Massachusetts had
caused to be made in response to the very numerous
petitions for land which had been laid before them.[2]
The speculators proved too grasping; because of the
great number of grants made, it was impossible to fulfill the conditions required by the General Court. Neither were there enough people in Massachusetts who
were willing to move into so unpopular a district, nor
could the grantees induce settlers to come from Eng-

---

[1] *Mass. Hist. Soc. Coll.*, 3d ser., ii, 274, 275. For instance, Narragansett
No. 7 (New Gorham, Maine) was granted to men of Barnstable, Yarmouth, Eastham, Sandwich, Plymouth, Tisbury, Abingdon, Duxbury, and
Scituate; nearly every Cape Cod town sent settlers to it ultimately. See
ibid., 279; and Pierce, *Gorham*, 36.

Buxton (Narragansett No. 1) was granted to inhabitants of Ipswich,
Newbury, Hampton, Berwick, and towns surrounding these. *Mass. Hist.
Soc. Coll.*, 3d ser., ii, 276.

[2] Hall's *Eastern Vermont*, 58. The terms of the grants made here are
interesting. Each settler had to give bonds in the sum of £40 as security
for performing the conditions imposed. Those who had not received grants
for the last seven years were given the preference, but in case not enough
of these applied, the next choice fell upon those who had fulfilled conditions elsewhere. On every lot there must be built a house eighteen by
eighteen feet, with at least seven feet stud; five acres had to be fenced
in and broken up for ploughing; and occupancy must take place within
three years. A meeting-house had to be built, and a minister settled. If
these conditions were not met, the land was forfeited. As usual, there
were sixty settlers' rights, one right for the first minister, and one for a
school; but the sixty-third right went to the second minister rather than
to the ministry, as was naturally the case. Each right was divided into a
houselot and an intervale lot.

land, though they evidently tried to do so.[1] Still the
growth of Massachusetts in those forty years is remarkable. In 1748 one hundred and forty towns had been
incorporated since the colony's founding, and of these
sixty-eight had received charters since 1692.[2] There was
little land left for new towns east of the Connecticut
River; about one third west of it had been taken up.
The pressure for new lands must very evidently lead to
emigration outside the boundaries of the colony, and
the frontier must be pushed out into the wilderness to
the north and west in order to furnish homes to those
who wished to establish themselves on farms of their
own, but were too poor to pay for higher-priced lands
lying about the older towns.

The acquisition of Maine by Massachusetts in 1677
had placed those lands at the disposal of the General
Court of the Bay Colony, and one would naturally look
for emigration into that territory. At the close of Queen
Anne's War more than one hundred miles of the Maine
coast lay unpeopled and desolate. When the old towns
were revived, it was thought advisable that for the safety
of the inhabitants no less than twenty or thirty families
should go at the same time and settle compactly near
the seaside on lots of three or four acres, with outlying
meadows about them. Upon these conditions the General Court authorized the resettlement of Saco, Falmouth,

---

[1] Hutchinson, *Hist. of Mass.*, ii, 299, 300. New Braintree shows how the
colony paid its debts for public services in land, — the commodity of which
at this time it had most. The tract was granted to certain persons of
Braintree for services rendered, and was long known as Braintree Farms.
See Barber, *Hist. Coll. of Mass.*, 588.

[2] Barry, *Mass.*, ii, 163. Also footnote on the same page.

and other towns.[1] Portland, Bath, and many other villages whose territory had lain waste for forty years were
now repeopled by the former inhabitants, or by their
children, who returned to lay claim to their former
homes. None grew rapidly : Bristol contained only a few
people in 1720; in that year Scarborough held its first
town-meeting; and Portland contained in 1726 but four
hundred people, the same population it had numbered
fifty-one years before; Cape Elizabeth had no church
for fifteen years after its revival. Between 1722 and
1725 the Indians of northern and eastern Maine and of
Nova Scotia, urged on by emissaries of the French government and by French sympathizers in the territory to
the east so recently acquired by the English, descended
again and again upon the reëstablished settlements.
Not until Captain John Lovewell (or Lovel) of Dunstable, Massachusetts, took the field with a small body
of volunteers did the Indians meet with any effectual
opposition. After Lovewell's death in the decisive fight
of the war, peace was concluded between representatives
of the Indians and the Massachusetts General Court,
ratified a little later by a larger body of Indians at Falmouth on the Maine coast. In spite of the treaty, it was
still evident that only dire necessity could induce men
to remove into the territory east of New Hampshire;
few towns were planted, and these grew but slowly, some
even being burned once before they were permanently
established. Of the Narragansett townships laid out by
Massachusetts, Gorham was settled in 1736, but the

---

[1] Williamson, *Maine*, ii, 80, 81. No one was allowed to undertake the
resettlement of a town without a license from the governor and council.

grantees of Buxton left their tract vacant until 1748, when King George's War was over. Topsham was planted by three families in 1718; it was destroyed four years later, and remained a waste for some time; in 1750 its inhabitants numbered eighteen families, — mostly Scotch-Irish, who have ever been Indian fighters and hence good stock for the frontier. New Gloucester, which took its pioneers and its name from the Massachusetts town, was able to show but nineteen frame houses after eight years of hardship; these were destroyed, and for twelve years the land lay desolate. Windham (called New Marblehead in its early days) had sixty proprietors who were Marblehead men, as were its first settlers; it had a long struggle before its growth was assured.[1] Maine had a severe struggle for existence for over a century after the first fishing-

---

[1] Williamson, *Maine*, ii, 365 ; also *ibid.*, 284. Warren and Thomaston were Scotch-Irish towns like Topsham ; Thomaston was begun by twenty-seven families who came together; they were later joined by a company of German immigrants. Compare Hanna, *Scotch-Irish in America*, ii, 25, with Williamson, ii, 238.

Waldoborough, settled in 1740, was depopulated during King George's War, but resettled immediately afterward. It had been at first a Scotch-Irish town ; in 1752–53 fifteen hundred Germans came in, but later removed to southwest Carolina because of threatening lawsuits regarding land-titles. See *Maine Hist. Soc. Coll.*, v, 403, 404 ; also Coolidge and Mansfield, 336.

Most of the towns laid out after 1733 had to have, as conditions of the grant, sixty actual settlers, each of whom must clear from five to eight acres for mowing and tillage, build a house at least eighteen feet square, with seven-foot posts. The families must together build a meeting-house within five or six years, settle a minister, and support him. Usually three lots were reserved for the ministry, schools, and the first minister ; later a fourth one for the "future disposition of government." See Williamson, *Maine*, ii, 180.

villages were planted on her shores in 1623. There was
not in 1720 a house between Berwick and Canada to the
north, nor between Georgetown and Annapolis Royal
in Nova Scotia, save a single fish-cabin on Damariscove
Island.[1] Even the invitation of Governor Dunbar, who
laid out three towns in his territory of Sagadahoc
and asked settlers to come, could only induce fifty or
sixty to make homes there. The Lieutenant-Governor
of Massachusetts stated that the two obstacles — and
he considered them "the principal and perhaps only
material" ones — which kept settlers away from Maine,
were the "exposed situation to the Indian enemy in
case of rupture," and the great disputes over titles, because of overlapping grants and consequent claims.[2]

The history of New Hampshire is quite different. In
1716 there were perhaps nine thousand persons in the
colony, settlements being confined almost entirely to a
radius of fifteen miles about the Piscataqua River. The
first large town planted was Londonderry, to which there
came, in 1719, fifty families, with ministers, from Londonderry, Ireland.[3] About the same year the inhabitants
of the older towns began to look out for new lands for
their children, and in 1721 a company of nearly one

[1] Williamson, *Maine*, ii, 77, n. ; also on 97 (from Commissioner's Report, 1811), testimony of P. Rogers, taken in 1773.

[2] Cited in Williamson, ii, 289. The speech was made June 12, 1753, to
the General Court. Pierce (*Hist. of Gorham*, 35) thinks the population of
Maine in 1736 could not have been more than seven thousand.

[3] Bedford was founded in 1737 from this same Londonderry, and was
the first of ten towns in New Hampshire planted by these Scotch-Irish
emigrants. Hanna, *Scotch-Irish in America*, ii, 18. Hanna says that Londonderry was also the mother of two Vermont towns and one in Pennsylvania.

hundred made up from Portsmouth, Exeter, and Haverhill, petitioned for a grant of land north of Londonderry.
Immediately, petitions were filed by persons from other
towns for lands contiguous to those asked for in the first
petition. The governor and council suspended the petitions while they had surveys made and four townships
laid out, and then gave permission for settlers to occupy
them. These grants, as well as those of Massachusetts
already mentioned (four of the so-called Narragansett
townships), were filled up more or less slowly, most of
the settlers coming from the nearby Massachusetts
towns. Thirty-six Haverhill men were among the list
of one hundred admitted settlers of Concord in 1725;
Billerica and Chelmsford families pushed up into Litchfield and Amherst, while others from Haverhill planted
Atkinson. Rochester, in a petition to the General Court
relative to settling a minister, gave sixty families as settlers in the seven years since the town was begun, but
reported that Indian troubles kept others away. Pembroke (Suncook), in a petition for a guard, recited how
peculiarly liable the people were to attacks from Indians,
since they were "eighteen or twenty miles from any
place":[1] Canterbury was threatened in the same way, as
were Bedford and Charlestown. Swanzey and Hillsborough were actually deserted for several years, as was New
Boston, upon which the proprietors had spent £2000 in
"promoting settlements and improvements," apparently
with little success.[2] The number of frontier towns in
1745 on the Connecticut River was six; on the Merrimac

---

[1] Hammond, *Town Papers*, xiii, 153, 154.
[2] See Cogswell, *New Boston*, 44.

River, the same number; and on the Piscataqua, three.[1]
The story of the New Hampshire frontier, then, was a
recital of hardship and often of danger, yet population
had perhaps doubled, and a map shows considerable expansion in the extent of settlement.[2]

The first pioneers in Vermont came during this
period, and five settlements were begun before 1754.
Fort Dummer had a few families in 1724; Vernon, then
a part of Hinsdale in New Hampshire, drew some settlers from Northampton and Northfield about 1744–45;
at both places there was a fort, under whose shadows
the first comers made shift to live. A few clearings had
been made at Westminster, but during King George's
War they were abandoned; when the settlement was
revived, fifty families came within a short time, mostly
from Northfield, and from Ashford and Middletown.[3]

The growth of Rhode Island consisted not in forming
new settlements, for all the land in the colony was already allotted to the various towns; but the population
was rapidly increasing in density. The figures are significant. From 7181 in 1708, the inhabitants increased
in number to 17,935 in 1730, and to 32,773 in 1748,

---

[1] Belknap, ii, 238, 239.

[2] Barstow, *New Hampshire*, 186. Barstow thinks it had doubled since
1731, and was in 1749 thirty thousand. This is evidently only a good guess.

[3] Thompson, *Hist. of Vermont*, pt. iii, 187 ; Coolidge and Mansfield, 939.
Dummerston had settlers from Worcester, Sturbridge, Petersham, Boston,
Rutland, Cambridge, and Deerfield, all in Massachusetts ; from Pomfret,
Connecticut ; and from Winchester in New Hampshire. All of these came
between 1754 and 1777. Rockingham was deserted during the French
and Indian War ; it had been begun in 1753. See D. L. Mansfield, in *Ver-
mont Hist. Gazetteer*, v, pt. ii, 70–73, 24, 33, 41, 58. Also Hall, *Eastern
Vermont*, 101.

an increase of over three hundred per cent in forty years.[1] Five counties had been erected by 1751, and old towns like Providence and Newport were divided to incorporate their outlying portions into new towns.[2] The final adjustment of the boundary between Massachusetts and Rhode Island had given to the latter the five towns lying below East Providence, — Bristol, Tiverton, Little Compton, Warren, and Cumberland, — thus increasing the colony's area quite materially, and adding about four thousand souls to its population.[3]

Connecticut settlers had been very active in moving up into western Massachusetts, following the Housatonic valley ; they were also going from all parts of the colony into their own undivided western lands. The population had been ready to swarm before the peace of Utrecht ; when the war was definitely ended, and the lands were clear for settlement, the movement to the west began. As in Massachusetts, the speculative element entered in, and grantees became proprietors, selling the lands the General Court had allotted to those who were willing to become actual settlers. Willington will illustrate the movement. A few families settled on the lands here

[1] The number for 1730 includes 985 Indians ; for 1748, 1257 Indians. How much of this was due to immigration it would of course be difficult to say. Besides this increase, settlers may have left to live in Narragansett townships, whose grantees included men from Rhode Island towns ; but it is probable that these grantees sold their shares, since no settlers are enumerated from that colony. See for figures, *R. I. Col. Rec.*, iv, 59 ; v, 270 ; Arnold, *Hist. of Rhode Island*, ii, 101.

[2] *R. I. Col. Rec.*, iv, 442, 443. Scituate, Gloucester, and Smithfield were set off from Providence. Middletown was incorporated from Newport. *Ibid.*, v, 66. Also Arnold, *Hist. of Rhode Island*, ii, 102.

[3] Greene, *Hist. of Rhode Island*, 168–169.

about 1715–20; in the latter year the tract (seven
by five miles) was sold by the colony for £510 to
Roger Wolcott of Windsor, John Burr of Fairfield,
John Riggs of Derby, two Milford men, and two from
Hartford, who evidently intended the purchase to be a
speculation. These proprietors secured " planters " from
various parts of New England, who moved to the land
one after another, in no organized company; but by
1728 there were twenty-eight ratable polls here, and a
minister was settled. Litchfield affords another typical
illustration. In 1718 sixty proprietors (chiefly from
Hartford, Windsor, and Lebanon) bought the tract
from the colony, and the next year settlement began.
A considerable number from Hartford and Windsor
went to the new town in 1721, with an organized company from Lebanon who took their minister with them.
There were sixty " rights " in the town,[1] three of them
for the church, the first minister, and the school. A few
years later, when the town was threatened by Indians,
thirty-two able-bodied men were sent by the council to
defend it. An order followed shortly that any person who
had left Litchfield and did not return within a month
of the close of the Assembly for that year must either
send a man for watch and ward, or forfeit his estate.[2]
Hartford and Windsor patentees received in 1729 a
grant of four towns in the northern part of the colony,
— Hartland, Winchester, Torrington, Barkhamstead,
Colebrook, New Hartford, and Harwinton. The last two

[1] *Conn. Col. Rec.*, vi, 126.

[2] *Conn. Col. Rec.*, vi, 126, 127, 471, 472, 500, 501. Also Barber, *Hist.
Coll. of Conn.*, 452–455. Sixty-one rights in the town were sold at auction.
Trumbull, *Connecticut*, ii, 89.

were settled shortly after from Hartford and Windsor ; Torrington a little later still (from Windsor), but Barkhamstead had but one settler till 1759.[1] Under an act of 1737 " for the ordering and directing the sale and settlement of all the townships in the Western lands," seven townships were laid out along the Housatonic, — five on the eastern side, and two on the western. These townships were then sold at auction in various towns of the colony ; bonds were required for double the purchase price, with one good surety. Six of the seven towns fulfilled the conditions upon which they had been granted, — that actual settlers be obtained who would build a house of required size within three years and live in it for three years afterward, and that the inhabitants collectively have within a specified time an organized church with a minister.[2]

Besides the settlement of these new towns, old communities were splitting up into new parishes, which in

---

[1] Trumbull, *Connecticut*, ii, 99–102, 104, 105, 111, 113.

[2] *Conn. Col. Rec.*, viii, 134–137. Salisbury and Norfolk were sold at Hartford, Goshen and Sharon at New Haven, Kent (including Warren) at Windham, Canaan at New London, and Cornwall at Fairfield. Goshen was settled by families not only from New Haven, but from Wallingford, Farmington, Litchfield, Durham, and Simsbury ; Kent, from Colchester, Fairfield, and Norwalk ; Sharon, from Colchester and Lebanon ; Cornwall, chiefly from Plainfield, but also from Litchfield, Colchester, Norwalk, Tolland, and Middlebury (Massachusetts). Barber, 463, 465, 467, 470, 481, 490.

Norfolk was forfeited because of non-fulfillment of the requirements, and was resold at Middletown in 1754, when but one shareholder claimed his grant on the ground of having had four families settled there before 1774. All of the settlers moved into these towns by way of the Housatonic or by way of New York. See Barber, 481. Also Trumbull, *Connecticut*, ii, 112. The proceeds of the sale of these townships went into Connecticut's school fund.

a few years came to be separate towns. In 1738 fourteen families, who lived in a distant part of the town of Woodbury, petitioned that they might have "winter privileges" for five months ; they complained of the distance which it was necessary for them to traverse on cold Sundays to get to the Woodbury church, and asked not only to be relieved from support of the old church for five months, but also to be allowed to have preaching of their own for that length of time. This petition was granted ; the next year saw a separate church, and though the district was not incorporated as the town of Bethlehem for many years, its separate existence was assured from the time it became a distinct parish. Washington, another outlying part of Woodbury, followed the example of Bethlehem, and became a separate society. The people of Canton (which had been settled by Simsbury families as part of that town and New Hartford) began to hold services of their own in 1741, but they did not withdraw definitely from the Simsbury church and have their own minister till six years later.[1] It was not until 1750, however, that a distinctly separate parish was made.

The population of Connecticut, estimated from replies to questions of the Board of Trade in England, were

[1] Phelps, *Simsbury*, 141. There are instances of the same sort in Massachusetts. Certain inhabitants of Brookfield, Palmer, and Brimfield, dissatisfied with the inconvenience they suffered because of their distance from churches and schools, petitioned the General Court that they be incorporated. Millbury was made a parish of Sutton in 1743, with a separate church, upon petition to the General Court. See W. T. Davis, "Warren," in *Hist. of Worcester Co.*, ii, 1185 ; J. C. Crane, "Millbury," in *ibid.*, 1092.

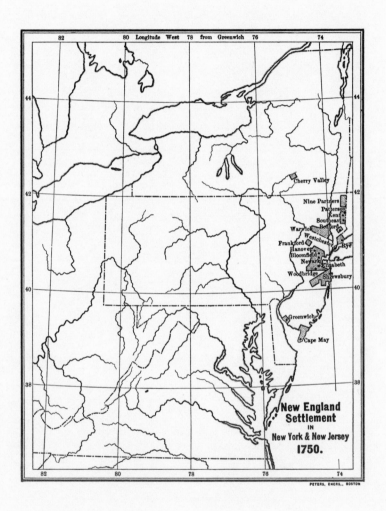

82   80   Longitude West   78   from Greenwich   76   74

44

Cherry Valley

42

Nine Partners
Patterson
Kent
Southeast
Bedford
Warwick
Westchester
Frankford   Rye
Hanover
Bloomfield
Newark   Elizabeth
Woodbridge   Shrewsbury

40

Greenwich

Cape May

38

**New England
Settlement**
IN
New York & New Jersey
1750.

82   80   78   76   74

given in 1730 as thirty-eight thousand; in 1749 the white population was reported to the same body as seventy thousand. By that time all of Connecticut had been laid off into towns and contained settlers, save three tracts on the Massachusetts border, west of the Connecticut River.

Long Island remained practically as it was in the preceding period; the only new settlement was made in 1730 at Sag Harbor, when a few cottages were erected for the convenience of the fisher-folk who had lived there temporarily. The older towns grew more populous, and the plantations, through the thrift of their inhabitants, became too limited for the increasing number of residents. A veritable swarming time came about 1740–50, when many families went to the eastern shore of New Jersey, a large number moving to Cape May County.[1] By far the largest emigration was to Westchester and to Dutchess County in New York, where in the Phillipse patent and the Nine Partners tract many former Long Islanders found new homes.[2] Putnam County on the Hudson was wild and unpopulated in 1740, when the first settlers came from Cape Cod and from Suffield in Connecticut.[3] In 1741 the first emigration to Delaware County, then far beyond the edge of settlement, took place, moving the frontier to a considerable distance

---

[1] See map opposite.

[2] Flint, *Early Long Island*, 337. New England families moved over into New York in this period also, but it is difficult to trace them.

[3] Blake, *Putnam County*, 288, 301, 322, 327, 328, 336. In the *Doane Family History*, 74, 75, one Elnathan Doane is given as an emigrant with his family from Eastham on Cape Cod to what is now Doanesburg in Putnam County, New York. He went about 1755.

west of the Hudson. The hardy Scotch-Irish who had
over twenty years before located homes in Londonderry,
New Hampshire, now furnished the pioneers to Cherry
Valley in Delaware County. In the latter part of the
decade 1740–50, settlers came from Connecticut,
Massachusetts, and Long Island to Orange County, giving a strong New England character especially to the
southern part.[1]

A movement farther afield has already been noted
in the Dorchester colony of South Carolina. In 1752,

when Georgia was
but a score of years
old, a committee
was sent from this
transplanted New
England town to
secure a new grant
in Oglethorpe's ter-
ritory. Two rea-
sons were alleged
for the project:
first, that there was not sufficient ungranted land in the
vicinity of the South Carolina settlement to provide new
homes for the sons and daughters just growing up:
and second, that the South Carolina site had never
been a healthy one. The required permission was
granted by the Georgia authorities, who allotted 22,400
acres to the newcomers. During the year 1752 it has
been estimated that over eight hundred men, women,
and children went to the new tract, called Medway.

[1] Eager, *Orange County*, 46, 47, 422. See map opposite p. 95.

Eventually almost all the colony moved to the new home, but in Colleton County of South Carolina there are still families of New England stock, as there doubtless are in other nearby towns.[1] The Medway settlement preserved its character as a Puritan community, even while it adapted itself to the necessities of Southern agriculture. At the time of the Revolution the sympathy of these transplanted New Englanders with their Massachusetts kinsfolk was so strong that they collected two hundred barrels of rice and £50 to send to the victims of the Boston Port Bill, renamed their district Liberty County, and made themselves obnoxious in other ways to Sir James Wright, their governor, who deplored "their strong tincture of . . . Oliverian principles."[2] Led by Dr. Lyman Hall, a native of Wallingford, Connecticut, who was numbered among the first emigrants to Medway, the Puritan colony in Liberty County did good service by inducing Georgia to ally herself with the patriot cause. It was this same Dr. Hall who signed the Declaration of Independence for Georgia, and who became governor of the new state in 1783.

The time had come when settlements had spread so far from the older towns that neither the natural highways which the rivers afforded, the Indian trails, nor the well-known roads like the old Connecticut path were

[1] McCrady, in his *South Carolina*, i, 326, 327, 707, 708, gives some history of this New England centre in the South. But apparently no one has made a detailed study of it.

[2] In a letter to the Earl of Dartmouth, dated April 24, 1775. It is cited in White's *Hist. Coll. of Georgia*, 523. The settlement was often called Midway.

sufficient for communication between the new towns and the older ones along the coast. The movement in all the colonies for public improvements like bridges and ferries indicates probably increased prosperity, since higher taxes were of course the outgrowth of legislation on the subject. But while money was expended upon bridges and ferries, the unscientific and uneconomic process of " working out " road taxes continued to be the usual method till much later, and is even at the present time approved in many rural districts throughout almost the entire country. Much of the so-called road-making about 1750 was merely cutting wider a long-used Indian trail. Rhode Island was especially active in building bridges, providing ferries, improving old roads and constructing new ones, so that all parts of the colony might be in communication with one another. A committee was chosen in Fitchburg, Massachusetts, in 1743, to " lay out and mark a way to the west line of the town, in order to answer the request . . . on behalf of Ipswich Canada [Winchendon], and to accommodate Dorchester Canada [Ashburnham] and the new towns above us." The road through Lunenburg and Fitchburg was a well-known thoroughfare; a part of it was the old " Crown Point Road," the famous Indian route from Canada to the Connecticut River and eastward.[1] Long a thoroughfare from the coast to Lake Champlain, the eastern end of it was now improved and made available for much traffic as far as Lunenburg. In New Hampshire a thirty-mile

[1] It ran from a point on Lake Champlain a few miles south of Brown Point through the woods to Otter Creek, up which it passed to the highlands, over these to West River, and down that stream and Black River to the Connecticut. See Hall, *Eastern Vermont*, 21.

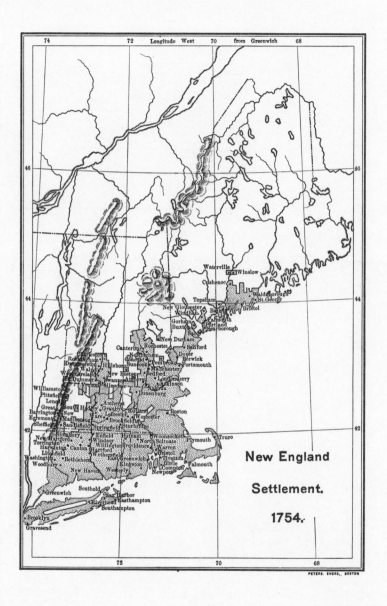

46   46

44   44

Waterville   Winslow

Cushenoc

Topsham   Waldoborough
         St. George
New Gloucester   Bath   Bristol
Windham
Gorham   Falmouth
Buxton   Portland
       Scarborough

New Durham
Canterbury   Rochester   Sanford
Charleston   Nottingham   Dover
Rochester   Chester   Berwick
Dunstable   Nottingham   Portsmouth
Walpole   Hillsboro   Suncook   Manchester
Westmoreland   New Boston   Bedford
Fort Dummer   Swanzey   Amherst   Londonderry
       Hinsdale   Atkinson
Williamstown   Lunenburg
Pittsfield
Lenox   Amherst
Great   South Hadley
Barrington   New   Granby   Rutland
Egremont   Marlborough   Leicester   Worcester   Boston
Sheffield   Sandisfield   Enfield   Brookfield
         Springfield   Sturbridge

42   New Hartford   Simsbury   Enfield   Woonsocket   Plymouth   Truro   42
Torrington   Canton   Windsor   Willington   Providence   North Scituate
Harwinton   Hartford   Putnam   Warren
Litchfield   Wethersfield   Bristol
Washington   Bethlehem   East   Greenwich   Tiverton
Woodbury   Kingston   Little   Falmouth
      New Haven   Weverly   Newport   Compton

Greenwich   Southold
       Sag Harbor
    Riverhead   Easthampton
Brooklyn   Southampton
Gravesend

New England

Settlement.

1754.

road was cut from Dover to Cocheco Falls. Such improvements were common in all the colonies except Maine, where the towns lay close to the shore or to rivers, so that the natural waterways furnished sufficient facilities for transportation and communication between the settlements. There was not in that district as yet sufficient indication of prosperity to warrant any increase of taxes or expenditures for public improvements.

Enough has been said of the progress of settlement to make it apparent that the years from 1713 to 1754 were characterized by conflicting tendencies: on the one hand was the pressure exerted by an increasingly dense population to thrust the less prosperous, the discontented, the ambitious, and the more adventurous elements out into the newer parts of the colonies.[1] The well-to-do classes, prosperous merchants, lawyers with lucrative practices, capitalists of all sorts, are always disinclined to move away from their homes; they are everywhere the conservative element in their community. They are also comparatively few; but their interests attach others to them, and only the more ambitious of their underworkers seek to establish themselves in business ventures of their own. Many will naturally move into the more recently planted towns; but there is always a more radical element which loves the unrestricted life of a pioneer community, and chafes under the restraints of a solidified economic and social condition. With this radical element there combines another made up commonly of young men (frequently unmarried) who have not the capital to buy a farm in the neighborhood in which they

[1] See map opposite.

were reared, but can gather together enough money to buy a tract in the wilderness. This they cultivate, to the new log cabins they bring their brides, and here they raise their families. Upon these elements was the pressure exerted which drove them out into the wilderness.

This pressure was, in the period under discussion, intensified by the development of a mania for speculation in wild lands. It has been shown how both Massachusetts and Connecticut felt this craze, and sold townships to grantees who never intended to occupy the lands so obtained, but meant to re-sell them and pocket the profits. Even in older communities, such as Boston, Hartford, and New Haven, there were not many enterprises which invited new capital, besides the stereotyped ones of lumbering, fishing, whaling, and trading occupations by sea, and the mercantile life in its various phases by land. Capital would undoubtedly have been attracted to manufacturing schemes had not the English Parliament suppressed any budding plan by repressive legislation. The manufacture of felt hats, of various commodities of iron, and of woolen cloth received attention at the hands of those British manufacturers who feared competition. The attitude of the mother country was by 1754 well known; — she would be invariably hostile to any movement which looked toward changing the character of the colonies from producers of raw materials and consumers of English manufactures.[1] Industry was thus kept comparatively little diversified,

[1] See G. L. Beer, *Commercial Policy of England toward the American Colonies*, in "Columbia University Studies in History and Political Science," vol. iii, no. 2.

and opportunities for the outlay of surplus capital were not numerous. In the unappropriated land of the colonies, however, lay an opportunity for investment upon which such men as Roger Wolcott had seized.[1] The time was as yet not ripe for success in these speculative enterprises; the grants made were too numerous, and the demand for settlers within the required three or seven years was too great to be met by the supply of those either here or abroad who were willing to go to a frontier threatened by hostile Indians. Yet these speculations added to the influences enumerated above, and exerted considerable pressure upon the families to move out into the unoccupied parts of the colonies.

The pressure outward was at the same time met by a counter-pressure which tended to keep back settlers. The Indians were still numerous and still hostile; the Peace of Utrecht was not, after all, to be a permanent assurance of safety. It was evident soon after 1713 that in the more remote settlements, though conditions were improved, life was still destined to be strenuous; that the farmer must plough with one hand and hold a gun in the other. As time went on, Maine, New Hampshire, and western Massachusetts towns were especially liable to attack from the northwest, for the Iroquois and their friends, held by only a slender leash, found forests no real barrier, and the Crown Point Road a convenient highway for occasional attack and retreat. Even Connecticut, a reasonably well-protected colony because of its compact settlement, had its trials

[1] See his purchase of Connecticut lands, page 92.

from Indians, who raided Litchfield in 1722. The
authorities of New France, who evidently carried out
instructions from Paris, had kept the Indians on the
alert ever since 1713; when the War of the Austrian
Succession brought France and England again face to
face in a struggle with colonial possessions for the
prize, the train had been laid ready for immediate
encounters. As before, the Indians were the foes most
dreaded, and these the French urged on. Maine, New
Hampshire, and Massachusetts all suffered; towns were
deserted, the families fleeing to the older settlements to
remain till peace was restored. The frontier line held in
the main, however; but it was not extended noticeably,
for it speedily became evident that the treaty of 1748
was but an armed truce, and that the conflict would be
renewed, and renewed speedily. Even the hardiest hes-
itated to plant a new home in the wilderness, when
massacre and fire threatened him at any moment, and
if he luckily escaped with his life, his labor was gone
for nothing in the pillage and desolation which were
sure to follow. Consequently, almost no new settlements were planted during the last ten years of the
period.

With fear of Indians was joined the difficulty of
getting clear titles to lands. Ignorance of the geography
of the country had resulted in overlapping grants of
various sorts, — in Maine to different individuals, in
the other colonies to indefinite boundaries set by the
charters; so that a grantee of a tract on the western
Connecticut border might go to his new possessions
only to find them occupied by a Dutch settler who held

his title from New York.[1] The settlement of Maine was retarded, also, because of these controversies over overlapping grants, and the consequent fear that all the toils and privations of beginning frontier homes would end at last in total loss. Life in the wilderness was not at all worth while unless one were sure that ultimately ownership with a clear transferable title would be the reward of years of labor.

Yet even a clear title did not make poor land attractive. Worcester County in Massachusetts had been passed over for nearly sixty years because of its uneven and intractable soil; pioneers left portions of it unoccupied while they moved on to take up the intervale lands in the Connecticut and the Housatonic valleys. It was only when the more fertile lands were wholly peopled that the later comers were willing to stop midway and cultivate farms where the land was more difficult to subdue. Ellington (in Connecticut), a well-wooded and timbered plain, was passed by for some seventy-five years, emigrants preferring the mountainous lands under the impression that they were more fertile.[2] Moreover, the lands contigouus to the rivers

---

[1] Such was the case of New Fairfield, the settlement of which was delayed about twenty years by the dispute between the two colonies over the boundary line. See Barber, *Hist. Coll. of Conn.*, 387. In Tolland the settlers had a long law suit with the heirs of the Indian sachem of whom they had purchased their land. *Ibid.*, 540.

[2] Stiles, *Ancient Windsor*, 263. Also Barber, *Hist. Coll. of Conn.*, 547. Ware, Massachusetts, had a similar history. The tract was granted to a military company from Narragansett, as a reward for driving out the Indians. The owners placed so little value upon it that they sold it soon after to John Reed of Boston for "two coppers" an acre. See Barber, *Hist. Coll. of Mass.*, 343.

were chosen because of the transportation facilities they offered, — a consideration of importance in a country where there are no roads.

The settlers in the wild lands were becoming more and more differentiated from those of the older towns. On the frontier men mingled from Connecticut and Massachusetts, as has been shown, especially in the Berkshire County towns, where they met Dutch settlers from New York as well. In many cases it was probably a second move for the family, or a third, and certain families were growing to be " pioneering families," who inherited, as it were, a longing for the open, for the free life of an unorganized community ; or else, chafing among conservatives who resented change of any sort, and therefore seemed intolerant to a radical, desired to organize a community where people might do as they pleased. Wethersfield had had a great number of such splittings off from the old church. It was only natural that such characters should impress themselves upon a new community, and that the frontier should be more radical than the seaboard. That the traditions of church and school were not forgotten even in the midst of overwhelming vicissitudes is evident from instances on record in Maine, where the province helped to pay the salary of at least two ministers, and the people of Kittery received from the provincial treasury £400 to help them build a new meeting-house.[1] But the case was not always so hopeful, for the absence of churches and schools in some parts of Maine and New Hampshire had left its mark upon the people, and had been re-

[1] Williamson, *Maine*, ii, 158, 159.

corded with unfavorable comment as early as 1754. Some towns which had been rebuilt three times alleged their poverty as an excuse for neglecting to support the educational and religious institutions upon which their fathers had set such store.[1]

While this differentiation was taking place between the more populous seaboard and the sparsely settled interior, it became evident in one interesting instance that England still regarded the whole of New England as an inexperienced and radical frontier. With the development of industry and commerce, banking projects of a simple character had been furthered by individuals in the older colonies such as Massachusetts and Rhode Island, but had met with opposition from the newer communities, whose inhabitants were usually of the debtor class or in sympathy with it. The most notable banking scheme was launched in 1740 in Massachusetts, where a bank was proposed on land security. Scarcely was it organized, when the English Parliament ordered its dissolution by applying the "Bubble Act," which had had its origin in the disasters of 1720. Thus did the English government express its disapproval of frontier finance.[2] But the floating of paper money, in the shape of bills of credit, was undisturbed, perhaps because the scarcity of specie in the colonies, even for paying direct taxes levied that Indian wars might

---

[1] Belknap, iii, 288–290, shows a sad state of affairs in New Hampshire, where poverty was made the excuse for persistent evasion of the school laws.

[2] The best account of this Land Bank is by A. M. Davis, *Currency and Banking in the Province of Massachusetts Bay*, in *Publications of Amer. Econ. Assn.*, 3d ser., ii, No. 2.

be carried on, made some form of credit an absolute necessity.

The close of the period 1713–54 shows France and England again face to face, waiting for some overt act to precipitate open warfare. The European questions at stake in the Seven Years' War do not concern this study. The issues in North America were those of expansion, of the future character of the frontier. It was to her American outposts, their inhabitants, and to pioneer methods of warfare that England looked to save the day in the last struggle with her ancient enemy.

BIBLIOGRAPHICAL NOTES

THE same general works mentioned for the previous chapters are again available here. Some other local histories have been called into requisition, as Rev. Samuel Orcutt's *History of Torrington, Connecticut* (Albany, 1878) ; Noah A. Phelps, *History of Simsbury, Granby, and Canton* (Hartford, 1845) ; William Hyde, *Address delivered at Ware, Massachusetts* (Brookfield, 1847) ; and Arthur Latham Perry, *Origins of Williamstown.* For Vermont, Coolidge and Mansfield duplicate Thompson's *Vermont* in many cases ; but B. H. Hall's *History of Eastern Vermont* (New York, 1858) contains much material not available elsewhere. Hiland Hall's *History of Vermont* (Albany, 1868) is a different work entirely. Charles A. Hanna, in *The Scotch-Irish* (2 vols., New York and London, 1902), is the authority for the Scotch-Irish settlements in New Hampshire and elsewhere.

There are several good county histories for New York which take up the period. Samuel W. Eager's *Outline History of Orange County* (Newburgh, 1846–47) ; Robert Bolton, Jr., *History of the County of Westchester* (2 vols., New York, 1848) ; William J. Blake, *History of Putnam County, New York* (New York, 1849) ; and a most interesting work of the capitalist Jay Gould in his early days, *The History of Delaware County* (Roxbury, 1856) — all these are excellent pieces of work.

For the Dorchester colony in its later history, see Rev. George White, *Historical Collections of Georgia* (3d edition, New York, 1855) ; C. C.

Jones, Jr., *History of Georgia* (2 vols., Boston, 1883) ; Rev. D. B. Hall, *The Halls of New England* (Albany, 1883) ; and T. P. Hall (compiler), *Genealogical Notes, relating to the families of Hon. Lyman Hall, of Georgia* [and others].

For economic conditions, reference has already been made to William A. Weeden's work. There are a few general works such as Professor E. L. Bogart's *Economic History of the United States*, Miss Katharine Coman's *Industrial History of the United States*, and Professor D. R. Dewey's *Financial History of the United States ;* but these take up the matter very briefly. Professor G. L. Beer has made the best study of the navigation acts in his *Commercial Policy of England towards the American Colonies* in *Columbia University Studies*, iii, No. 2. Professor Beer's newest books, — *British Colonial Policy, 1754–1765* (N. Y. 1907), and *Origins of the British Colonial System, 1578–1660* (N. Y. 1908), are also admirable. A. M. Davis has done the best work on currency and banking in Massachusetts Bay Colony.

CHAPTER V

THE FRONTIER IN WAR AND IN PEACE

1754–1781

As early as 1750 it was evident that the treaty of Aix-la-Chapelle was merely an armed truce, and that within a few years there must inevitably ensue a life-and-death struggle between England and France for the possession of New France, including the Ohio valley, and the unknown, unexplored regions stretching westward to the mountains and the Pacific. To the victors in this struggle the colonies would be the prize, and hence they were forced to take sides not merely to decide under what government they should continue, but in some cases actually to struggle for their very existence. The Indians were held by the slightest leash, and even tried and seasoned frontiersmen were unwilling to carve new homes out of the forest until the outcome of the struggle should be known.

In 1754, two years before the European contest began, the representatives of the British government, in the persons of General Braddock and the young frontiersman George Washington, began the struggle with the French and Indians at Fort DuQuesne. Between that year and 1760, when the hardest fighting was over, there was but little shifting of the frontier line. In western Massachusetts the depopulation of Williamstown and Becket was but temporary, but not a new town was planted within the borders of the colony till the actual warfare was over. In Connecticut conditions were similar : one man lived alone in Barkhamstead from 1749 to 1759 ; and the single family in Hartland moved back to civilization in 1754 after a year of pioneering, but returned the following year with three families from Lyme. From 1658 until 1762 not a new settlement was planted. No extension of the settled area in New Hampshire took place till 1758, nor in Maine till 1759. A family which had already tried pioneering in Charlestown, New Hampshire, who had come originally from Shirley, Massachusetts, moved to Putney, Vermont, in 1755, and found three families there before them.[1] Until 1761 no new settlers moved into any other part of Vermont.

With the fall of Quebec in 1758, the war in America was practically over, though the contests in Europe continued five years longer. The pent-up population was ready to swarm by 1760, and as soon as hostilities ceased, the unappropriated lands were taken up. A few Massachusetts towns will serve to illustrate the movement. Lee[2] drew its pioneers of 1760 from Tolland and New Haven, Connecticut ; from Barnstable, Sandwich, Falmouth, and Great Barrington, in Massachusetts. Huntington, whose first settlers called their new home Norwich from the Connecticut town they had left, sent back twenty years after for a minister from the old home.[3] To

[1] Rev. Amos Foster, " Putney," in *Vermont Hist. Gaz.*, v, pt. ii, 219. The families after 1761 came from Canterbury, Connecticut, and from Rehoboth, Massachusetts. A little later others came from Athol, Manchester, and Oxford, Massachusetts. *Ibid.*, 220, 240, 243, 244.

[2] Barber, *Hist. Coll. of Mass.*, 77. In 1770 thirteen families were here. Amory Gale, *Lee*, 4.   [3] J. H. Bisbee, *Huntington*, 7, 26, 27.

Chesterfield there moved sixty families between 1760 and 1765, twenty-one of whom came from Scituate, the others from seven Massachusetts towns.[1] New Ashford had pioneer families from Rhode Island and Connecticut, as had Hancock, Hinsdale, and Cheshire.[2] Richmond contained settlers from Long Island and Connecticut, Clarksburg drew its inhabitants from Long Island and Rhode Island, while Williamsburg's pioneers were from Martha's Vineyard and central Massachusetts. Thus the population of the most recently settled towns was made up of diverse elements which were seeking new homes in any New England territory as yet unoccupied. Besides granting lands in the usual way, upon the request of would-be proprietors, the colonial government of Massachusetts took the initiative on June 2, 1762, by offering for sale at public auction nine townships lying near the western border of the colony. The township of Adams brought into the colonial treasury £3200, Windsor £1430, Peru £1460.[3] The three proprietors of Adams laid out forty-eight settling lots of one hundred acres each, to which they later added twenty lots of the same size, and admitted settlers to the number of sixty, on condition that they build a meeting-house and settle a minister according to the requirements of the General Court. In

[1] Holland, *West. Mass.*, ii, 183. The towns were Cohasset, Dudley, Sutton, Charlton, Pembroke, Pelham, and Northampton.

[2] Barber, 83, 73, 75. The first settler of Hancock came with his seven sons, who all settled about him. All four of these towns are strongly Baptist, as were their Rhode Island pioneers.

[3] Adams was seven by five miles, as was Windsor; Peru was six by four and one half. This makes Adams bring about seventy cents an acre, Windsor about thirty-three cents, and Peru about thirty-seven cents.

1768 the rest of the land was divided into tracts containing two hundred acres each.[1] Windsor, another of these auction townships, was settled by Connecticut and Hadley families; Peru drew its first family from New Jersey, later ones from Connecticut and eastern Massachusetts.[2]

Connecticut settlers had, as has been shown, gone in considerable numbers to western Massachusetts. They also filled up what little unoccupied land was left in their own colony. Barkhamstead, whose settlers came from Enfield, Suffield, Simsbury, Hamden, Hartford, and East Haddam;[3] Hartland, which was a younger Lyme;[4] Colebrook, whose pioneers were Windsor and East Windsor people — these, with Winchester, provided homes for a few. The whole of the colony was thus laid out in townships, and the history of settlement within the borders of Connecticut was ended, as was that of Rhode Island and Massachusetts. But yet there were many families in all these colonies restless and unsatisfied. For such adventurous spirits lay the vacant lands beyond the frontier line of northern New England. During the French and Indian War soldiers had passed continually through the territory along both sides of the Connecticut River, and when peace was restored, they were eager to possess the fertile tracts which they had coveted on their marches. Governor Wentworth of New Hampshire and his council ordered that a survey be made, and that townships six miles square be laid out. During 1761 sixty townships

[1] Barber, 61, 62. The first settlers were mostly from Litchfield, Woodbury, and Wallingford, Connecticut ; they very soon sold to Quakers from Rhode Island, and the population changed in character entirely.

[2] Holland, *Western Mass.*, ii, 615, 616, 543, 544.

[3] Barber, *Hist. Coll. of Conn.*, 460.   [4] Trumbull, *Connecticut*, ii, 112.

were granted on the west side, and eighteen on the east
side of the river, in each of which there were reserved
lots for "public purposes," and five hundred acres for
the governor, the reservation being free of all fees and
charges. Altogether one hundred and thirty-eight grants
were made, and the proprietors sought settlers in all the
colonies.[1] Rhode Islanders were going to western Massachusetts and Pennsylvania, others moved to New Hampshire, where a new Richmond perpetuated the memory
of the old one of 1669. Marlow was granted in 1761 to
seventy men, mostly of Lyme, Connecticut, who brought
twenty-eight families here in ten years. Lebanon is a child
of Lebanon and Mansfield, Connecticut; Claremont's
pioneers were from Hebron, Farmington, and other
Connecticut towns, Hebron also contributing families to
Gilsum. Plainfield is but Plainfield, Connecticut, transplanted, Lyme but an offshoot of the older Lyme. Families from East Haddam founded Campton, others from
Hebron and Lebanon began Orford. From North Killingworth six men went in 1765 to Newport and spent the
winter; the next year their wives and children followed,
and the permanence of the town was assured. The number of Connecticut settlers who began New Hampshire
towns was not small, and examples might be multiplied.

Massachusetts also did her part in founding New
Hampshire towns. To Lancaster, Plymouth, Weare, Corn-
ish, Croydon, Stoddard, Bradford — to these and other

---

[1] Belknap, *Hist. of New Hampshire*, ii, 312, 313.

[2] Edmund Wheeler, *Croydon Celebration*, 73–157. Most of the first
settlers came from Plymouth County or from Sutton. Later ones were
from Royalston, Boston, Worcester, Brimfield, and Hingham.

towns moved many Massachusetts families. To some of the new towns went also families from eastern New Hampshire,[1] so that four colonies mingled on the northern frontier. The growth of New Hampshire was remarkable: one hundred towns were planted in fifteen years following 1760, all of them by families from Connecticut, Massachusetts, Rhode Island, or the older New Hampshire towns.

Nor do these one hundred towns represent all the northern emigration, for Maine claimed a share. During the early part of the French and Indian War, towns along the frontier were harassed by the savages, and until the fall of Quebec the whole eastern section remained a wilderness. Tentative beginnings had been made in several towns in 1760, while in 1761 twelve townships were granted east of the Penobscot River. To these there moved, within the next few years, settlers from Haverhill, Andover, Concord (New Hampshire), and the western towns of Maine, such as York and Georgetown.[2] Other towns were founded under proprietors, as Belfast, whose grantees were inhabitants of Londonderry, New Hampshire. They purchased of the heirs of General Waldo (founder of Waldoborough) 15,000 acres,

[1] To Wolfeborough from Portsmouth, New Durham, Suncook, and other towns. See B. F. Parker, *Wolfeborough*, 105–111, 114. Also to Middletown from Lee and Rochester. See *Mass. Hist. Soc. Coll.*, 2d. ser., iii, 121. The ratable polls in New Hampshire in 1753 were 6392 ; in 1767, 11,964 ; in 1773, 13,853. See Bouton, *Provincial Papers*, vii, 723. Belknap gives the whole population in 1767 as 52,700 ; in 1775, 82,200. See his *Hist. of New Hampshire*, iii, 234.

[2] Williamson, *Maine*, ii, 544. Coolidge and Mansfield, 151, 165, 310, 343. Land sold here, before 1784, for thirteen cents an acre; after that, for thirty cents. See letter quoted in Williamson, ii, 608, n.

which they divided into fifty-one rights and resold to Scotch-Irish families of Londonderry and the surrounding towns. A company laid out Augusta in 1761–62, and in five years had disposed of all rights but five to people from Boston and the surrounding towns. Indeed, Massachusetts supplied most of the settlers to the ninety-four Maine towns which were founded between 1759 and 1776. A few villages will illustrate all. To Vassalborough went Cape Cod families, ten in the eight years after 1760; five families from Beverly and Andover moved to Bluehill, 1762–65; five Haverhill families began Bucksport; Concord (Massachusetts) families settled four towns, Bloomfield, Canaan, Norridgewock, Baldwin; while Cape Cod had three to her credit, — Hampden, Manchester, and China, — though some families came also from Nantucket. Plymouth County sent emigrants to Hebron. Several families often banded together to go to the wilderness, as the four families who moved from Rowley to Waterford. The usual conditions — that thirty families be settled within six years — were not often fulfilled; but the emigration was certainly a large one. In 1772 there were forty-two towns in the Penobscot district alone, and 2638 families.[1]

[1] Williamson, *Maine*, ii, 373, gives a census report of 1764 which he says is neither very thorough nor very correct. He gives the following figures : —

	White Persons.
York County	11,145
Cumberland County	8,195
Lincoln County	4,247
Total	23,587
	332 negroes.
	23,919

Still other new lands were awaiting inhabitants. To the people of eastern Massachusetts, Maine had been most accessible ; to those in the central part, New Hampshire had offered an alluring prospect; but to the people of the western counties of the Bay colony, Vermont lands were too easily reached to be passed by for tracts to the eastward. Up to 1761 the danger of fire and tomahawk was too great to be risked; with that fear set at rest, there was no restraint upon those who wanted new homes. Even the conflicting claims to the territory which were set up by New York and New Hampshire could not stem the tide that surged northward, though usually the frontiersman was wary about building upon the chance of being dispossessed in a few years. New Hampshire had made large grants on the Vermont side of the Connecticut, and the patentees had gone into all parts of the other colonies to get settlers for the new lands. Seventy-four new towns were planted in the fifteen years just preceding 1776, to whose origin every colony in New England, save Maine, which had enough vacant land within easy reach, contributed many families. Rhode Island was represented in Marlborough, Bennington, Shaftsbury, Danby, Londonderry, and probably others ; Smithfield was the town which sent the most families. Weathersfield in Vermont suggests by its name Connecticut origin ; [1] many of the proprietors were New Haven men. Norwich was a town which attracted Preston and Mansfield settlers, while Middletown, Suffield, and Strafford emigrants settled in Marlborough with many from western Massachusetts towns, and some

[1] Thompson, *Hist. of Vermont*, pt. iii, 184. The spelling differs, however.

Smithfield (Rhode Island) families. Arlington was the home which Connecticut Episcopalians chose; eleven families from Newtown arrived in 1764, — almost a whole congregation, as was the group of families which joined them from New Milford. Nor did the families come singly. Hartford's pioneers were from Lebanon, Connecticut; in two years it had more than twelve families established. Eight families moved from Salisbury to Tinmouth. Vergennes, Thetford, Rupert, Strafford, Pittsford — dozens of towns had Connecticut representatives, side by side with families from most western Massachusetts towns, and sometimes from Dutchess County and Nine Partners, New York.[1] From the very names of most towns one may often see their origin, — as in Pomfret, Wallingford, Salisbury, Newbury, and Londonderry.

Bennington will serve as a type of the old methods of planting towns, combined with new features. There was an organized emigration to Bennington from Hardwick, Massachusetts, in 1761. Captain Samuel Robinson, a Hardwick resident, was returning from the French and Indian War when he lost his way, and in endeavoring to get home through the wilderness, passed through the country about Bennington. He found the land so attractive that he determined to make for himself a new home, and gathering a company of twenty-two people, set off for Vermont. By winter some thirty families from

[1] Dutchess County and Nine Partners had had accessions from New Jersey, as has been shown; New Jersey had been settled from Long Island, and Connecticut and Long Island from Connecticut. The pioneering spirit had evidently not been diminished in the moving. See A. M. Caverly, *Pittsford*, 26–52.

Massachusetts towns, and a few others from Connecticut, had arrived. The Hardwick emigration was distinctly a religious movement; the people had gone " to gain greater freedom in ecclesiastical affairs." [1] A church was organized in 1762 with fifty-seven members. For many of the settlers it was a second or a third remove: one man had gone from Cambridge to Hardwick, thence to Bennington; another had begun life in Concord, but had lived in Hardwick and Amherst; another had moved from Guilford to Roxbury, thence to Bennington; a fourth came directly from Charlemont, Massachusetts, but had been born in Norwich, Connecticut. There was a family from Newark, New Jersey, one from Portsmouth, England, and one from Troy, New York, mingled with those from the New England colonies.[2]

A few figures are significant. In 1771 the population of Cumberland and Gloucester counties was 4669, — 3947 in the former and 722 in the latter; the population of the whole of Vermont was about 7000,[3] and this number had been very considerably augmented by 1776.

The course which expansion had taken after 1763

[1] L. R. Paige, *Hardwick*, 56, n.

[2] Jennings, *Memorials of a Century*, 20–22, 33, 205–317. One of the settlers from Hardwick, Massachusetts, on his way to Bennington in 1761, passed through Charlemont, Massachusetts, as a tavern-bill is preserved by the family showing his expense at that place. *Ibid.*, 23. Hardwick parted with another company in 1775, who went under the leadership of Asa Whitcomb to plant Barnard, Vermont ; this was not, however, a distinctly religious movement. L. R. Paige, *Hardwick*, 55, 56.

[3] Thompson, pt. ii, 30. R. S. Taft (in *Vermont Hist. Gaz.*, i, 492) thinks that what contributed largely to the rapid settlement of Chittenden County just before the Revolution was the fact that there a clear title could be obtained, whereas in the southern part, the conflicting claims of New York and New Hampshire interfered greatly with any possibility of

was directed somewhat by the terms of the English proclamation of that year. France had at last been driven from the New World, and by the Peace of Paris England had come into undisputed possession of all the land from Hudson's Bay to the Gulf of Mexico. The government of these tracts was provided for[1] by a proclamation erecting the territories of Quebec, East Florida, West Florida, and Grenada, leaving the whole interior of the country bounded by the Great Lakes and Florida, the Appalachian Mountains and the Mississippi River, to the Indians and the fur-trade, with specific injunctions that settlement should be kept out. Thus the area open to settlement was very definitely restricted. Northern New England had been filling rapidly since 1760, and the three southern colonies were entirely divided off into townships.[2] But there was still land east of the limit laid down by the property line of 1764, and by the boundaries defined at Fort Stanwix in 1768. Towards one of these tracts much of Connecticut's surplus population turned. The territory of the Delaware and Susquehanna Companies in northeastern Pennsylvania

getting a secure title. Settlers in Windham, Windham County, bought land in 1773 for three or four English shillings an acre ; this was in the disputed tracts. See Mrs. L. B. Wood, " Windham," in *Vermont Hist. Gaz.*, v, pt. iii, 5.

[1] The document is given in its entirety in Macdonald, *Select Charters*, 267–272.

[2] There is no room in this study for the investigation of the New England migrations to Canada following the French and Indian War. Fishermen from Cape Cod and Nantucket took advantage of the proclamation of the Governor of Nova Scotia in 1756, and as early as 1757 the movement to Cape Sable began. In 1761–62 a number of families founded Barrington. See *The Doane Family*, 75, 76.

was the great district to which hundreds of families now moved. The Delaware Company was a Connecticut organization which purchased lands of the Indians on the Delaware River, with the sanction of Connecticut, the claimant of the lands under her charter. They invited settlers to that tract, where the proprietors announced in October, 1760, that they had erected three townships, each extending ten miles along the Delaware and eight miles inland. They had also laid out a large town of eighty lots in the middle township, and had built thirty cabins, three loghouses, a grist-mill, and a sawmill. Twenty men were reported as being on their land, and one hundred families were expected in the spring. The lands were parceled out in two-hundred-acre lots, twelve of which were to be cleared and improved and a house built on each within three years, on pain of forfeiture.[1] Two years later there were sixteen families settled on the river, their farms spreading over seven miles. Forty men were in the settlement, living in loghouses, and claiming their lands under title from Connecticut.[2]

The Susquehanna Company, also a Connecticut association, was formed by eight hundred and fifty Connecticut men who in 1755 bought the lands claimed by the Six Nations in northern Pennsylvania, in accordance

[1] *Report of the Sheriff and Justices of Northampton County* (to the Governor of Pennsylvania), October 15, 1760. See *Pennsylvania Colonial Records*, viii, 565. Also Miner, *Hist. of Wyoming*, 70.

[2] Memorandum of John Williamson, *Pa. Archives*, iv, 83, 84. The names given are Thomas, Tracey, Jones, Kimball, Cash, Parks, Tyler, and Cummins, — all of them Connecticut or Massachusetts names. This was called the Cushetunck settlement, and is probably the later Cochecton in Wayne County.

with colonial practice. The tract was twenty miles in extent from north to south, and covered two degrees of longitude from a line just west of the Susquehanna River.[1] In 1762 the Company sent two hundred persons into the beautiful Wyoming Valley, whose intervale lands and luxuriant woods offered richest prospects for new homes.[2] The Company had made a regulation requiring that the emigrants should support a minister, and one went with the band in 1762. Many of these first settlers went back to Connecticut for the winter, returning in the spring of 1763 to the Wyoming Valley with their families.[3] In October the Indians fell upon the settlement; many were massacred, among them their minister, and the rest fell back to Connecticut. For six years the valley lay desolate; then a second company, taking with them a minister, was sent out. Feeling assured that this time the enterprise would be successful, the Company apportioned in each township three shares of land, each containing about three hundred acres, — one for schools, one for the erection of a church and parsonage, and one for the support of a pastor. When the forty persons who set out from Connecticut arrived, they found that Pennsylvania had determined to make good her claim to the Susquehanna Company's lands, and had also sent settlers into the territory. All the settlers stayed, however, and by April, 1769, there were

[1] *Conn. Col. Rec.*, x, 378. The assembly acquiesced in the proposed colony to be planted by the Susquehanna Company if His Majesty approved.

[2] Sherman Day, *Hist. Col. of Pa.*, 434.

[3] Stewart Pearce, *Annals of Luzerne County*, 277. This settlement was just below Wilkesbarre.

two hundred and seventy or eighty able-bodied men here. In September the Pennsylvanians drove out the Connecticut men, and forced them again to their old homes.[1] Not daunted by their expulsion from their lands, they returned in small squads in 1770, only to be again driven out in the fall. Two families seem to have settled in Plymouth, and were joined by others in 1771–72.[2] From that time on, settlers came in increasing numbers. Wilkesbarre (its name indicative of colonial sympathy with English parliamentary affairs) was a typical New England town. Surveyed in 1770, it had two hundred acres divided into eight squares of twenty-five acres each, these into six lots, each of which contained (after the streets were taken off) nearly four acres. A central square was laid off for the town buildings, mills and ferries were provided, and "with true pilgrim zeal, attention was immediately turned to the subject of a gospel ministry, and the establishment of schools." In 1772 the first town-meeting was held. It is evident that such a village is merely a transplanted Connecticut town, in settlers, traditions, and institutions. A tax of threepence in the pound was levied in 1773 for the support of a free school in each township of the tract, and the following year was appointed the first

[1] Miner, *Hist. of Wyoming*, 70, 104, 105, 107–113. The five townships settled at this time were Wilkesbarre, Hanover, Kingston, Plymouth, and Pittston. Obadiah Gore and his seven sons went from Norwich with the first company in 1769. Very few settlers brought their families.

[2] H. B. Wright, *Hist. Sketches of Plymouth*, 38, 361, 371, 373. There were about eighty men here in 1777 who were able to bear arms. *Ibid.*, 66. Plymouth, Pennsylvania, was named from Plymouth, Connecticut, which had been named for Plymouth, Massachusetts, from which its first settlers came. Pearce, *Annals of Luzerne County*, 215.

school committee, with power to erect schoolhouses and employ teachers.[1]

At a meeting in Hartford on June 2, 1773, the Susquehanna Company drew up a set of articles which was accepted by the settlers who went into Pennsylvania.[2] The preamble of the articles set forth that since the lands into which the Connecticut people were about to move were claimed by both Pennsylvania and Connecticut, and advices had not been received from Great Britain as to which had the real title, therefore no civil authority existed in said settlement, and all sorts of disorders were liable to arise. The first article professed allegiance to the king; the second bound the signers to obey the laws of Connecticut as faithfully as if they actually resided within the borders of that colony. By the third article the settlers in each town promised to choose immediately after their arrival three directors to take upon themselves the regulation of town affairs, subject to the general orders of the Susquehanna Company, and one person was to be chosen as constable, with the same powers that such an officer would have in Connecticut. These directors were to meet once a month or oftener for the transaction of business and to impose fines and punishments on offenders as might be needed. The directors of all the towns were ordered to meet once in three months for conference, and to act as a sort of court of appeal from the decisions of the

[1] Judea, Charleston, and Muncy, three towns planted on the west bank of the Susquehanna, were all broken up by the Pennsylvania government in 1775.

[2] Miner, *Hist of Wyoming*, 146–150.

directors of any one town; and there was to be no appeal from these directors in general conference to the Susquehanna Company save in land disputes. The directors at
this meeting were also to elect a sheriff for the whole settlement, to whom the inhabitants were to submit as to the
high sheriff in a Connecticut county. For serious crimes
the offender was to be banished and his goods confiscated
by the town wherein the offense was committed. The
tenth and eleventh articles provided for the election of
constables and directors by male settlers twenty-one
years of age and one proprietor in each town; for the
preparation by the directors of lists of ratable polls and
estates, and for general taxation according to such
schedules. Finally these twelve articles are declared
binding "until the colony of Connecticut shall annex
us to one of the counties of this colony, or make us a
distinct county, or we obtain from the said colony, or
from his Gracious Majesty, King George the Third,
whose true and loyal subjects we are, powers of government in some more permanent method." All settlers
were required to sign these articles as a warrant of
their acceptance of them. This agreement is most significant as an instance of the removal of institutions
hand in hand with the removal of the people who were
to live under them; and of the fact that the new colony
was regarded as but an extension of the older one, later
to be incorporated under its general government. This
incorporation was accomplished by an act of January,
1774, by which the General Assembly of Connecticut
erected all the territory within her charter limits, from
the Delaware River to a line fifteen miles west of the

Susquehanna, into a town, with all the powers of a corporate town in Connecticut. It was to be called Westmoreland, and be attached to Litchfield County. Two
justices of the peace were commissioned and directed
to call a town-meeting for the purpose of electing local
officers. The whole town, which was about seventy
miles square, was redivided into townships five or six
miles square, each of which was to make rules and by-
laws for itself by which its internal affairs should be
regulated. The Connecticut programme was carried out
exactly as it was planned: Westmoreland, which now
contained 1922 inhabitants, held its first town-meeting,
and subdivided the town into eight districts shortly
after.[1] That year seven other town-meetings were held,
and the organization was completed. Selectmen, a treasurer, constables, a surveyor of highways, fence viewers,
grand jurors, — all these and the rest of the officers of
a Connecticut town were elected; and in April four
deputies were chosen to go to the General Assembly at
Hartford, regardless of the distance and the intervening
colonies.[2] Westmoreland was in the minds of the Con-

[1] Miner, *Hist. of Wyoming*, 152–156. The eight sub-townships were
Wilkesbarre, Hanover, Plymouth, Kingston, Pittston, the North district
(containing Exeter and Providence), the Lackaway district (with three
settlements), and the East district (comprising Cushetunck, and all the
settlements on the Delaware).

[2] Miner, *Hist. of Wyoming*, 156–159. The names of some of the officers chosen are Connecticut ones, — Haskel, Tracey, Gaylord, Sills, Butler,
and Chapman. The names of the Westmoreland towns are interesting
to study : Exeter, Kingston, Providence, and Newport suggest Rhode
Island pioneers. Lebanon, Colchester, Plainfield, Lyme, Kent, Norwich,
Voluntown, and a dozen more Connecticut towns had sent settlers into
Westmoreland before 1773. See Pearce, *Annals of Luzerne County*, 184–
218 ; and Miner, *Hist. of Wyoming*, App., 12–61.

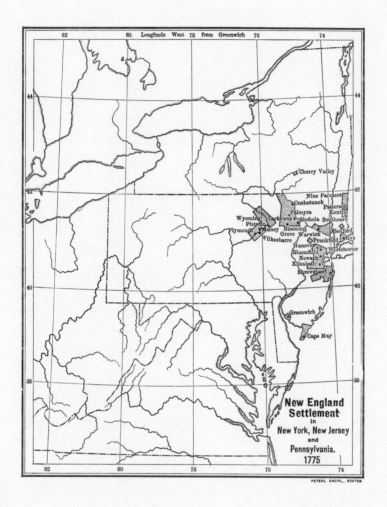

Longitude West from Greenwich

Cherry Valley

Nine Partners
Cushetunck
Palmyra Patterson
Kent
Wyoming ckway Shohola Southeast
Pittston Blooming
Plymouth Muncy Grove Warwick Bedford
Wilkesbarre Frankford Lo?re
Hanover Westchester
Bloomfield
Newark
Elizabeth
Shrewsbury

Greenwich

Cape May

New England
Settlement
in
New York, New Jersey
and
Pennsylvania.
1775

necticut people quite as much a part of the old colony as if it had lain on her border : it was but an extension of her lands to take it in.[1]

The Lackaway settlement deserves a word. Here came Connecticut settlers in 1774, to settle the townships of Lackaway and Bozrah. A fort was erected at once, with a blockhouse inside it; then a civil, military, and ecclesiastical form of government was chosen. A justice of the peace, who had a commission supposedly from Connecticut, was selected first; then a constable and a tithing-man. After four years the settlement was broken up, and the settlers fled either to Orange County, New York, to Connecticut, or to the Delaware. After the Revolution, however, the original settlers returned and again took up their old homes.[2]

An enterprise allied with the Susquehanna Company's project was that of the so-called Phineas Lyman colony. Phineas Lyman of Suffield, Connecticut, had been a member of the Susquehanna Company when in 1755

---

[1] See map opposite.

[2] Miner, *Hist. of Wyoming*, 466–475. Their descendants are said to have retained to this day the peculiar features of person and character which distinguished the first settlers. *Ibid.*, 476. Pennsylvania local history, except where the Germans are concerned, has had but slight attention. One cannot help feeling that if more work were done, the extent of the Connecticut settlement would be found to be much greater than this investigation shows. A glance at the map reveals a Canaan, a Lebanon, a Berlin, a Preston, a New Milford, a Warren, a Windham, a Litchfield, a Granville, a Shrewsbury, a Union, a Brookfield, a Farmington, a Westfield, — every one the name of a Connecticut town ; to say nothing of a Salem, a Smithfield, a Lenox, a Canton, — all of which immediately suggest either Rhode Island or Massachusetts. The coincidences are too numerous to be accidental ; yet data are lacking from which one can prove the New England origin of these towns and others.

that body had petitioned the General Assembly of Connecticut for a grant of land in northeastern Pennsylvania. Lyman had served in the French and Indian War, and about 1763 went to England to solicit recognition and reward for the services he with his fellow officers and soldiers had rendered. In the name of a company called the "Military Adventurers" he petitioned for a grant of land in Mississippi on the Yazoo River. It is not certain that he actually obtained a grant, but he evidently thought the promises made him were sufficiently encouraging to warrant him in returning to America and setting his colonization schemes on foot.[1] Rufus Putnam, surveyor for the new colony and later prominently connected with a great emigration to southern Ohio, in his account of the exploration made in 1773 by a committee acting for the company, says their report as to the character of the soil and climate was so favorable that in the fall of that year several hundred families from Connecticut and Massachusetts departed for Mississippi. During 1773–74 more than four hundred families made the journey, some going by sea, others by flatboats down the Ohio, and still others through Tennessee. Nearly every town up and down the Connecticut River furnished families for the enterprise, and the passenger lists given by Phelps in his memoir are in the nature of a directory of well-known Connecticut and Massachusetts names; — for instance,

---

[1] Justin Winsor (*Westward Movement*, 28, 42) says that General Lyman had a plan, which he laid before Lord Shelburne, for establishing colonies all along the Mississippi River from West Florida to St. Anthony's Falls.

New England
Settlement
in the South.
1781

Comstock, Sheldon, Wolcott, Weed, Crane, Bowen, Knapp, Phelps, Bradley, Case, Hotchkiss, and Ellsworth. Suffield, Windsor, Hartford, Springfield, Wethersfield, Middletown, Northampton, and many other towns were represented. The colony moved in the traditional manner, with a minister at their head. Between the time of their departure from New England and their arrival in the Gulf of Mexico, an order from the king in council was received by the governor of West Florida, in whose jurisdiction they intended to live, forbidding the grant of more land, either by family right or by purchase, until further orders. As a consequence, the emigrants were dismayed to find upon their arrival that they could occupy land only as " squatters," with every chance of being dispossessed later. They finally determined to carry out their project, and seventeen miles up the Big Black River, above the old French town of Natchez, the site for a town was selected.[1] Illness overtook many, among them General Lyman himself, and the outbreak of the Revolution put an end to further additions to the colony. There are, however, many families of New England origin in and about Natchez to-day.[2]

Still another emigration to the south belongs to the years just preceding the Revolution. About 1760 the settlement of Guilford County, North Carolina, was be-

[1] See map opposite.
[2] S. P. Hildreth, *Pioneer Settlers of Ohio*, 53, says : " In the year 1802, the survivors of that company [the Military Adventurers] about one hundred in number, reorganized themselves, and petitioned Congress for a confirmation of their old grant, but it does not appear that anything was done for them ; and thus ended this famous land adventure, which at the time caused a good deal of excitement in New England."

gun [1] in the southern and western parts by Quakers from
Pennsylvania and from Nantucket Island. The family
of William Starbuck left Nantucket in 1771; several
families, among them at least one named Coffin, settled
in New Garden in 1773, and Elihu Swain's family came
in 1776.[2] At that time there was no slavery in the western counties of North Carolina ; as the institution began
to spread inland, the Quakers, who hated it, moved
gradually to the west, — to Jefferson, Blount, Greene, and
Sevier counties, on the eastern border of Tennessee;
and later to Ohio and to Indiana.[3]

Such was the history of the frontier line up to the
time when the Revolutionary War called forth many an
able-bodied young man who in the time of peace would
have set off for the wilderness to make a clearing and
build a log-cabin. Ethan Allen of Vermont and his
" Green Mountain boys" formed but one of the many
bands of backwoodsmen who enlisted on the side of
the colonies in what was essentially a frontier struggle.
For England and the English Parliament were still of
the opinion that a conservative administration of the

[1] It then included the present counties of Randolph and Rockingham.
See Wheeler, *North Carolina*, ii (bound with i), 170.

[2] Some of the Quaker branch of the Doane family, originally from
Massachusetts, but at this time living in Pennsylvania, moved to Cane
Creek, Chatham County, North Carolina, in 1753. See *The Doane Fam-
ily*, 123, 124, 223, 224.

[3] The literature of this movement is to be found largely in the best
genealogies of the families concerned in it. See Levi Coffin, *Reminiscences*
(Cincinnati, 1876), in the Howe Collection, Indianapolis (Indiana) Public
Library. See, also, *The Doane Family*, and Tucker's *History of Randolph
County, Indiana*, where sketches of the early settlers are given. See map
on page 199.

whole kingdom (including such outlying portions as those in North America) could be best carried out from London by means of virtual representation. More than two centuries of local government by their own delegates had made the acceptance of such a policy impossible to the colonies; and when with this grievance were combined others of an undeniably frontier character, — economic as well as social, — the inevitable result was a resort to arms. As in the French and Indian wars of the preceding century, so again in the Revolution, it was the outlying districts which felt the hard fortunes of war. In Vermont the people of the village of Panton were either made prisoners, or had to return to their former homes in Cornwall or the Nine Partners tract on the Hudson River. Other towns — Whiting, Middlebury, Monkton, Brandon, and their neighbors in the north and west — were abandoned, or so threatened with misfortunes that no new settlers came in. On the other hand, settlement did not wholly cease even amid the uncertainties of war. Four new towns in Vermont were actually begun in 1776; five in 1777–78; and six in 1779.[1] A company was formed in 1778 at Hanover, New Hampshire, to purchase the township of Randolph, and secured settlers from Vermont, New Hampshire, Massachusetts, and Connecticut towns. Another com-

[1] Tunbridge was begun by New Hampshire men who did not bring their families for several months; Peacham had settlers from Haverhill, Hollis, and Concord, New Hampshire; Andover was a new home for Enfield emigrants; and Colchester harbored New London and Woodbury settlers, who departed between 1776 and 1783, but returned in the latter year and renewed the town. Three families moved from Hardwick to Somerset in 1777, and eighteen farms in Brookline were laid off between

pany, also from Hanover, in the same year petitioned for and received a grant of Bethel. Evidently there were able-bodied men who had managed to escape the horrors of warfare and who kept on in their ordinary walks of life, bettering their condition rather than suffering from the hard times. All the colonies suffered, however. Several Maine towns were abandoned, and many were retarded by the war. Belfast was a waste from 1779 till 1785; Brewer, from 1779 to 1784; Hampden, from 1779 to 1783. Yet here, as in Vermont, settlement went on, — three towns were planted in 1776, three in 1777, four in 1779. In New Hampshire four new towns were begun.

Upon the Wyoming Valley settlements in Pennsylvania fell the most terrible blow of all, — the massacre of 1778, laying waste the beautiful lands which had been settled in 1773, and which the labor of the pioneers had rendered even more productive than they were by nature. Those who escaped fled in every direction, — to New York State, to Connecticut, to southern Pennsylvania, — leaving only a few families in the whole Westmoreland tract. Slowly, in 1779–80, the survivors crept back to rebuild their houses and to retill the soil. Sullivan's campaign, which was undertaken as a punishment for the Indians, made his soldiers acquainted with the region, and after 1780 many who began homes here under the Connecticut title were joined

1777 and 1780, the first settler paying twenty cents an acre for his tract. Hollis Town in *Vermont Hist. Gaz.*, v, pt. ii, 530 (article on Somerset), says the first settler paid about $640 for 670 acres, but this may have been in depreciated currency. The statement quoted is C. P. Stickney's in "Brookline," *Vermont Hist. Gaz.*, v, pt. ii, 377.

by settlers from New York, some of whom were only
"squatters." The roads which were opened up hastened
the tide of incoming migration from New England, as
well as from Bedford, Luzerne, and other Pennsylvania
counties.

By 1780 the tide, which had only ebbed during the
preceding four years, flowed out again to the north as
well as to the west. Nine new Maine towns begun in
1780, two the next year, show the tendency. Only three
New Hampshire towns were planted in 1780–81; but
twelve Vermont villages in 1780, four in 1781,—these
mark the turning of the tide. The coming of peace merely
accelerated the flow which actual warfare had but temporarily and partially checked. A new era of prosperity seemed just dawning, and with the removal of such
restraints as the English acts of 1763 and 1774 had imposed, to say nothing of the overlapping titles of the in-
accurate colonial charters, there came a veritable rush of
pioneering to the north and (a still more important phase)
to the Far West. Beyond the Alleghanies such adventurers as Daniel Boone[1] had led the march before the
Revolution; now the more conservative New Englanders
followed in their wake.

A few phases of the aftermath of the Revolution are
an interesting study. With the hard life incident to frontier conditions, there had grown up in some parts of New
England a carelessness concerning some institutions

---

[1] Ex-president Theodore Roosevelt, in his studies of pioneering, *The
Winning of the West* (4 vols.), has taken up the pre-Revolutionary movement in a most interesting way. Justin Winsor, in *The Westward Movement*, covers somewhat the same ground.

which were traditionally very dear to the descendant of
the Puritans. New Hampshire, for example, had become
notoriously remiss concerning the enforcement of her
laws for education. The old laws had been those of
Massachusetts, and made the requirement that every
town of one hundred families support a grammar school.
When the towns were few, care was taken to fulfill the
requirement; but some towns stood out conspicuously as
being uniformly negligent in the matter of education.
In 1722 some frontier towns petitioned to be relieved
from supporting a grammar school during the war. During the Revolution, not only those, but many large and
prosperous towns, were for a long time without any schools
whatever, and the result is said to have been disastrous
alike to education and to moral standards.[1] In 1781
Phillips Exeter Academy was founded, very largely because of the woeful neglect of education in New Hampshire. Its effect was to stimulate education, and by its
success to induce the foundation of others, like those at
New Ipswich, Amherst, Atkinson, and Concord.[2] But a

[1] Belknap, *Hist. of New Hampshire*, iii, 289, 290.

[2] *Ibid.*, 290–293. Connecticut men also began to establish academies, not
because education was neglected, but rather to stimulate it, especially in
the matter of raising the standard of instruction. Hitherto, while public
schools had been encouraged, any attempt to open a school which would
not be under colonial inspection was decidedly frowned down. Toward the
end of its pre-Revolutionary history, however, private academies began to
spring up ; the academy at Lebanon, established in 1743 by Governor
Trumbull, was kept by a Harvard graduate, Nathaniel Tisdale, for more
than thirty years. Under an act of incorporation from the General Court,
twelve proprietors opened the "Union School of New London" in 1774,
to fit young men for college. Nathan Hale was its principal when the war
broke out, and from his schoolroom he went to give his life for the patriot
cause. See B. C. Steiner, *Hist. of Education in Connecticut*, 31, 32, 34.

sign which was even more hopeful for the future development of New Hampshire on the educational side was the founding of Dartmouth College. It was but fitting that in a colony where so great a number of the inhabitants were originally from Connecticut, Yale College should contribute a large share to the founding and the history of a new institution which was bound to be more or less like that at New Haven. The founder of Dartmouth, Rev. Eleazar Wheelock, was a Windham (Connecticut) boy, who was also a Yale graduate.[1] As early as 1763 Wheelock had besought General Phineas Lyman to include a tract for a college in the Natchez grant, but in 1770, after a varied history, the college was established at Hanover, New Hampshire, where fifty-five of the sixty-eight shares in the town had been assigned to settlers from Windham, Connecticut. In its early years Dartmouth College graduates were often Connecticut youths; in 1772 both graduates came from that colony; in 1773 five of the six in the class; in 1774, two in eight; in 1775, eight in eleven; in 1779, eleven in seventeen; in 1785, nine in nineteen. "In all, of the 284 graduates up to 1790, 121 came from Connecticut, and 22 from the town of Lebanon alone, where Wheelock had formerly preached." But the majority of the students were from New Hampshire, and into the history of that state the traditions and ideals of Dartmouth are woven.

The years just preceding the Revolution were fruitful ones in developing a spirit of liberty in all the colonies, but most radically upon the frontier, where

[1] Frederick Chase, *Hist. of Dartmouth College*, 1.

the settlers were unhampered by conventional views. Troubles arose in new towns of New Hampshire, Vermont, and Massachusetts between proprietors and settlers, the latter complaining that the former were absentees, and, not knowing local conditions, had refused to help pay for improvements such as roads and bridges. The inhabitants of Gilmanton in 1770 petitioned the General Court relative to a road, complaining that the proprietors had not aided in making it.[1] Those of New Chester asked leave to tax non-resident proprietors for the repairing of a road,[2] as did Hillsborough, Lyman, and Warren.[3] The grantees of Maidstone, Vermont, were all Connecticut men, not one of whom ever became an inhabitant of the town ; complaints were frequent, especially concerning the necessity of going to Connecticut or New York if a prospective settler wanted to buy land. Finally, the matter was adjusted by holding proprietary meetings by proxy in Maidstone after 1779, by the allotment of lands a few years later, and by the appointment of agents resident in Maidstone who were competent to transact business for the absentee landlords.[4]

The trouble at Westminster, Massachusetts, deserves notice at length.[5] Here some of the proprietors were also settlers, but the majority were non-resident, and refused either to make the improvements which the

---

[1] Hammond, *Town Papers*, xii, 3, 4.

[2] *Ibid.*, 200. The town is now called Hill.

[3] *Ibid.*, 206, 499 ; xiii, 625.

[4] *Vermont Hist. Gaz.*, i, 1026.

[5] W. S. Heywood, "Westminster," in *Hist. of Worcester Co.*, ii, 1148, 1149.

settlers demanded, or to induce outsiders to take up
homes on their land. For ten years the struggle was
waged, with the victories on the side of the non-residents, who held their meetings in Cambridge or nearby
towns, where the residents of Westminster could not
go, but where the non-residents were at home. Many
proposals which seemed to the settlers essential to their
comfort and prosperity were voted down at Cambridge;
and any attempt to hold meetings at Westminster was
as promptly checked. Finally, the last resort was
reached, and an appeal for redress was made to the
legislature by the resident proprietors. The petition
was granted, and meetings were ordered to be held in
the township after 1749. Thereafter the residents were
in the majority, as the non-residents could not go to
Westminster for the meetings. Most of the officers of
the proprietary organization were now elected from the
inhabitants of the town, and improvements were pushed
rapidly, especially the making of roads. From 130 in
1750, the population increased to 350 in 1760. But as
soon as the population had grown to that number, the
desire to be altogether free of non-resident proprietors
and to be a corporate town led to the drawing up of
a petition signed by thirty-two men, asking the General
Court for incorporation. The act was passed on October
20, 1759, and the strife between proprietors and settlers
was at an end.

A similar struggle, this time between a state and
a district which aspired to statehood, came between
New York and Vermont. Originally claimed by all
three of her neighbors, — New York, New Hampshire,

and Massachusetts, — the history of Vermont had been one of conflicting titles and an uncertain future. When, in July, 1777, it became necessa y to set up some form of government, Vermont aspired to independent statehood, and made her grievances known along with her determination to be free of her previous restrictions. Her declaration of independence (for so it may be called) is strongly suggestive of the national document of 1776, which was probably a powerful incentive to Vermont to assert her freedom.[1]

Maine, Vermont, New Hampshire, Pennsylvania, North Carolina, Mississippi, — all these states had afforded homes to emigrants from their neighbor states, and their growth in the thirty years ending in 1781 was little short of marvelous.[2] Although the history of settlement since 1754 had been one of alternate flow and ebb of the tide of population, the period had upon the whole been one of expansion. People, churches, town-meetings, schools, had traveled in company, giving to new towns a lasting resemblance to the old ones along the coast. Yet differences were becoming more and more apparent; Vermont owed much of its increase of population to New York, whose emigrants were unlike the Connecticut frontiersmen whose log cabins stood next to their own. Although the household from Nine Partners had in its family history the names of ancestors who had lived in Connecticut, Long Island, and New Jersey, and traditions of New England still sur-

[1] A good summary of this document is given by Professor Max Farrand in an article in the *Yale Review*, May, 1908, entitled "The West and the Principles of the Revolution."

[2] See map opposite.

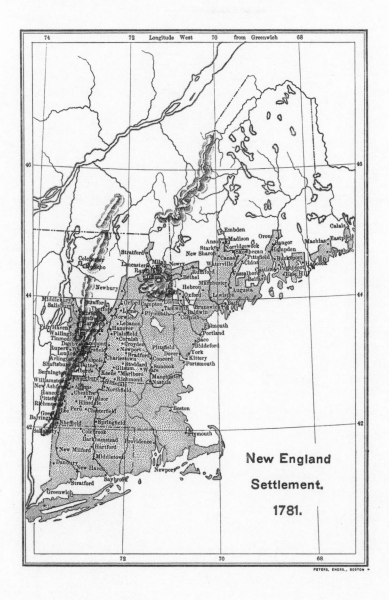

New England

Settlement.

1781.

vived many transplantings, nevertheless, the generations
of frontier life in four different colonies must have left
their impress and given the Vermont youth an outlook
not exactly like that of the lad from Connecticut who
had always lived under the shadow of the old colony
church and school. It was on this common ground that
the diverse elements could meet, — they could all work
together to form a new state upon the lines which
conservatism and radicalism combined should dic-
tate; and altogether they could move on again to join
other workers in the wilderness stretching out into the
west.

BIBLIOGRAPHICAL NOTES

THE sources of Vermont history have been enumerated for the most
part in preceding notes. A few local histories ought, however, to be enumerated especially : A. M. Caverly, *History of . . . Pittsford* (Rutland,
1872) ; H. S. Dana, *History of Woodstock* (Boston and New York, 1889);
Isaac Jennings, *Memorials of a Century* (the early history of Bennington);
Rev. Silas McKeen, *History of Bradford* (Montpelier, 1875); and Samuel
Swift, *History of . . . Middlebury* (Middlebury, 1859.)

The story of New England in Pennsylvania will be found in Sherman
Day's *Historical Collections . . . of Pennsylvania*, which is on the plan of
Barber's work for Massachusetts and Connecticut, but is not so good.
Charles Miner's *History of Wyoming* (Philadelphia, 1845), though not
well organized, is the standard for the territory it covers. W. H. Egle,
Illustrated History of the Commonwealth of Pennsylvania (Harrisburg,
1876), has good material on local history. *The Pennsylvania Archives*
(First Series, 12 vols., Philadelphia, 1852–1856) contains documents which
can be well supplemented from the *Connecticut Colonial Records* and from
the *Minutes of the Provincial Council of Pennsylvania* (cited usually as
Colonial Records), in 16 vols., with an index volume (Philadelphia and
Harrisburg, 1851–60). Stewart Pearce's *Annals of Luzerne County* and
H. B. Wright's *Historical Sketches of Plymouth, Luzerne County*, con-
tain material not found elsewhere. On the whole, the historians of Penn-

sylvania have been more interested in the story of Germans, Quakers, and Scotch-Irish than in that of the Puritans.

For the Lyman colony the following are the chief sources of information : *Pennsylvania Archives*, ii, 303, for Lyman's connection with the Susquehanna Company ; Dr. S. P. Hildreth, *Biographical and Historical Memoirs of the Early Pioneer Settlers of Ohio*, gives Rufus Putnam's graphic account of the colony ; Dr. Lyman Coleman, *Genealogy of the Lyman Family* (Albany, 1872) ; Timothy Dwight, *Travels in New England and New York* (4 vols., New Haven, 1821–22), in his first volume gives his account of Lyman's scheme ; and Anthony Haswell's edition of the *Memoirs and Adventures of Captain Matthew Phelps* (Bennington, Vermont, 1802) is by a member of the ill-fated expedition.

The somewhat meagre material on the emigration from Nantucket to North Carolina has been indicated in a footnote.

CHAPTER VI

THE BEGINNING OF THE GREAT MIGRATIONS FROM NEW ENGLAND TOWARD THE WEST
1781–1812

IT was evident by 1782 that the war between England and her American colonies was, to all practical intents, a victory for the latter, and that the time intervening between the defeat of Cornwallis and the making of a treaty of peace would be employed only in arranging details as to the final settlement of territorial claims. That the new nation just forming as the United States of America would extend to the Mississippi River was not a foregone conclusion, yet there seemed to be no reason why emigrants should be restrained any longer from settling on the lands just ceded to the general government as the price of a constitution. Expansion had not ceased during the struggle between the armies of the mother country and the colonies; new towns had been planted farther north each year, though settlements on the very edge of civilization had been temporarily depopulated; but the movement away from the more densely peopled states of Massachusetts, Connecticut, and Rhode Island was greatly accelerated by the cessation of hostilities and the enforced peace which drove the Indians back beyond the borders of cultivated land.

In all directions the stream of emigration from the settled portions of New England poured forth in 1782,

— to the north, the northeast, to the west, all at the same time, from the same sources, and for the same reasons. It was natural that the first expansion should follow rather closely the movement of the old, and one finds new towns first planted beyond the ones last settled, in the states just north of Massachusetts.[1] There was little unoccupied land in New Hampshire, and that little gave but small promise of future fertility; yet all the most rugged and mountainous tracts were settled slowly. Bethlehem, for example, was uninhabited in May, 1798, when the petition for a grant was signed; in November of the same year the request for the incorporation gave the number of settlers as forty.[2] Whitefield, in Coos County, though granted in 1774, was not settled for twenty-seven years, but was incorporated three years after it was settled.[3] Over Pittsburgh in the same county the British government exercised jurisdiction till the Webster-Ashburton treaty adjusted the boundary; fifty-five people settled here in 1810, each claiming two hundred acres of land, some of it consisting of rich intervales. Cambridge and Dummer, granted in 1773, were for fifty years quite unoccupied by reason of the poor soil, the former having in 1850 but thirty-five inhabitants. The population of the whole state was, in 1790, 141,885; in 1810, 234,460.[4]

In Maine the population increased from 96,540 in

[1] Florida was the only new town settled in Massachusetts; — Erving, Monroe, and Webster were but extensions of older ones. See Holland, *West. Mass.*, ii, 362, 393, 489. See map opposite.

[2] Hammond, *Town Papers*, xi, 190–192.

[3] *Ibid.*, xiii, 648.

[4] *Ninth Census Report*, i, 48.

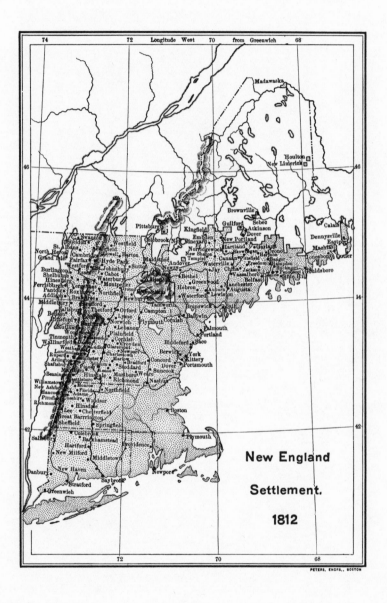

New England

Settlement.

1812

1790 to 151,719 in 1800, and to 228,705 in 1810.[1] Many of the pioneers in the new towns came from the oldest parts of Massachusetts, from Plymouth County and Cape Cod; but Andover and Denward perpetuated Andover in Massachusetts.[2] Dennysville is a Hingham town ; New Vineyard was peopled from Martha's Vineyard ; Kingfield from Weymouth and Kingston. Jay was given to sixty-four persons in payment for service in the French and Indian War.[3] New Hampshire families also contributed to Maine towns; [4] — New Portland, Hermon, Freedom, Temple, Garland, Dexter, Atkinson, Sebec, Hartland, and other towns were peopled directly from New Hampshire, and Exeter was named by its first settlers from their former home. Maine towns sent some of their own people as pioneers to plant new homes in Cutler, Auburn, Gouldsborough, Pittsfield, Jackson, Garland, Brooks, Greenwood, and many other villages. Where land was but twelve and one half cents an acre there was little need to go far from home in search of a new farm.[5] On the northern and eastern boundaries immigration turned from Canada south, to settle cheap

[1] *Ibid.*, 35.

[2] Nine tenths of the first settlers of Andover, Maine, were from Andover, Massachusetts. MS. letter of J. A. Poor, in Williamson, *Maine*, ii, 599, n.

[3] Coolidge and Mansfield, 164. It long bore the name of Phips's Canada, from Captain Phips, one of the grantees. When it was laid out in 1785, it was divided into 400-acre shares, of which one was reserved for Harvard College, one for the first minister, one for the ministry, and one for schools.

[4] The material on Maine is found almost entirely in Coolidge and Mansfield.

[5] This was the price of land in Palmyra in 1800. MS. letter of Samuel Lancy, Williamson, *Maine*, ii, 609 n.

lands, as at Madawaska Plantation, which was begun in 1784 by French Canadians.[1]

It was over the Wolfborough road, the "old Brookfield road," the Coos road, and by blazed trees that settlers found their way into central and northern Vermont. The Wolfborough post-road had been of use during the Revolution,[2] and doubtless had led the way for emigrants who heard from returning soldiers of the country it opened up before the troops. One would expect Wethersfield people as "chronic pioneers" to follow up the Connecticut to begin a new town; and to Middlesex they moved in 1783. The ten families who had gone to Addison and Panton from Connecticut in 1770 had been driven away during the war and their homes burned; in 1783 most of them returned and were followed speedily by others.[3] From Suffield, Litchfield, Glastenbury, Wethersfield, and Hartford, settlers went to Benson.[4]

[1] Coolidge and Mansfield, 969. In 1794 nineteen new towns were incorporated, fifteen of which had been plantations, "every new town being supposed to contain when incorporated at least 500 inhabitants, though in some instances the number was less." See Williamson, *Maine*, ii, 564.

[2] Letter from John Wentworth to T. W. Waldron, October 25, 1774, *Belknap Papers*, pt. iii, 56–59 (*Mass. Hist. Soc. Coll.*, 6th ser., vol. iv). The "Old Brookfield road" ran to Berlin from the south, and then on to Montpelier, and the Coos road from the Connecticut River to Burlington. See S. F. Nye, in *Vermont Hist. Gaz.*, iv, 53. From Burlington settlers went north by following blazed trees. See B. A. Kingsley, *ibid.*, ii, 201.

[3] Coolidge and Mansfield, 731, 870. For a description of the "Hazen road," a great thoroughfare for Vermont settlers going to the north, see Thomas Goodwillie, in *Vermont Hist. Gaz.*, i, 266. Originally a road over which to convey troops during the Revolution, it was lengthened and repaired by General Hazen, until it extended to Westfield. Afterwards branch roads were made on either side of it.

[4] Their children formed part of a colony to DuPage County, Illinois, later. See Kellogg, in *Vermont Hist. Gaz.*, iii, 408. Also Blanchard, *Hist. of DuPage County*, 84, 85, 197.

To Essex, North Hero, Shelburne, Sheldon, Fairfax, Ferrisburgh, Northfield; to Waterbury, from older Waterbury, to Fairfield, and a dozen other villages swarmed families from most of the Connecticut towns. Nor was Massachusetts behind her neighbor as the mother of new Vermont settlements. Braintree is the child of Braintree on the bay; West Springfield settlers made homes beside families from Litchfield, Connecticut, and organized Williston; Worcester County towns had representatives in Cabot and Stratton; a family which had started from Cape Ann and had halted for a few years in New Hampshire at Hooksett, now joined with Connecticut, Rhode Island, and New York people to found Grand Isle. Between 1784 and 1787 fifty-three families moved to Hinesburgh, and two years later joined in organizing a Congregational church; of these fifty-three, two from Canaan, Connecticut, had built cabins here in 1775, had been driven away during the war, and when they returned were reinforced shortly by one household from Rutland, another from Williamstown, Massachusetts, ten others from New Milford and Stonington, Connecticut, while still more came from Lanesborough, Williamstown, and Worthington. To Westford, Massachusetts, New Hampshire, and Rhode Island sent men to plant the town. Ludlow is a Massachusetts town. Swanton had many pioneers from Hardwick, Lanesborough, Richmond, Holden, and Barre. Westfield, Lowell, — many other towns derived first inhabitants from towns in the old "Bay State." [1]

[1] Pittsfield and Groton were named for the Massachusetts towns; Rutland, for the Bay State Rutland. See W. R. Blossom, "Pittsfield," *Vermont Hist. Gaz.*, iii, 935; A. H. Hill, "Groton," *ibid.*, iv, 1146.

Nor did Connecticut and Massachusetts send out all the pioneers there were in Vermont. Rhode Island contributed some, as has been shown; three families went to Northfield; a company of grantees headed by Jonathan Arnold obtained in 1786 the grant of St. Johnsbury, settled it the same year, and organized it in 1790, when it had a population of 143. Burrillville families were among the founders of Sutton, Providence people among those of Barton, a Glocester man at Westfield. New Hampshire towns were swarming also; — Piermont sent pioneers to Cambridge, Fairfax, and Johnson; while Claremont, Alstead, Bath, Plaistow, Rumney, and many others were represented from one end of the state to the other. The older towns in Vermont, like Bennington and Westminster, were now planting new towns, — Groton, Hyde Park, Morristown, and many more. From Dutchess County, New York, emigrants moved east into Burlington and Huntington, while some of the grantees of Waterbury were from Newark, New Jersey.[1] Maine towns were sending out their settlers, and some helped plant Worcester, Vermont.

There were still unoccupied tracts in New Hampshire and Vermont in 1812 as there were in Maine; but they were barren soil, from which a mere pittance could be wrung after months of toil, and though there were men who were willing to make a trial of their strength in overcoming the difficulties of agriculture on such terms,

---

[1] C. C. Parker, "Waterbury," *Vermont Hist. Gaz.*, iv, 813. Settlers from Morris County, New Jersey, went to Vermont in considerable numbers at this time.

they were few in number and often easily discouraged. Searsburg, in Bennington County, Vermont, had one family within its limits from 1812 to 1815; in 1820 its population was nine, but " one moved away." Four years later one family came to stay, as did another which had come since 1820; in 1830 the census reported forty people in the town.[1] James Elliot, the first man in Victory, Vermont, stayed but three or four years, and for a number of years after his departure the town had no inhabitants at all. Finally, Deacon Asa Wells, who had been born in Bolton, Connecticut, and had lived in Tolland, Massachusetts, in Lunenburg, and then in Granby, Vermont, came to Victory and made his home here for the rest of his life.[2] Success, in New Hampshire, had but two inhabitants for many years, and Kilkenny had in 1850 a population of nineteen.[3] The same story may be repeated for Maine, which still had good land for farming though no one had purchased it. Into the counties of Aroostook, Penobscot, Washington, and Piscataquis, settlers finally moved, from the older portions of Maine or the British Provinces chiefly, with here and there a Massachusetts family, as in Bradley. Some towns grew rapidly; Lee, incorporated in 1832 with its four hundred people, had been settled since 1824. The older towns were filling up, however, and the population, which in 1820 was 298,269, had leaped in 1850 to 583,169.[4]

---

[1] George J. Bond, " Searsburg," in *Vermont Hist. Gaz.*, i, 231.
[2] Loomis Wells, " Deacon Asa Wells," in *Vermont Hist. Gaz.*, i, 1048.
[3] Coolidge and Mansfield, 545, 658.
[4] *Ninth Census Report*, i, 35. See frontispiece.

The settlement in northern New England after 1781 is illustrative of several points: first, the heterogeneous elements which went to make up a town in which five states were represented; second, how the lines of emigration crossed and recrossed, as when Newark and New York settlers came to Vermont, while Vermont settlers moved, as we shall see later, to New York; and third, how for many families the Vermont home was the third or fourth which had been planted in a wilderness. Again and again there are found such data as this: a man from Providence (Rhode Island) had moved to Clarendon, Vermont, where he remained for a few years, and then took up a new abode in Swanton with the rest of the pioneer families; another from Lebanon, Connecticut, removed to Hartland, then to Roxbury, Vermont; still another from Preston, Connecticut, to Plainfield, New Hampshire, thence to Morristown, Vermont; or from Hadley to Worthington, Massachusetts, then to Morristown. The writer of the history of Bloomfield said frankly, "But few of the early settlers remained in town for any great length of time."[1] When Timothy Dwight traveled through Vermont in 1805, he noted the radical and unconventional ideas of the inhabitants, as evidenced in their conversation, their constitution, and their educational and religious views. He was continually contrasting the condition of affairs in the towns through which he passed with the more settled order of things in Connecticut, to the disadvantage of Vermont. The tendency to go into politics and law seemed to him remarkable; for us it foreshadows the later prominence

---

[1] William Burbank, "Bloomfield," *Vermont Hist. Gaz.*, i, 950.

of the Vermonter in Wisconsin and Michigan politics, and upon the bench in the West as well.

One observation made by Mr. Dwight in commenting upon northern New England was the low moral tone which he found prevailing, and which he greatly deplored. He attributed it in large part to indifference regarding churches and schools, and cited instances to prove his charge in Vermont, in New Hampshire, and in Maine.[1] A little earlier, however, the first college in Maine had been founded at Brunswick, and named for the French refugee, Peter Bowdoin. Its original endowment was five townships of land, and from 1812 to 1831 it received three thousand dollars annually from the general treasury.[2] The people of Maine were apparently conscious of the lack of educational advantages for their children, and were determined to perpetuate Puritan traditions when they were able.

The figures of increasing population in northern New England seem significant; but the greatest emigrations after 1781 were outside the New England States, to Pennsylvania, New York, and Ohio, where the history of the old states on the Atlantic was to be continued in

[1] See Dwight, *Travels*, ii, 456–475. He cited New Hampshire towns as neglecting church and school. "It is a very great evil to . . . [Wolfborough, Middleton, Tuftonborough and] many others in New Hampshire, that they are, and for a considerable length of time have been, destitute of well-educated ministers of the gospel. The last minister of Wolfborough died about fourteen years ago: and the reluctance to be at the necessary expense has prevented the inhabitants from settling another. This is an extensive calamity in New Hampshire." *Ibid.*, iv, 173–175. He found the same true in Maine, because of the poverty and weakness of new settlements. See *ibid.*, ii, 237.

[2] See Williamson, *Maine*, ii, 562, 563.

the newer states their children founded. A differentiation of three kinds of pioneers became quite apparent with this movement to the West, — to Pennsylvania, to the Genesee country in New York, to Ohio, Indiana, and Illinois.[1] In the vanguard moved a few restless spirits, trappers and hunters primarily, who had lived perhaps on the edge of civilization in Vermont or New Hampshire, and now moved to the newer "West," a region ever shifting before an oncoming army of settlers. These pioneers built for themselves rude cabins just at the danger line, but made no effort to cultivate more than a garden-patch about the rude loghouse which served merely as a shelter from rain or snow. They were rough men who usually disliked any restraint of law or order, and cared not for church or school; men to whom an advancing wave of the next class of pioneers was a sign of a country too densely peopled and a warning for the hunter to move on farther west. Therefore, these forerunners of civilization, who had merely "squatted" on the piece of ground they had appropriated, sold a shadowy claim to the representatives of the second class of frontiersmen, and moved on to a new forest, to go through the same process of building a temporary home, and again selling out and wandering from the newer New England townships.

[1] Dwight, *Travels*, ii, 459 ff. Mr. Dwight noted this classification in Vermont, New Hampshire, and New York in 1805–20. James Flint, in *Letters from America*, 203–209, gives almost exactly the same idea of the people he found in Ohio, Indiana, and Illinois. He found in 1820 the third class most prominent in Pennsylvania and the earlier settled parts of Ohio ; the second in the later settled parts of Ohio and Kentucky ; and the first in Indiana and Illinois.

The next class was made up of farmers who either appropriated the hunters' cabins, or built new loghouses of their own, — men who through poverty or discontent had taken up the search for a new home; or maybe they had the roving spirit which is born in many an Anglo-Saxon, and which drives a man to seek new lands and explore the wilderness which lies beyond his horizon. These farmers cultivated the soil to a limited extent; they "girdled" the trees and burned them instead of felling them, and their crops were raised on the ground still bristling with the stumps of a charred forest. Of this class some were ambitious and faded into the third class of thrifty farmers; but others soon became restless, and gathering into a covered wagon their few household effects and a group of ragged children, sold at a slight profit the lands they had purchased of the hunter or at second hand from a company of proprietors, and moved on again toward the setting sun.

The lands thus vacated were bought by the representatives of the third and best class of pioneers, — those who were young, ambitious, who had a little capital with which to buy a farm and rear a family, — capital too limited to purchase a home in the East, where land had become more dear than suited the purse of a farmer's son just beginning his life independently of his father's family. To the new home the young man brought his bride, and together they saved and planned and toiled till the log cabin was replaced by a substantial house, barns clustered about the home-lot, and from this group of buildings stretched away the acres of wheat and corn. The farmer's chief desire at this stage

was to raise more than enough produce for his immediate needs; the surplus he sold, and the profits he
invested in new lands about his home-farm. It is this
class which brings the church, the school, the town-
meeting; this class which dreams of a college which
shall reproduce Harvard, Yale, or Dartmouth; this class
which "aims at a seat in the legislature or the guber-
natorial chair."[1]

Not always were these three classes distinct; the first
might fade into the second, the second into the third,
and one man might exemplify in his own person all three
types. But the distinction was there, and shrewd travelers
like Dwight saw it and commented upon it. The first
two made but little lasting impression upon a new community; temporarily they gave it a hard, rough character, "with a reputation for recklessness and low morals."
The third gave tone to a mixed population, and to these
workers in the wilderness the Western States owe their
character of to-day. To this character all the elements
contributed; — the Southern man, the Pennsylvanian,
the Kentuckian, each gave his share and lent his traditions to the building of a new commonwealth; but though
recognizing the part each played, this study concerns
itself with New England's share in planting new states
outside the confines of her own original territory.

Emigration to Pennsylvania, begun on a large scale
before the Revolution, was continued on a far greater
plan after the conflict. The terrible massacre of 1778
had laid the Wyoming country waste; but General Sul-

---

[1] James Flint says they are "Congressmen, politicians in the legislature, or justices of the peace." See *Letters from America*, 209.

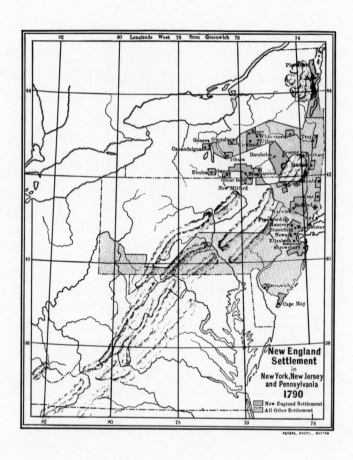

New England
Settlement
in
New York, New Jersey
and Pennsylvania
1790

New England Settlement
All Other Settlement

PETERS, ENGRS., BOSTON

livan's expedition had made the tracts in northern Pennsylvania again habitable, and as soon as the war was over, the settlers who had fled to Orange County, New York, to Connecticut, or to the Delaware, returned to begin life anew.[1] Into all the northeastern counties, into the newer counties of Elk, Erie, Crawford, Bradford, McKean, Schuylkill, Tioga, Susquehanna, Venango, Warren, and Allegheny, poured a stream of New Englanders and New Yorkers, with a sprinkling of New Jersey men, Scotch-Irish, and Germans. The Susquehanna Company, not disposed to surrender the Westmoreland country without a struggle, appointed at a meeting in Hartford in December, 1786, twenty-one commissioners as a provisional government to be set up over the new states they hoped to form by dismembering Pennsylvania. A constitution was drawn up and officers appointed, but the scheme crumbled when Pennsylvania erected Luzerne County in 1787–89, established courts and introduced laws.[2] The settlers now moved in under a clear title, and made permanent homes. Erie County became more like New York than Pennsylvania, with its Connecticut, Rhode Island, and Maine settlers, several of whom had tried pioneering in New York.[3] A Congregational church organized in Poultney, Vermont, moved bodily to East Smithfield, in Bradford County. With the opening of a rough wagon road to

[1] Charles Miner, *Hist. of Wyoming*, 469–475.

[2] *Ibid.*, 401–412. Oliver Wolcott is said to have drawn up the constitution ; Major William Judd of Farmington, Connecticut, was to have been governor, and Colonel John Franklin of Wyoming, lieutenant-governor. H. M. Hoyt, *Brief of a title . . . in . . . Luzerne*, 73.

[3] Sherman Day, *Hist. Coll. of Pa.*, 309. See map opposite.

the source of the Tioga River, New England and New York people poured over the Alleghany Mountains, — hitherto a barrier to settlement. They filled up Tioga County, — " the pleasant front yards, gardens, and green blinds indicating the origin of the population." [1] The town of Honesdale, in Wayne County, laid out around the court house square, with its shade trees, white houses with green blinds, set gable-end to the street "after the fashion of New England," and the front yards filled with flowers and shrubbery, attested the traditions of the Eastern States. Luzerne County was furthermore a veritable hotbed of Federalism, true in its political adherence to its Connecticut tradition.

Crawford County, which had but 2346 inhabitants in 1800, numbered 16,030 in 1830. Here were mingled Germans, Scotch-Irish, New Yorkers, and New Englanders.[2] Alleghany College was incorporated at Meadville in this county in 1817; its first president was Timothy Alden; one of its first donors was Isaiah Thomas of Worcester, a clergyman of Salem, and its first accession of rare books was the gift of Judge Winthrop of Massachusetts.[3] In these ways did the Bay State pass on her traditions of higher education.[4]

---

[1] Day, 624–627. This was said of Wellsborough, but it was a description which might have been applied to a number of towns similarly founded.

[2] Bates, "Crawford County," in W. H. Egle, *Hist. of Pennsylvania*, 610.

[3] Day, *Hist. Coll. of Pa.*, 257, 258.

[4] The reason why the areas of New England settlement in eastern and central Pennsylvania differ in the map opposite page 155, and those opposite pages 159 and 168, is that often the New England element came late either into the towns and there made up the merchant and professional class, or into the country to buy up farms already settled in order to increase their productiveness. See Day, *Hist. Coll. of Pa.*, 233, 504, 603; Emily C. Blackman, "Susquehanna County," in Egle, *Hist. of Pa.*, 1093.

But the greatest emigration of all those directly following the Revolution took its way into New York, the more conservative element staying nearer the eastern boundary, the venturesome ones going out into the wilderness. A strong current set out in 1783–84 from the New England States, and speedily the western shore of Lake Champlain and the older towns on the Hudson felt the influence of the newcomers.[1] This sort of emigration is represented in Troy, which had been founded before the Revolution, but was now filled up with home-seekers from west of the Green Mountains and the Connecticut River, who were looking for a favorable location for trade. They were followed by professional men, mechanics, and manufacturers, who saw the opportunity which a rapidly increasing population north of Albany offered to the "speculative" and "migrating" New Englander.[2]

But the great opportunities for expansion lay beyond the Hudson, in the central and western portions of the state. Pioneers poured into these regions from three directions: those from Pennsylvania, especially the New Englanders transplanted to the Wyoming Valley and driven out from that territory in 1778, pushed up the Susquehanna to Tioga Point, from which they diverged east and west; those who came directly from New England crossed the Hudson River, proceeded to Unadilla, thence down the Susquehanna into Chemung or up to the Genesee country; while a third stream from either New England, the eastern New York counties, or New

---

[1] W. C. Watson, *Essex County*, 203.
[2] A. T. Weise, *Hist. of Troy*, 19.

Jersey went out through the Mohawk Valley to the upper part of the Genesee country, emerging at Buffalo about 1800.[1]

The first settlers had often become acquainted with the lands personally through the campaigns of the Revolution, or through stories of returning soldiers. During the early years of the war, perhaps in 1776, seven pairs of brothers, from seven families in Plymouth, Connecticut, enlisted in the army, were marched westward, and stationed at various times at Forts Herkimer, Schuyler, and Stanwix, where the surrounding country seemed to them especially attractive. At the close of the war they went immediately to make homes in the vicinity of Kirkland.[2] Doubtless others were led in the same direction by the reports of returning soldiers. Judge Hugh White of Middletown, Connecticut, a proprietor of lands in Oneida County, New York, moved with four grown sons (but one of whom was married) to his new possessions in 1784.[3] To induce his neighbors in Connecticut to follow him, he was accustomed to send back, when he found opportunity, the largest stalks of corn, oats, and wheat, with samples of his best potatoes and onions, that his old friends might judge for themselves how productive was Oneida County soil. "These so far excelled anything they had been accustomed to see, that very soon many came to see the country, and in general, were so

[1] H. C. Goodwin, *Cortland County*, 93.

[2] Rev. A. D. Gridley, *Hist. of Kirkland, New York*, 19, quotes this from an historical address by Judge Williams at some celebration in the town.

[3] Pomroy Jones, *Annals of Oneida County*, 790. Also Barber and Howe, *Hist. Coll. of New York*, 27.

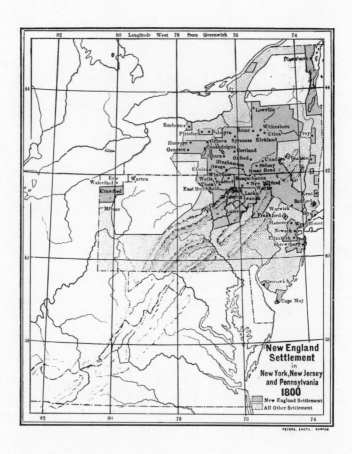

New England
Settlement
in
New York, New Jersey
and Pennsylvania
1800

New England Settlement
All Other Settlement

PETERS, ENGVS., BOSTON

well pleased that they located in the vicinity," — and Whitestown became distinctly a Connecticut settlement.[1]

The history of Binghamton is a little different from others which have been mentioned. In 1787 a native of Plymouth, Massachusetts, who had survived the massacre of Wyoming Valley in 1778 and a later flood of the Susquehanna, was told by a fur-trader of the fertile land about the site of the future Binghamton, and moved there. Only a few weeks elapsed before he was joined by two men, natives of Connecticut, who had tried pioneering in Vermont and in the Wyoming Valley. Others who came in from Massachusetts and Connecticut found no roads after crossing the Hudson, and made their way through the woods. By 1815 settlers were here from seven Connecticut towns and one New Hampshire village, one Vermont family had built a home, while still others were from Massachusetts.[2]

The familiar mode of movement by neighborhoods which was as old as the first town in New England was exemplified again in the settlement of Hudson, New York, by an association of thirty Quaker fishermen from Nantucket and Martha's Vineyard, who combined at Providence in the purchase of lands for a new home and began the town of Hudson in 1783.[3] A company formed at Dighton purchased 46,000 acres in what is now Richmond, and planted that town.[4]

An enterprise which followed the old lines of purchase

[1] See map opposite.
[2] J. B. Wilkinson, *Annals of Binghamton*, 44, 45, 60, 92, 176–210.
[3] S. B. Miller, *Hist. Sketches of Hudson*, 6–8, 85.
[4] O. Turner, *Phelps-Gorham Purchase*, 198, 199.

by proprietors who sold to settlers was the speculative
plan of Phelps and Gorham, a scheme on a far larger
scale than had ever been the case before the Revolution.
In 1786 the State of New York, in order to settle the
claim to a portion of her territory which Massachusetts
had based upon the ancient limits of her charter, ceded
to the latter without any equivalent a large tract consisting of vacant lands in the west central part of the
state.[1] The lands having been turned over to Massachusetts, Oliver Phelps of Granville and Nathaniel Gorham,
also of the Bay State, bought the preëmptive rights to
the lands in western New York for $100,000, payable
in three installments. The following year the Indian title
to over two million acres was extinguished by treaty,
and the Massachusetts Legislature confirmed the grant.
Thereupon, Phelps and Gorham had their purchase
divided into townships six miles square, and then subdivided into 160-acre tracts; a land-office was opened at
Canandaigua, and about one third of the whole purchase
was sold to actual settlers or to speculators who sold
later to settlers.[2] Because of the superiority of the soil
and the exceptional excellence of title, pioneers fairly
swarmed to the "Genesee country." James Wadsworth,
a native of Durham, Connecticut, who with his brother
was traveling west, noted in a letter to his family in 1790

[1] Barber and Howe, *Hist. Coll. of New York*, 40. There were two tracts
in the cession, one called indefinitely "The Genesee Country," the other
including the counties of Browne and Tioga. It was the first which Phelps
and Gorham bought.

[2] The rest was sold to Robert Morris of Philadelphia, who sold it to an
Englishman, and the land was sold by the latter in land offices at Geneva
and Bath. Rev. J. H. Hotchkin, *Western New York*, 8-10.

that there had arrived that day two vessels from Rhode
Island, laden the one with twenty-eight passengers, the
other with thirty, all bound " full speed for the Genesee
country," and added, " The imigrations [*sic*] to the westward are almost beyond belief." [1] Out to the wilderness
by way of the Mohawk from Albany, up the valleys
from the Susquehanna, overland from Vermont, settlers
poured into every western county by single families,
by twos and threes, and by whole colonies. In reading
the local histories, one feels that Connecticut must have
been beggared of inhabitants, so fast did hundreds of
her families make their way into New York; many who
came from western Massachusetts, eastern New York,
and from Vermont, had been in those states but for a
short time, and were Connecticut men by birth.[2] Durham, New York, is but one instance of a village settled
from a Connecticut town, whose pioneers preserved the
memory of the old home east of the Hudson in the name
of the new.[3]

When in 1796 the British evacuated Fort Oswego,

[1] O. Turner, *Phelps-Gorham Purchase*, 331. Barber says that winter was
chosen by many as a time to migrate because of the fine sleighing and consequent ease with which goods could be hauled. See *Hist. Coll. of New York*,
40.

[2] Berkshire, Tioga County, was named for Berkshire County, Massachusetts, from which its first settlers came ; Berkshire County had been
settled from Connecticut, as has been shown in this study. W. B. Gay, *Tioga
County*, 113 ; also Jones, *Annals of Oneida County*, 13, and Turner, *Phelps-
Gorham Purchase*, 164–182.

[3] W. C. Fowler, *Hist. of Durham* (Connecticut), 214, 215, gives the
names of thirty emigrants from Durham, Connecticut, to Durham,
New York, in a letter of Rev. Mr. Timothy Williston, January 26,
1848.

settlement immediately began upon that site; the next
year or two saw families building homes in Lewis and
Jefferson counties; by 1800 the hamlets which stretched
from Utica to the Genesee River were mostly connected
with one another by extensions of the main thoroughfare, and from that time dates the influence of the western
counties in the councils of New York.[1] To learn the
nature of this enormous movement, one has but to study
the history of a few representative towns. A semi-cen-
tennial celebration in Lowville, Lewis County, was held
in 1826, in which fifty-five old settlers took part. Of
these, twenty-two had come from Connecticut, eight
from Massachusetts, sixteen from New York, and one
each from Rhode Island, Vermont, and New Jersey.
The twenty-two Connecticut settlers represented fourteen towns in every part of the state, while the Massachusetts men represented seven places, including Boston, West Springfield, and others lying between the
two.[2] Thirty-eight persons from Wolcott, New Hampshire, went in 1803 to Genesee;[3] Augusta in Oneida
County, was a Litchfield County, Connecticut, town,
Farmington was settled by emigrants from Adams,[4] and
indeed all of Berkshire County was a veritable hive,

---

[1] Barber, *Hist. Coll. of N. Y.*, 40.

[2] F. B. Hough, *Lewis County*, 297, 298.

[3] As if settlers were not moving in fast enough, a settler in the Genesee country went to Wolcott, New Hampshire, in 1803, called a public
meeting, gave a description of the New York lands, and urged Wolcott
people to emigrate. Five families and three unmarried men, thirty-eight
persons in all, did so at once, in seven wagons. They were twenty-one
days on the road. See Turner, *Phelps-Gorham Purchase*, 511.

[4] Turner, *Phelps-Gorham Purchase*, 217-222.

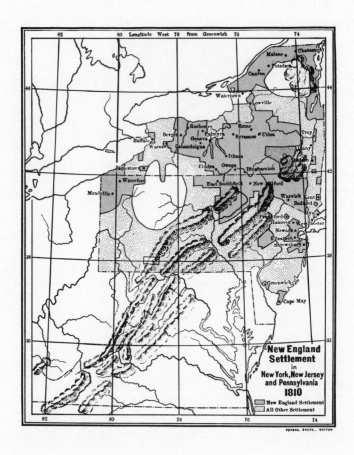

New England
Settlement
in
New York, New Jersey
and Pennsylvania
1810

New England Settlement
All Other Settlement

from which workers swarmed into the Phelps-Gorham Purchase.[1]

Kirkland, in Oneida County, was a typical New England settlement. The preliminary surveys having been made in 1786–87, five families from Plymouth, Connecticut, came the following spring from German Flats, then the outpost of the region, where they had lived for several years. By April the little clearing had thirteen families living there, by winter twenty more were established within its boundaries. On April 8, 1787, in the unfinished house of Captain Moses Foot, leader of the colony, the first church services were held.[2] The settlers, feeling their isolation and their lack of organization, determined to draw up a sort of compact for the regulation of affairs in their little settlement.[3] They all signed an agreement that they would abide by its terms. They were to choose a secretary as soon as possible; he was to keep a record of the papers, votes, etc., of the settlement. The draft preserved is but a rough one; but it bears an interesting resemblance to other agreements among settlers as to the distribution of land, and the necessity in all town business of conforming to the will of the majority.

[1] Turner, *Phelps-Gorham Purchase*, 222. A list of sixty-one settlers in Rochester between 1794 and 1819 gives twenty-eight Connecticut men, nineteen from Massachusetts, twenty-five from New York, three from Vermont, eleven from New Hampshire, one from Rhode Island, and one from Scotland. *Proc. of Rochester Pioneer Society.* 3, 4, 11. See map opposite.

[2] Rev. A. D. Gridley, *Hist. of Kirkland*, 19–58.

[3] P. Jones, *Annals of Oneida County*, 167, 170, 171. The next year twenty more families arrived; those who came together from Brimfield, Massachusetts, settled along one street known ever since as "Brimfield Street."

A few instances will show the trend of many similar personal histories. A young Irishman and his wife left the north of Ireland in 1740, and made a new home in Plainfield, Connecticut, where they became very well-to-do. In 1765 they found it necessary to provide new farms and homes for their nine sons and only daughter, and as Vermont was then the "new country," where cheap lands beckoned the pioneer on, the family moved — father, mother, and children — to Windsor, Vermont. From this town eight of the nine sons entered the Revolutionary Army. But after the war was over, thinking Vermont offered too few opportunities to the enterprising farmer, four of the sons moved to Marcy, Oneida County, New York, in 1793–94, and became early settlers in that town.[1] The story might be reproduced in many a case.

It was no wonder that the resemblance of central and western New York to New England was so striking as to excite comment. Timothy Dwight, in traveling west from Schenectady, entered New Hartford, — "the first New England settlement which we found in this region." He noted the neat church with its "pretty steeple," the houses built in "New England manner," the "sprightliness, thrift, and beauty" of the settlement.[2] He recognized Durham as a New England town by its schoolhouses and churches. The eastern immigrants took with them improved methods of agriculture, enterprise, ingenuity, and social habits; by 1813 the newcomers were rapidly gaining an ascendancy in the

[1] Jones, *Annals of Oneida County*, 237, 238.
[2] Dwight, *Travels*, iii, 179 ; iv, 17.

state.[1] Azariah Smith was a typical pioneer; born in Middlefield, Massachusetts, in 1784, he taught school winters and worked on his father's farm summers, till a cousin in business in New York induced him in 1807 to move to Onondaga County, where three years after his arrival he owned a small store. He was always remarkable for the interest he manifested in the local village affairs; — he was solicitous for the welfare of education, for Sunday schools, was a trustee of the village school in Manlius, of Manlius Academy, of Hamilton College, and of Auburn Theological Seminary. But he went beyond his native town, and served in the state legislature from 1839 until 1841, where he was placed on the committee on prisons and penitentiaries, and suggested many valuable reforms in the administration of those institutions.[2] The biography of Samuel Miles Hopkins, who was born in Waterbury, Connecticut, and lived in Geneva, New York, shows the same philanthropic zeal mingled with shrewd judgment.[3]

The phase of character which most writers on the local history of New York towns emphasize is the strongly marked tendency of the New Englanders to establish public worship as soon as they arrived. Jay Gould, in speaking of the company of twenty heads of families and two single men who came in 1799 to Stamford, Delaware County, from Fairfield County, Connecticut,

---

[1] H. C. Spafford, *Gazetteer of . . . N. Y.*, 36. In 1803 six families from Orwell, Vermont, settled Stockholm, St. Lawrence County. They brought with them fifty sheep, the first flock in the county. F. B. Hough, *St. Lawrence and Franklin Counties*, 473.

[2] J. V. H. Clark, *Onondaga*, ii, 194–199.

[3] S. M. Hopkins, *Autobiography*, 9–41, in *Rochester Hist. Soc. Pub.*, no. ii.

notes especially that these pioneers kept Sunday by meeting at some house in the neighborhood which was cen-
trally located, and listening to some old sermon read by
the deacon of the settlement.[1] At Bergen, the Guilford, Connecticut, emigrants " set up public worship at
once ";[2] Deacon Patchin, from Connecticut, used from
the time of his arrival in Newfield to open his house
every Sunday for worship, and maintained it almost
alone for ten years.[3] The settlers of Marcellus were
gathered from Massachusetts, Vermont, and Connecticut; they were noted for the anxiety they showed in
providing for the religious and intellectual education
of their children, and for their establishment of a school
two years after their arrival.[4] A Congregational church
was formed in Lafayette by members from Berkshire
and Hampshire counties in Massachusetts in 1804, services having been held previously in the house of a Congregationalist from Norwich, Connecticut.[5] Public worship was instituted by a pioneer of Genoa immediately
after his arrival; six years later the church of sixteen
members was organized.[6] Several colonies in Essex
County brought their ministers with them.[7]

One significant change was wrought in church organization by the process of transplanting from New Eng-

[1] Jay Gould, *History of Delaware County*, 197–202.

[2] Rev. J. H. Hotchkin, *Western New York*, 502.

[3] *Ibid.*, 414.

[4] J. V. H. Clark, *Onondaga*, ii, 290. Also W. C. Watson, *Essex Co.*, 210,
speaks of voluntary support of schools.

[5] Clark, *Onondaga*, ii, 283–286.

[6] Hotchkin, *Western New York*, 355, 356.

[7] Watson, *Essex County*, 310.

land. Congregationalism had been the prevailing form
of church government in Massachusetts and Connecticut, and the emigrants from those states had taken
their individualistic administration with them to their
new homes in the wilderness. But poverty stared the
pioneers in the face; although they wanted the benefits
of churches and public worship for themselves and for
their children, they were often too poor and too few in
numbers to support a minister for themselves. Presbyteries were established early in western New York, and
under these organizations many weak Congregational
churches placed themselves, under an " accommodation
system," by which they retained most of their own
peculiar administrative forms and their own creed, yet
had the advantage of united support from their neighbor
churches. The Congregational Church of Florence,
Oneida County, was organized in 1816 with ten members, but soon joined the Presbytery on the " accommodation system " ; [1] the Congregational Church of Candor,
organized in 1808, became Presbyterian in 1821; the
First Presbyterian Church of Owego was organized in
1817 as a Congregational church, was soon taken under
the care of the Cayuga and Tioga Presbyteries, and in
1831 abandoned Congregationalism and adopted the
Presbyterian form of government in full.[2] Seventy years
after its establishment the Congregational Church of
Kirkland became Presbyterian because the Congregationalists had become weak in that region, and the

---

[1] Jones, *Annals of Oneida County*, 150.
[2] W. B. Gay, *Tioga County*, 402, 403. In 1850 forty-six members withdrew, and formed a Congregational church.

Presbyterians comparatively strong.[1] In Marcellus, Congregationalists, Presbyterians, and Baptists worshiped together for twenty years, — a witness to frontier toleration and a spirit of mutual forbearance born of wilderness life.[2]

The need for preachers in the new settlements reacted upon the older states by fostering anew the missionary spirit which had led the Puritans in their early history to an endeavor to rescue the souls of the Indians from "a heathen doom." The Presbyterians and Congregationalists of New England sent before 1800 at least thirty-seven ministers either to report the spiritual necessities of the frontiersmen, or to labor in the wilderness.[3] A missionary society organized in 1779 in Massachusetts, began operations in 1800 in the Genesee country;[4] the Hampshire Missionary Society of Northampton, Massachusetts, directed its attention for twenty years to the settlers of western New York, as did the society of Hopkinton, New Hampshire. The Connecticut Society worked on a different basis, for their missionaries were usually on leave of absence from their own congregations for three or four months, during which time they ministered to the needs of the New York settlers.

The New Englanders carried with them, also, their town-meeting. In Canandaigua, the first assemblage of settlers was held in 1791, two years after the first comers arrived. Up to 1805–06, there was no govern-

---

[1] A. D. Gridley, *History of Kirkland*, 98.
[2] Clark, *Onondaga*, ii, 290, 291.
[3] E. H. Roberts, *New York*, ii, 486.
[4] Hotchkin, *Western New York*, 184, 186, 187, 188.

ment in western New York save such town organization as the early settlers had established; the whole
of the territory west of the Genesee River was included in the town of Northampton, but the vicinity
of Buffalo lay beyond the pale of the county system. In
1808 the legislature organized Niagara County, with
Buffalo as the county seat, on condition that the Holland Land Company (which owned the tract so organized) should build a courthouse and jail, and convey
them to the county.[1] But the final arrangement was not
that of the New England town-meeting as it had existed
in Massachusetts or Connecticut, for in New York the
mixed system of county and town government had
obtained ever since the Duke's Laws of 1664 had been
promulgated. Whenever a new town was erected, four
justices of the peace were chosen at the first election,
and these presided at a town-meeting where the town
officers were chosen: the usual New England ones with
the addition of a supervisor to receive and pay out town
moneys, keep accounts, sue in the name of the town,
and cause town surveys to be made. This supervisor is
to-day as he was then, — the link between town and
county; he meets once a year with supervisors from
every other town in the county, and represents his town
on the board so formed, to make laws for the corporate
property of the county, have charge of its accounts, and
audit debts and bills of all officers and other persons
outstanding against the towns. In addition to the board
of supervisors, the county has its treasurer, clerk, sher-

[1] Wm. Ketchum, *History of Buffalo*, ii, 230, 231.

iff, coroner, surrogate, and district attorney.[1] Thus the town government of New England takes a subordinate place when upon it is superimposed the county government as in the New York system.

The settlement of western New York is typical of the later emigration into the Northwest Territory, and so deserves a general résumé. The restless and discontented elements moved first; among the pioneers who emigrated to the Genesee country in 1788–89, before the Indian title was extinguished, were Jemima Wilkinson and the followers she had secured to practice her peculiar religious ideas, — ideas which could not be tolerated in their New England homes.[2] But the next settlers went for good, cheap land; therefore a very considerable portion of those who emigrated to western New York were farmers in the " meridian of life," whose children, acquaintances, and relatives made up the settlements. Generally they were supplied with enough money not only to buy their farms, but also to make improvements, and therefore were exempt from the privations of the earliest pioneers who had sold out to these later comers and emigrated west. Mechanics followed farmers, in the hope of attaining greater prosperity than they had enjoyed in their old homes, " by adding the business of a farm to their mechanic employment." Mills were erected, and the whole community took on an appearance of permanence which it had lacked in the earlier days.[3] Here, however, in conse-

[1] Rev. Statutes of New York, i, 110, 339–342, 365–367.

[2] O. Turner, Phelps-Gorham Purchase, 153–162.

[3] Hotchkin, Western New York, 25; also Jones, Annals of Oneida Co., 639, 640.

quence of the intermixture of emigrants, diversity in thought and taste were apparent, and the churches, town-meetings, and schools were no longer precisely of the Puritan type, though the traditions of all were preserved in the new institutions.[1] With the arrival of the first emigrants from New England, in the early days of New York, the incoming missionaries had been a great stimulus to education, churches had also flourished, and the interior of the state found an attraction in the field offered, and churches were widely extended as the population increased. "Every new method in religion, every new suggestion in theology, found hospitable reception there,"[2] though the theories were not always sane or practical. The Oneida community is but one illustration; Mormonism, whose founder was by birth a Vermont man, as was its first great president, Brigham Young, shows a phase of peculiar religious enthusiasm associated with communal ideas.[3]

[1] Samuel Hopkins noted the difference between the state of society in his native town of Goshen, Connecticut, and that of his new home in New York. He had never seen in his native town a person of "competent age to read and write, who could not do both." He testified to the high grade of general intelligence in Connecticut, and found a sharp contrast in western New York. See S. M. Hopkins, *Autobiography*, 19, in *Rochester Hist. Soc. Pub.*, no. ii.

[2] E. H. Roberts, *New York*, ii, 559.

[3] Warsaw will serve as a type of the growth of a town in New York between 1812 and 1837. Settled in 1803–04 from Vermont by way of Granville, it had not many inhabitants in its early years. One of the early settlers who arrived at the age of forty had already moved six times since in his childhood his parents had left his birthplace of Bozrah, Connecticut. In Colchester and in Hebron, in Sandisfield and Great Barrington, in Green River and Genesee, he had tried his luck, and finally settled in Warsaw. His neighbors came from Londonderry, Bath, Poplin, Lebanon, and Richmond, New Hampshire; from Bennington, Pawlet, Hub-

After 1812 the interest in settlement centres elsewhere ; "the West" now moved on into western Ohio,
Indiana, and Illinois. The overflow still carried settlers
to New York and Pennsylvania, but the process was
now one of filling in states whose organization was per-
fected, and their institutions no longer in the formative
stage.[1] The emigrants from New England took their
thrift and enterprise with them, and contributed substantially to the prosperity of their adopted homes. It
seemed to Timothy Dwight that the inhabitants of New
York and New England were substantially one people,
"with the same interests of every kind inseparably
united."[2] When this observant traveler made a journey

bardton, Fair Haven, and Shaftsbury, Vermont ; from Attleborough,
Barnstable, Rehoboth, Wilbraham, and Hanover, Massachusetts ; from
Canaan, Lebanon, Canterbury, Cheshire, Hartford, Warren, Guilford,
Hartland, and Colchester, Connecticut ; and from Scituate, Rhode Island ;
— arriving from 1804 to 1833. Much of Chautauqua County, settled after
1804 (and quickly after 1812), shows the same influx of population from
all over New England during the thirty years following the war. See
A. W. Young, *Hist. of Warsaw*, 234–236, 257 ; also *id.*, *Hist. of Chautauqua
County*, 350–364.

[1] P. A. Hamilton, in an article on "Some Southern Yankees," in the
American Historical Magazine, iii (Oct., 1898), 304–309, gives some interesting illustrations of the migrations of New Englanders from 1795 to
1817. Lewis Judson of Stratford, Connecticut, founded in Mobile, Alabama, soon after 1795, the trading establishment of John Forbes and Co.
Peter Hobart, a Vermonter, had about the same year a mill in Mobile.
Cyrus Sibley of Massachusetts came by way of the Natchez settlement to
Mobile. Josiah Blakeley of New Haven moved to Mobile about 1806,
after six years' residence in Santiago de Cuba. President Jefferson assisted
the movement, according to Mr. Hamilton, by the distribution of Southern offices to Northern men. Although St. Stephens, the new capital of
Alabama, was founded in 1817 by a large number of Southern men, there
was one Silas Dinsmore of New Hampshire among them.

[2] Dwight, *Travels*, iv, 527. See map opposite.

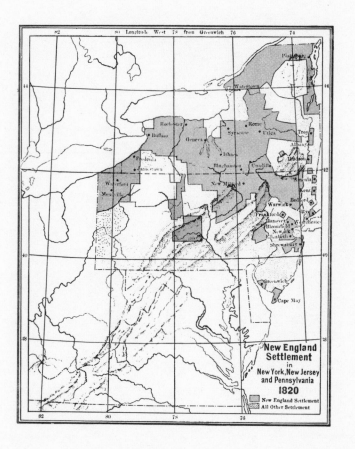

New England
Settlement
in
New York, New Jersey
and Pennsylvania
1820

New England Settlement
All Other Settlement

in 1821 to Niagara, he noted the increase in New
York's population from 1790, when it was 340,120,
through 1810, when it was 484,620, till 1820, when it
had reached 959,220. He estimated that from three
fifths to two thirds of this increase had originated from
New England, and thought the population increasing
continually; he considered New York would be ultimately but "a colony from New England," whose
inhabitants crowded in for commercial as well as for
agricultural betterment.[1]

Into the history of New York, and to a less degree
into that of Pennsylvania, are woven strands which only
New England could have contributed. From 1783,
when the great movement into central New York began,
down to 1820, when its climax was reached, the history
of New York was largely one of immigration, of new
settlements, of frontier influences, shaping the future
of the larger half of the state. By 1820 our interest
lies elsewhere; the movement has lost its distinctively
pioneer features, and one must follow the flood farther
west, there to find the story repeated, — the same, yet
ever varying.

[1] *Ibid.*, iii, 266, 267. There was also at the close of the Revolution a
decided movement towards the Canadian lands just over the border, especially from Pennsylvania, New Jersey, and Vermont. Children of these
pioneers often in the '40's and '50's moved back into the "States," settling in Michigan and Wisconsin. See Wm. Ketchum, *Hist. of Buffalo*, ii,
142 ; and John Maude, *Visit to Niagara*, 60, 120, 127, 133.

BIBLIOGRAPHICAL NOTES

The sources for Pennsylvania history are not very different from those mentioned in the notes on Chapter V. There are a few good articles, such as H. M. Hoyt's "Brief of a title in the seventeen townships in the county of Luzerne," available in the *Pennsylvania Historical Publications*. Miss L. C. Sanford's *History of Erie County, Pennsylvania*, was useful. But the great mass of literature on Pennsylvania local history deals with the Germans, Quaker, or Scotch-Irish settlement, or with the obvious New England towns in the Westmoreland district.

For New York history there is almost an embarrassment of riches. Such local histories as these are accurate and excellent : J. V. H. Clark, *Onondaga* (2 vols., Syracuse, 1849) ; Rev. J. H. Hotchkin, *A History of the Purchase and Settlement of Western New York* (written by a missionary to that part of the state) ; O. Turner, *Pioneer History of the Holland Purchase of Western New York* (Buffalo, 1849), and his other work, *History of the Pioneer Settlement of Phelps and Gorham's Purchase, and Morris' Reserve* (the latter having a supplement giving the history of Monroe County) ; Rev. A. D. Gridley, *History of Kirkland*. There are also some good county histories, notably the following : W. B. Gay (editor), *Historical Gazetteer of Tioga County, New York*, 1785–1888; H. C. Goodwin, *Pioneer History of Cortland County. . .* ; F. B. Hough, *History of Lewis County*, and another work by the same author, *A History of St. Lawrence and Franklin Counties ;* W. C. Watson, *The Military and Civil History of the County of Essex ;* A. W. Young, *History of Chautauqua County*, and his earlier work, *History of the Town of Warsaw*. Reference has also been made to the *Publications* of the Rochester Historical Society, and to the *Proceedings* of the Pioneer Society of Rochester. Ellis H. Robert's *New York* (2 vols.), in the American Commonwealth Series, is popular, like all of that series, but is useful at times for special study.

Timothy Dwight's shrewd observations in his carefully compiled *Travels in New England and New York* (4 vols., New Haven, 1821), can be drawn upon again and again. He not only conversed with people wherever he went, but made keen deductions from his information. James Flint's *Letters from America* (Edinburgh, 1822) is a work much like Timothy Dwight's, but from quite a different standpoint. It is especially valuable for observations on Ohio, Indiana, and Illinois. John Maude, *Visit to the Falls of Niagara in 1800* (London, 1826), published his book at first anonymously. It contains much material on western New York towns in 1800.

CHAPTER VII

THE PLANTING OF A SECOND NEW ENGLAND

1787–1865

THE years just succeeding the Revolution had been characterized, as has been shown in the preceding chapter, by unprecedentedly large emigrations from all of New England into the unsettled parts of New York and Pennsylvania, as well as to the still unoccupied portions of Maine, New Hampshire, and Vermont. But even these immense tracts were insufficient to satisfy those who were in quest of new homes, and the pressure exerted upon the frontier line everywhere was greater than it had ever been before. The dangers looming large before the would-be pioneer were the same ones that his ancestors had met; but of them all, the danger of hostilities begun by the dispossessed Indians was greatest. One of the first duties of the new government just forming was to make habitable those regions beyond the Appalachian Mountains where was destined to be planted a second New England.

The story of the settlement of Ohio has many points of resemblance to the history of the beginnings in the coast states; yet in one feature there lies an essential difference. The states that had been settled as English colonies had each had their own lands, granted with more or less indefinite boundaries by some English king. These lands were at the disposal of the colonial legislatures, which made preëmptive grants to settlers or to a group of proprietors, by whom the Indian title was extinguished, generally by purchase. If the transaction had been made by proprietors, they often sold the lands to actual settlers, and pocketed the gains. After the Declaration of Independence had transformed the colonies into states, the situation as to unappropriated lands lying within the boundaries of those states was quite unchanged, and the process of settling unoccupied tracts was not essentially different from what it had been before 1776. Even in New York the termination of the dispute between that state and Massachusetts over the lands beyond the Hudson River which both claimed did not alter the mode of disposing of vacant lands; the story of settlement in the Phelps-Gorham tract and in the Holland Purchase is not at all unlike the story of settlement in the preceding century, save that it took place on a far larger scale and far more rapidly than had seemed possible before that time.

But with the cession of Western lands to the general government in 1781, the whole situation was changed; now the seller of lands beyond the western boundaries of New York, Pennsylvania, and the coast states to the territory of Florida, was the United States, — not any one state. From that time until the present day the Federal government has had at its disposal large areas of land, — prairie, timber, salt, and mining tracts, — all of which it has been ready to sell at the lowest possible terms to actual settlers. So far as the United States has been concerned, there has not been any speculative scheme in mind, no desire to make money

out of the prospective emigrant; when speculation has
taken place, it has been possible only after the tracts
have passed out of the hands of the general government.
To the federal authorities, moreover, there passed, with
the cession of the land, the responsibility for quieting
the Indians, and the treaties which followed the close
of the Revolution form the basis for settlement west of
Pennsylvania and New York. The new nation had no
money in its treasury, but it had plenty of land; and
the first payments of the officers and soldiers who had
won the struggle which ended in the formation of a
new nation were made in the only commodity available
for the purpose,— tracts of unoccupied soil. In order
to make these bounty lands and military tracts habitable, a series of Indian treaties was entered into, beginning with that of Fort Stanwix in 1784, followed by
the Fort McIntosh peace of 1785, and made definite
and effectual by the treaty of Greenville of 1794, when
settlement had been progressing for seven years under
the Ordinance of 1787. By the peace of Greenville the
Indian tribes concerned gave up absolutely all title to
the greater part of what is now the State of Ohio. By
1805 settlement had pressed up to the very edge of the
land ceded in 1794; thereupon a succession of new
treaties opened up the rest of the State of Ohio as well
as lands beyond the western boundary for the outgoing
flood of emigration.[1] The new part of the process, then,
is the part played by the Federal government. The only
place where old methods still obtained was in that

[1] These treaties are well summarized in Howe, *Historical Collections of
Ohio*, i, 36–43 (ed. 1904).

district extending westward halfway across the State
of Ohio, and occupying approximately an eighth of the
whole area of that state, — the district known as the
Western Reserve, which Connecticut had specifically
retained at the time of the general cessions. Here the
process of peopling the new country was exactly like
the old method whereby Connecticut herself, and later
her extensive Westmoreland, had been covered with
towns and farms. It is significant and interesting, moreover, to note that the proceeds of sales in the Western
Reserve went to swell the school fund of the mother state.

Beginning in 1787, the tide of emigration poured out
beyond the borders of the thirteen original states, into
a practically unknown and unbroken wilderness. By
wagons, by rafts, hundreds of families from New England, along with their neighbors in the Middle States,
followed the Mohawk Valley or the old Braddock
Road, or floated down the Ohio,[1] to plant a new state
which should be but a younger New England on the
shores of Lake Erie and on the banks of the Muskingum.
The process of emigration was for their descendants
what it had been for the Puritans themselves; — from
those early days when the Rev. Mr. Hooker and his
congregation had made their way from Newtowne to the
Connecticut River, until the time, two centuries later,
when the Rev. Mr. Shipherd took his colony to plant
a new town and a college at Oberlin, thousands of New
Englanders had carried their ideals and their traditions

[1] Professor A. B. Hulbert, *Historic Highways of America* (16 vols.,
1902–05), has given much detail as to the routes to the West. Another
admirable collection is that of Dr. R. G. Thwaites, *Early Western Travels*
(32 vols., 1904–07).

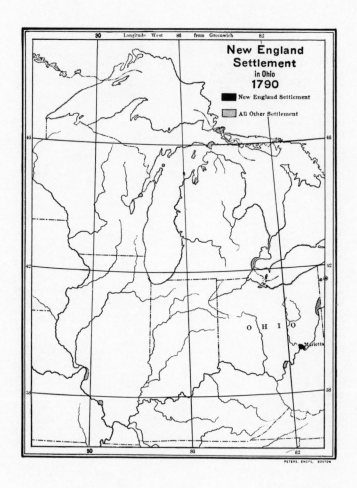

New England
Settlement
in Ohio
1790

■ New England Settlement

▨ All Other Settlement

Longitude West from Greenwich

O H I O

Marietta

PETERS. ENGRS. BOSTON

into the wilderness. There, time after time, had they organized church and school side by side, in a community where each settler had a voice in the control of local affairs, and might impress his individuality upon a new commonwealth in such measure as was possible from his training and ability. Whether the descendant of the Puritan emigrated to the shores of the Connecticut River, or to Ohio, he emigrated in the same way, with the same ideals steadfastly set before his eyes.

The first New England settlement in the Northwest Territory was made on the Ohio River, at Marietta, by officers and men of the Massachusetts, Rhode Island, and Connecticut line.[1] These soldiers had, on March 1, 1786, met at the "Bunch of Grapes" Tavern in Boston, in response to a call which General Rufus Putnam and General Benjamin Tupper had issued to every county in Massachusetts, asking that one or two delegates be sent to the appointed place on that day. Only eleven persons responded, but the Ohio Land Company was formed then and there.[2] Through one of the directors, the Rev. Manasseh Cutler of Salem, Massachusetts, purchase was made of a large tract in southeastern Ohio; shares were distributed to the proprietors according to the amount each paid in, with a reservation of one section (640 acres) for schools, one section for religious institutions, and two townships for a college. In 1786 the town of Marietta was laid out and the first settlers arrived. A Congregational church was formed at once with thirty-one members, fourteen from Massachusetts, sixteen from

[1] See map opposite.
[2] J. H. Perkins, *Annals of the West*, 283, 284.

Connecticut, and one from Linlithgow, Scotland.[1] In 1797 Muskingum Academy, the mother of the later Marietta College, was founded, — eleven years after the first settler had arrived in Marietta.

The pioneers of Marietta represented very accurately the New England movement to the West. Rufus Putnam, the leader of the enterprise, had served his apprenticeship in the wilderness, first with Phineas Lyman as a surveyor of the Mississippi tract, then as a general in the Revolution, and later as surveyor-general of the district of Maine.[2] Upon his return to his home in Rutland, Massachusetts, he wrote to General Washington urging that bounty lands be granted in Ohio, as there "are thousands in this quarter who will migrate" — as soon as settlements could be made with safety.[3] The first company left Danvers on the first day of December, 1787; the second left Hartford one month later. Putnam himself was after his removal in 1790 identified with every movement in Ohio: he was one of the first trustees of Ohio University, active in forming a Bible society, a supporter of schools, and a member of the constitutional convention of Ohio in 1803. "The impress of his character is strongly marked on the population of Marietta, in their buildings, institutions, and manners."[4] Among

[1] Rev. C. E. Dickinson, *First Congregational Church of Marietta*, 164. The Massachusetts members were from Boston, Middleton, Brookfield, Chester, Conway, Rutland, Westborough, and Chesterfield; those from Connecticut had lived in Colchester, Canaan, Lyme, Lebanon, North Lyme, Saybrook, and Middletown. *Ibid.*, 120.

[2] See Williamson, *Maine*, ii, 507.

[3] Dr. S. P. Hildreth, *Biographical and Historical Memoirs of the Early Pioneer Settlers of Ohio*, 14, 95, 96.

[4] *Ibid.*, 119.

his Massachusetts comrades were James Varnum of
Dracut; General Benjamin Tupper of Stoughton; Colonel Ebenezer Sproat of Middleborough; Rev. Daniel
Story of Boston, the first minister of the Marietta colony;
Captain William Dana of Cambridge; Captain Robert
Oliver of Boston, president of the Ohio legislative council, 1800 to 1803; and Major Robert Bradford, a lineal
descendant of the governor of the Plymouth colony. The
movement was not, however, wholly a Massachusetts
venture, though the initiative had come from that state:
— there were men from Rhode Island, Connecticut, and
New Hampshire, whose names are inseparably connected
with the story of Marietta. Such an one was Abraham
Whipple, of Rhode Island, who had been involved in
the Gaspee affair;[1] Jonathan Devol of Tiverton, in the
same state, and Griffin Greene of Warwick. From New
Hampshire came two Gilmans of Exeter, and Dr. Jabez
True of Hampstead, the first physician in Marietta. From
Middletown, Connecticut, the pioneers took Return Jonathan Meigs as surveyor for their company. Of such Puritan stuff were the early inhabitants of southeastern Ohio.[2]

[1] Hildreth, *Pioneer Settlers*, 127. Whipple was born in Providence,
Rhode Island, in 1733. After the burning of the Gaspee, he received the
following note from Sir James Wallace, commander of the frigate Rose,
in Newport harbor : —

"You, Abraham Whipple, on the 17th of June, 1772, burned his majesty's vessel, the Grape, and I will hang you at the yard-arm.

JAMES WALLACE."

The following was Whipple's reply : —

"To SIR JAMES WALLACE:

SIR, — Always catch a man before you hang him.

ABRAHAM WHIPPLE."

[2] Hildreth, *Pioneer Settlers*, gives lives of twenty-six Marietta pioneers,
every one with a Puritan name and a record of service to his country.

While these settlers were planting New England traditions on the Ohio River, their friends and neighbors
were beginning homes in the wilderness on the shores
of Lake Erie. From Conneaut,[1] the wave of settlement
flowed over northeastern Ohio. In 1800 settlements had
been begun in thirty-five of the one hundred and three
townships of the Western Reserve east of the Cuyahoga,
and one thousand people had settled there.[2] By 1812
nearly half the state was dotted with towns and farms.
To Plymouth, Ohio, from Plymouth, Connecticut ; to
the new Norwalk from the old ; to Greenwich from
Greenwich on Long Island Sound, — the very names of
the towns indicate the origin of their founders. It was
said of the first settler of Butler County, who came in
1801 from Chelmsford, Massachusetts, that he was in

C. M. Walker, *Athens County*, 371, 372, corrects the story of the "coon-
skin library," which had stated that the first library in Ohio was provided
at Amestown by the sale of coonskins in Boston and the purchase of books
with the proceeds. Jacob Burnet, in *Notes on the Early Settlement of the
Northwestern Territory*, 44, comments upon the retention by these settlers
of many of the customs and habits of their Puritan ancestors; he notes
their "veneration" for the "institution of religion, literature, and moral-
ity," as illustrated by their immediate organization of a church and a
school. In both the Ohio Purchase and the Symmes Purchase (made for
men of the New Jersey line in the southwestern corner of Ohio), section 29
was reserved regularly in each township for the support of a minister.
There was also in each a reservation of land for a college. Doubtless
many of the Symmes company and the later settlers were of New England stock. See Howe, *Hist. Coll. of Ohio*, 562.

    [1] Settled in 1796. See A. B. Hinsdale, *Old Northwest*, 362. In 1796 Ohio
had five bodies of population : Massachusetts was stationed at Marietta,
New Jersey about Cincinnati, Virginia at Chillicothe, Connecticut in
Western Reserve, and the "seven ranges" on the east from Pennsylvania
and Virginia. See Alfred Mathews, *Ohio*, 232, 233. In 1798 the population
of the territory was five thousand. See Burnet, *Notes*, 288.

    [2] J. H. Perkins, *Annals of the West*, 473. See map opposite.

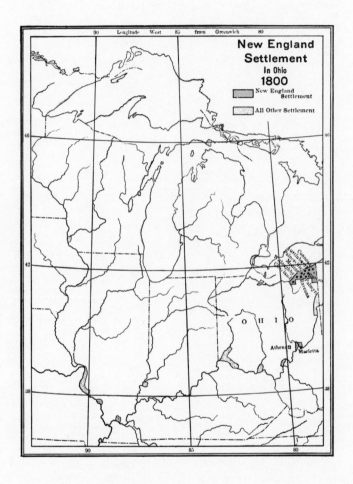

New England
Settlement
In Ohio
1800

New England Settlement

All Other Settlement

every way fitted for pioneer life, since his forefathers
had suffered just such toil and hardship as he was to
meet, when they helped settle Massachusetts, New Hampshire, and Maine.[1] The first settlers in Ashtabula County
towns, in Conneaut and Austinsburgh, were from Connecticut, as were those in Burton (Geauga County).
Some families went from Buffalo by water, whereas
others struck out through the wilderness. Although the
pioneer settlers arrived only in 1798 and 1799, the first
church in the Western Reserve was formed in 1801.
The nearest mill was forty miles away. The founders of
Palmyra, Deerfield, and Ravenna, in Portage County,
were from Connecticut and Massachusetts, as were the
pioneers of Lake County. General Edward Paine, who
began the village of Painesville, was born in Bolton,
Connecticut, had served in the Revolutionary War, and
at the age of fifty-four removed with a company of sixty-
six people from his New York home. Ellsworth, in Ma-
honing County, was settled by Connecticut people with
a few families from Maryland and Pennsylvania.

A typical pioneer was James Kilbourne of Granby,
Connecticut, who formed in 1802 a company with seven
associates to move to the Northwest Territory. Kilbourne was sent on ahead to explore the country and
pick out a tract for forty families; upon his return a
"Scioto Company" was formed, forty persons admitted,
and articles of association signed.[2] In 1803 a school-

---

[1] This was Jeremiah Betterfield. J. McBride, *Pioneer Biography of
Butler County*, ii, 161, 170.

[2] This is not the famous Scioto Company of 1787, which sold land to
the ill-fated Frenchmen who founded Gallipolis; for that company, see

house, a log church, a blacksmith shop, and twelve cabins were erected where Worthington now stands, and one hundred persons had arrived at their new homes. Here was formed the first Episcopal church in Ohio, and Worthington College was chartered in 1817, with Mr. Kilbourne as President. Nor did that energetic pioneer confine his labors to his own town, Worthington; he served in Congress and in the Ohio legislature, and early formed an abolition society.[1]

When the people of Granville, Massachusetts, decided to move, their first care was to select that "peculiar blending of hill and valley" to which they were accustomed. Avoiding swamps, bottomlands were chosen, and Granville, a New England town in central Ohio, was founded. The Congregational church of twenty-four members was organized in the old home and transplanted, pastor, deacons, and members, with the colony.[2] They drew up a sort of compact and a constitution by which their material well-being was to be regulated, — documents which bear a striking similarity to the Springfield compact of 1636, though they were formulated a century and a half after William Pynchon and his comrades moved to the Connecticut River. Having organized their church and drawn up their compact, the colony of one hundred and seventy-six persons took leave of their Massachusetts home, and for forty-six days made

Ohio Arch. and Hist. Soc. Pub., iii, 107–136. Joel Barlow's name is inseparably connected with that speculation.

[1] *Ohio Arch. and Hist. Pub.*, iv, 31–43.

[2] Rev. Benj. Talbot in *Papers of the Ohio Church History Society*, v, 30. A coeducational college was formed here in 1827. See N. N. Hill, Jr. (ed.), *Licking County*, 449.

their way toward the West. When they arrived at the
site of their proposed town, they released their oxen
from the wagons, and then listened to a sermon by their
pastor. The scene takes one back two centuries, to the
planting of Plymouth or of Hartford; the two hundred
years had altered marvelously little the Puritan concep-
tion of the emigrant's first duties in his new home. To
the north, the Becket Land Company, of Becket, Berkshire County, Massachusetts, purchased a township in
Portage County, Ohio, and there planted the town of
Windham between 1811 and 1817. The two upper tiers
of townships in Portage County were so like New England that the fact was remarkable, and a native of any
other state was rarely to be found there; in the southern part of the country was a mingling of New Englanders and Pennsylvanians, with here and there a family
from Virginia, Maryland, or the Carolinas.[1] Many a
country in the central and southern part of the state
had the same heterogeneous population; but the Western Reserve was almost pure Connecticut stock, save
in the southeastern portion, where might be found such
a mixture of elements as that which has been described
in Portage County.

By 1810 the frontier line in Ohio extended in a curve
from the shore of Lake Erie to the western border of
the state, leaving nearly half the whole area unoccupied.

[1] R. C. Brown, in *Hist. of Portage County*, 229, 238, 572. One can see
the difficulty of drawing a line between New England stock and New
Jersey stock in Ohio, as when Newark, Ohio, was laid out by a Newark,
New Jersey, man on the plan of his old home; but the older Newark
was a New England town, and the new Newark is very like its near
neighbor, Granville, which reproduced Granville in the Bay State.

Southerners from Virginia and Kentucky had pushed
their way north from the Ohio River, Pennsylvanians
and New Yorkers had worked inland from the eastern
border, while New England men and women had built
homes in half of the Western Reserve, in the Marietta
region, and were scattered here and there in the central
and southern portions of the state as well.[1] The war of
1812 affected outlying settlements, like those in the
northwestern portion of the state, where the occupation
of such counties as Medina was directly retarded by
fear of the Indians.[2] The return of peace meant opening up new lands, for the savages now had no British
allies to fall back upon for support, and were gradually
pushed farther and farther away into the lands across
the Mississippi. But in the east certain economic conditions attendant upon the war also stimulated emigration. The last years of the conflict had borne hard upon
the population of the New England coast, what with
invasions like that of Falmouth and Portland, and the
seizure of numbers of coasting vessels. Prices had risen

[1] See map on the opposite page. The opening of even such rude trails
as "Zane's Trace" had an enormous influence in developing Ohio. Ebenezer Zane blazed this trail in 1796, from Wheeling, through what is now
Lancaster in Ohio, to Maysville, Kentucky. Congress gave him the pre-
emption right to three tracts of lands for his service in making the road,
one of which he located in Lancaster. By 1797 many settlers were attracted from both north and south by the advantages which the path
offered, and betook themselves and their families to Ohio. See Howe,
Hist. Coll. of Ohio, ii, 328.

[2] N. B. Northrup, *Pioneer Hist. of Medina County*, 7. Its settlement
was begun in 1811–12, but the war checked the accession of newcomers
till 1814. Some of the pioneers of 1811 were from Ira, Vermont, Litchfield County, Connecticut, and Southbury, Connecticut. Other families
came in 1816 from Vermont. See *ibid.*, 32, 88, 95, 125, 212.

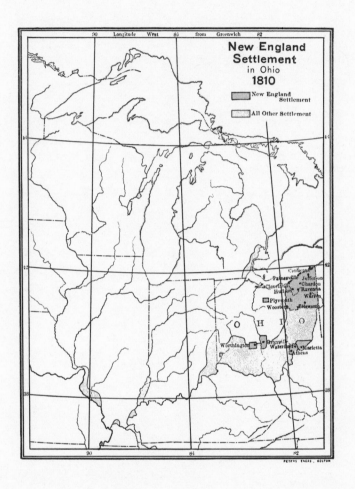

New England
Settlement
in Ohio
1810

New England
Settlement

All Other Settlement

Longitude   West   from   Greenwich

O H I O

Conneaut
Painesville Jefferson
Cleveland Chardon
Hudson Ravenna
Warren
Plymouth Ellsworth
Wooster

Worthington Granville
Waterford Marietta
Athens

in consequence of the war as well as of a succession of poor seasons for agriculture. The debtor class had increased greatly, and many persons who had been fairly prosperous in Jefferson's day found themselves beggared and forced to begin life anew. The years 1815 and 1816 saw hundreds of families setting off for the Ohio and Kentucky country, afflicted (so the newspapers of Maine asserted) with "the Ohio fever." [1] Stimulated by the reports of returning settlers and travelers, emigrants hastened again into the wilderness, pushing the frontier line out to the Mississippi. The sales of public lands were greatly increased up to 1819, when the panic of that year caused a decline temporarily; from 1822 on, the sales again increased, the speculations reaching a climax just before the panic of 1837. The abandonment by the government of the credit system of sales in 1821 probably affected the New England emigrants but little, for they were accustomed to pay for their lands at once, and to make improvements with their remaining capital. From 1814 until 1837 a ceaseless stream of pioneers took their way from the coast, by lake, river, road, and trail, to people the prairie lands of the Northwest Terri' ,ry.

After the Peace of Ghent in 1815, Ohio developed more rapidly than before, but along the lines .etermined before the war, — to the north and west on a New England foundation, to the south on Virginia-New-Jersey-New-England lines, while all these elements met in the centre, with Pennsylvanians and New Yorkers added. Timothy Flint, writing in 1828,[2] saw an essential dis-

[1] Williamson, *Maine*, ii, 664, 665.
[2] Timothy Flint, *Geography and History of the Western States*, ii, 350, 351.

tinction between the different parts of the state, although he admitted that the history of one log cabin and one clearing was substantially that of "an hundred thousand." The emigrants from the Northern and Middle States he found were mostly young people, recently married, with caution so ingrained that they rarely moved into the newer lands without having first investigated the proposed site, either in person, or by some trusted agent. Very infrequently did such immigrants take flocks and herds farther than into the eastern or southern counties of Ohio, but a load of furniture, a gun, and a dog comprised the equipment of hundreds. Flint estimated that his description applied to three-fourths of the ingoing settlers of Ohio and Indiana. The Southerners he found were mostly middle-aged, with families, and frequently "large establishments" of flocks, herds, swine, horses, and slaves. Each pioneer sought land like that which he had known in his old home to be most productive. The uplands, which are now known to be more fertile than any other regions of Ohio, were an unknown quantity to any of the first settlers; they were suspicious of the spacious prairies which are the distinguishing feature of the Mississippi Valley. Therefore the first comers here, like their fellow emigrants who moved later to Illinois and Indiana, chose the bottom or valley lands, and avoided the tracts which now produce most abundantly the staple cereals of that region.[1]

The Western Reserve filled up rapidly with Connecticut people, who not only gave old names to new homes,

[1] H. S. Knapp, *Ashland County*, 24.

but also the distinct character of their earlier abode. Flint found there a large and compact population, distinct from any other in Ohio, and noted especially the "equal dispersion of farms over the surface," the tendency to support schools and churches, — "exceedingly like the parent people from which they sprung."[1] The Connecticut settlers of Medina County who had been used to making dairying a prominent feature of their farming, introduced it very early; in 1847 a native of Vermont began the industry on a large scale, and it has been a chief source of revenue to the county ever since. Agricultural societies, to which the settlers had been used at home, "in the East," grew up here quite as a matter of course. By 1833 the people who had before met rather informally to show the best cattle and products and compare their merits, had begun to have such societies intermittently; the permanent organization dates from 1845.[2]

Oberlin, in Lorain County, deserves more than passing mention. In 1833, when the site of the future town was still a wilderness, a tract three miles square was secured, very level, with a rather stiff clay soil, covered with beech and maple trees. Here a number of families,

---

[1] Timothy Flint, *Geography and History of the Western States*, ii, 362. Note the names of towns in northern Ohio, — New Lyme, Orwell, Colebrook, Windsor, Farmington, Newton, Northfield, Amherst, New Haven, Andover, Hartford, and many more which call to mind their New England prototypes.

[2] Perrin, Battle, and Goodspeed (compilers), *Hist. of Medina County*, 206–210. No author is assigned for this article. It is not certain that the Southerners did not introduce county fairs as early as the New Englanders did. The subject ought to be investigated, for the movement is an interesting and profitable one.

mostly from New England, with a few from New York and northeastern Ohio, gathered to plant a town, a church, and a college, with homes for themselves and their children. Rev. John Shipherd, born in New York, but a Vermonter by training, and his friend Philo Stewart, also reared in Vermont, but born in Connecticut, were the leaders in this movement, which was designed especially to be a missionary enterprise to impress itself upon the surrounding country, and train laborers to work in lands across the ocean for the Christian cause. Mr. Stewart was especially anxious that a school be founded where study and labor might be combined: where students might defray their expenses by manual labor, and yet keep on with their studies. He had been educated in the academy of Pawlet, Vermont, where he had studied and worked in odd moments in his uncle's shop. In that academy, too, young men and young women had worked and studied side by side; his school must, then, include manual training and coeducation.[1]

Having secured the land from its New Haven owners, together with a five-hundred-acre tract for a "Manual Labor School," Mr. Shipherd gathered together colonists, who were all asked to subscribe to a covenant which had been drawn up. Here the settlers vowed themselves to a life of simplicity, to especial devotion to church and school, and to earnest labor in the missionary cause. All were Whigs, feeling it "almost as necessary to be Whigs as to be Christians."[2] Their early political affiliations did not prevent them later from

---

[1] J. H. Fairchild, *Oberlin*, 9–16.   [2] *Ibid.*, 109.

being thoroughgoing abolitionists; they voted with the Liberty party in 1840 and 1844, with the Freesoilers in 1848, and ever after 1854 with the Republicans.

Nor were the Oberlin settlers content with one missionary enterprise; Olivet College in Michigan, founded in 1844, is a child of Oberlin, as is Tabor College, founded in 1851 in Iowa. Oberlin graduates helped to build Hinsdale College in Michigan; Ripon College in Wisconsin; Iowa College in Grinnell, Iowa; Drury College in Springfield, Missouri; and Carleton College in Northfield, Minnesota. President Fairchild says that the impulse of a new college, growing from small beginnings, has seemed to impress many Oberlin students, and they have gone forth with the thought of undertaking a similar enterprise. He believes that such an impulse would hardly be a factor among the students of an old, solidly established college. " It comes when college-building is a part of the education." [1]

The church at Oberlin was organized in 1834, with sixty-two members; its confession of faith was of the New England Calvinistic type, but the church nevertheless connected itself with the Cleveland Presbytery, under the "Plan of Union" already familiar to students of New York church history. The same plan was followed by practically all the early settlers of the Western Reserve, whose churches, while Congregational in their constitution and confession, maintained their

---

[1] *Ibid.*, 152, 153. John Brown's father was a trustee of Oberlin as early as 1835 and his younger brothers and sisters were students here, while Brown himself helped survey some of the college lands in West Virginia. *Ibid.*, 157.

outward fellowship through connection with some presbytery. The Congregational Church of Granville, which
had been organized in Granville, Massachusetts, and
had been transplanted with the settlers, had become
involved in a church quarrel, which led in 1827 to the
division of the old church into two Presbyterian congregations, while the Congregational Church continued
its own existence with a remnant of its former membership. A little later an Episcopal church was the result
of another quarrel. In about a year after their division,
the two Presbyterian churches and the Congregational
one reunited under a " Plan of Union," and joined the
Licking County conference because the church was isolated in Christian fellowship. This church also became
a practically total abstinence organization, for after 1831
it admitted no one who " drank, bought, sold, or
manufactured ardent spirits, except for medicinal or
mechanical purposes." [1]

When Ohio was admitted as a state, one condition
was made which formed a precedent followed by most
states ever since. In every township one whole section
was to be set apart for the support of schools; — in
this state, as in most others, section sixteen of each
township was so reserved.[2] Thus the government put
itself on record as the advocate of public education, and
a precedent was established which has given character
not only to the states admitted after 1803, but to the
whole nation as well.

[1] Rev. Henry Bushnell, *Granville, Ohio*, 130, 210, 213.
[2] Beginning with the admission of Wisconsin in 1848, section 36 has
been reserved as well as section 16.

Although provision was made thus early for Ohio schools, nevertheless, all education before 1821 was purely voluntary, no public school system having been evolved. The legislature simply authorized the formation of school companies, and passed some regulations as to the universities of Oxford and Miami. In 1821, however, a recommendatory law was passed providing for the support of common schools; four years later the law was changed to a compulsory statute, the alteration being largely the work of Judge Ephraim Cutler, a member of the state legislature sent by constituents in the Western Reserve. Harvey Rice, born in Conway, Massachusetts, who had moved to Cleveland in 1824, was in 1851 made chairman of the committee on schools in the State Senate, and here he prepared and introduced a bill organizing the common school system of Ohio as it is to-day.[1]

With the story of the founding of Yale College and of Dartmouth in mind, it would be surprising not to find in its early history an institution of higher learning in northern Ohio. Western Reserve College, chartered in 1826, was modeled after Yale, both in its course of study and in the organization of its governing board, where the majority was to be made up of clergymen in both cases. In the beginning this majority had four out of seven men from Yale. Its first president was Dr. George E. Pierce, a graduate of the New Haven institution in 1816, who was said to have been thoroughly imbued with the Connecticut idea of a college.

[1] "Autobiography of Harvey Rice," in *Annals of the Early Settlers' Association of Cuyahoga County*, iii, 34–39.

Most of his faculty were Yale men, and for years the new college followed the lines of the old in every detail of its organization, administration, and courses of study. It has been from the first a practice for Yale and Western Reserve to have from time to time what one may almost call an interchange of instructors, for Yale graduates teach in the western college and graduates of Western Reserve are called to Yale, to help in carrying out the work of their own college's Alma Mater. Thus the two colleges have kept in closest touch with one another, — the old Yale in the old Connecticut, the new Yale in Connecticut's Western Reserve.[1]

In the matter of town and county organization, Ohio shows a development related more nearly to New York than it is to either New England or Virginia. It was but natural that a state in which the population was so mixed as it was in Ohio should adopt a compromise between the Virginia county and the New England town; the New York system showed a middle way which would preserve both organizations in harmony. Moreover, the counties of Ohio were erected in advance of any settlement save that of the most haphazard and isolated sort; only after the people had made very considerable headway in taking up lands and planting towns was any other civil administration required than that afforded by the county organization.

The county organization was in 1831 based upon the election of three county commissioners,[2] whose term was

[1] For the close connection between the two colleges, see Dr. Northrup, "Yale in its Relation to the Development of the Country," in the *Record of the Bicentennial Celebration of Yale University*, 307–309.

[2] *Laws of Ohio, 1831*, 44, 267–280, 315, 316, 344, 413, 484, 485.

three years, and who held annual sessions. These commissioners were to erect in their county a courthouse, of which the county sheriff was to have charge, and a poorhouse, for whose oversight they appointed three directors; besides these duties, they were to examine county accounts, administer oaths, etc. To these officers was intrusted the matter of erecting townships, and calling for the election of township officers, — three trustees, a clerk, two overseers of the poor, a treasurer, three fence viewers, a constable, and supervisors of highways. The township trustees have charge of the work of laying off school districts; the electors then choose the school officers. By the county judges of the court of common pleas is determined the number of justices of the peace for each township; when this number is settled upon, the electors choose them. The county government comprises, besides the commissioners and judges already mentioned, an assessor, prosecuting attorney, auditor, recorder, treasurer, sheriff, and coroner. There are, therefore, the two complete local administrative and judicial bodies, the county taking precedence of the township, which is subordinate to it, as the county is subordinate to the state. The matter of roads shows the same administrative divisions, for there are state roads, with their own commissioners; county roads, with their own viewers and surveyors; and township roads, with their own officers. Thus the development, while not deviating far from the New York pattern, has not followed exactly the New England system, which it nevertheless recalls.

Enough has been said to show the nature of Ohio

settlement. A frontier built by New Englanders at the North joined one constructed by Southerners, New Jersey men and their neighbors from the South, till the whole state, save only the Western Reserve and such localities as Granville and Marietta, had assumed a composite character which differentiated it from any of the old states. Yet New England tradition had been impressed upon Ohio; it had crystallized in the New Connecticut, and reproduced itself in Granville. Into the new West the school, the church, and the town-meeting had been carried; they were changed, for here, as in New York, the man from Massachusetts or Connecticut had been forced to compromise with his neighbor from Pennsylvania or Virginia whose ideas of institutions differed from those of the Puritan. But the change had not concealed the original type, nor obscured the ideal which lay at the foundations of all three institutions.[1]

[1] See maps opposite pages 206, 210, 236, 246.

Professor Chamberlain, of Vassar College, has drawn the author's attention to a little volume by Rev. Josiah Strong, entitled *Our Country*, published about 1885 by the American Home Missionary Society (New York, n. d.). Dr. Strong, on pages 145 and 146 of that volume, gives a curious story of two adjoining townships in the Western Reserve. One was founded by a home missionary with high ideals, who drew about him a selected body of settlers. At the centre of the township, where eight roads met, was set a church, and soon afterward "followed the school-house and the public library," with an academy a little later on. In this township (which Dr. Strong does not name, but which has been identified as Talmadge township of Summit County) was opened the first school for the deaf in Ohio.

The other township (not named by Dr. Strong, but identified as Stow township in Summit County) was first settled by an infidel who "expressed the desire that there might never be a Christian Church in the township." Dr. Strong says that to his knowledge there has never been one. He then draws inferences distinctly unfavorable to Stow township.

By 1840 Ohio's vacant land was all occupied, and the state had passed out of the pioneer stage; it had no longer a frontier, it had ceased to be the "far west," for that ever receding region had moved on to Illinois and the lands beyond the Mississippi. The population had become comparatively dense; as the number of inhabitants increased, the whole state became more homogeneous, and New Englanders were found everywhere, side by side with New York men, families from Pennsylvania, and settlers from Virginia. Cincinnati had in 1841 representatives of many states, besides a large percentage of immigrants of foreign birth.[1] The census of 1850 showed that 23,000 of Ohio's people had emigrated from Connecticut, 19,000 from Massachusetts, 14,000 from Vermont, 84,000 from New York, and

[1] A population including 12,292 males was made up as follows (excluding 46 per cent of foreigners ; only 54 per cent were of American birth, — a significant fact to be noted when one recalls the large German element in Cincinnati's population to-day) : —

Pennsylvania	1210
Ohio	1112
New Jersey	795
New York	672
Virginia	519
Maryland	537
Massachusetts	414
Kentucky	349
Connecticut	230
Vermont	118
Maine	96
Delaware	90
New Hampshire	70
Rhode Island	62

(The rest scattering)

See Charles Cist, *Cincinnati in 1841*, 38, 39.

9000 from Maine, Rhode Island, and New Hampshire. A decade later, the proportions had changed, though Ohio still counted 53,000 New England born men and women among her inhabitants. The emigrants from the coast had aided not a little in the labor of building a new state; by 1860 their sons and daughters had joined a host of other pioneers from New England to repeat the work their fathers had done, this time upon a new frontier far across the Mississippi, beyond the Rocky Mountains.

BIBLIOGRAPHICAL NOTES

HERE, as in all the preceding chapters, many more sources of information have gone into the preparation of the maps illustrating the text than can be cited in the footnotes or enumerated here. The most careful work on Ohio local history has been done in the New England centres, where the self-consciousness of the settlers has tended to full records of their life, as it had done in the case of their ancestors.

A good starting-point is Henry Howe's *Historical Collections of Ohio*, new edition, 2 vols., 1904. The *Annals* of the "Cuyahoga County Early Settlers' Association" (3 vols.) is distinctly like the work of Massachusetts historians. The State Archæological and Historical Society has thirteen volumes of *Publications* which are very good. Two county histories for which no person assumes the responsibility as editor or compiler are, nevertheless, of some value : *The History of Portage County, Ohio* (Chicago, 1885), and *The History of Medina County and Ohio* (Chicago, 1881). N. B. Northrup also has a good *Pioneer History of Medina County* (Medina, 1861). H. N. Hill, Jr., has compiled a *History of Licking County* (Newark, Ohio, 1881) ; H. S. Knapp has done a good piece of work in compiling *A History of the Pioneer and Modern Times of Ashland County* (Philadelphia, 1863). Alfred Mathews's *Ohio and her Western Reserve* is a rather popular study, but suggestive for the work of New Englanders in Ohio. James McBride has a *Pioneer Biography* (sketches of the lives of early settlers in Butler County) in two volumes, which is a good piece of work. Dr. S. P. Hildreth's *Biographical and Historical Memoirs of the Early Pioneer Settlers* of Ohio gives an excellent idea of Marietta, its settlers, and its institutions. Rev. Henry Bushnell's *History of Granville* and President James Fairchild's *Oberlin* are indispensable, and the standard for their towns. Rev. Dr. C. E. Dickinson's *Century of Church Life* gives the history of the Marietta church founded by the pioneers. Charles Cist has a good volume on *Cincinnati in 1841*.

The Laws of Ohio (Columbus, 1831) are the source for the town and county system.

The work of Timothy Flint which is referred to in the text is *A Condensed Geography and History of the Western States* (2 vols., Cincinnati, 1828), — a storehouse of information. J. H. Perkins's *Annals of the West* (Cincinnati, 1846) is full of anecdotes for Ohio, Indiana, and Illinois. Jacob Burnet, in *Notes on the Early Settlement of the Northwestern Territory* (New York, 1847), makes many shrewd comments on the character of early settlers. J. M. Peck's *Guide for Emigrants* (Boston, 1831) is very suggestive. Professor B. A. Hinsdale's *Old Northwest* is still of value.

Professor A. B. Hulbert's work, *Historic Highways* (16 vols.), referred to in this chapter, supplements with much detail the very general statements made in this chapter on routes to Ohio from the east, as do Dr. R. G. Thwaites's collections in 32 vols., — *Early Western Travels*.

The New England Magazine (New Series, 1889–1908) has a number of articles of varying excellence, which gives information of New Englanders in the West.

CHAPTER VIII

THE JOINING OF TWO FRONTIERS: INDIANA AND ILLINOIS

1809-1865

THE census of 1800 gave Illinois two hundred and fifteen inhabitants, and Indiana about the same number. These inhabitants were either the French at Vincennes, and at the forts upon the Mississippi and the Ohio, or the few trappers and hunters of the Daniel Boone type who had crossed the river from Kentucky or Virginia. Between the beginning of the nineteenth century and the opening of hostilities in 1812, the population had increased about the three centres, — Vincennes and the two forts, — but the two territories were still, to all intents and purposes, a wilderness. Yet here and there among the forerunners of incoming settlement might even then be found a venturesome New Englander. In 1805 a native of Connecticut who had tried frontier life in Kentucky pushed with his family into the woods of Gibson County, Indiana;[1] and Joshua Atwater, born in Westfield, Massachusetts, took his "New England habits and education" with him to Madison County, Illinois, where he taught school, and founded in 1809 what was probably the first charitable institution in that territory.[2] But such cases were the exceptional ones; men like these formed only the vanguard of the advancing army

[1] J. T. Tarte, compiler, *Hist. of Gibson County*, 55. See map opposite page 182.

[2] J. T. Hair, compiler, *Gazetteer of Madison County*, 136, n.

of those settlers, who, once the treaty of Ghent had
opened the way, resumed their march westward and
passed beyond the confines of Ohio to the prairies and
woods of Indiana and Illinois. Indiana, however, never
received any large accession of New Englanders; the
typical " Hoosier" of to-day is far more like a Kentuckian
or a Carolinian than he is like a New Yorker or a man
from the Bay State. In Illinois the Puritan element is
found chiefly in the northern third of the state. The
history of settlement in both regions is, however, the
history of a frontier pushed north by Southerners, and
of settlement by Puritan stock working down from the
North toward the centre, where both met and strove for
supremacy in state councils.

Throughout the territorial period there was " nothing
like a New England town " in Indiana,[1] nor was there
any appreciable number of New England settlers. The
tide from the East was up to 1816 flowing into western
New York, Pennsylvania, and Ohio; and although
southern Indiana was filling up with farms and towns,
the new population was chiefly from Kentucky, Ten-

[1] Introduction to the *Executive Journal of Indiana Territory*, 78. (In
Indiana State Hist. Soc. Pub., vol. iii). There were, however, at least
two attempts to plant such towns. In the *Annals of Congress*, 1804 – 05,
page 872, is a petition of Benjamin Strong of Vermont, for a tract of
land six miles square in Indiana Territory for a colony. In the *State Papers*,
vol. i on *Public Lands*, page 288, is a petition of December 1806, from
inhabitants of Ovid, New York, for the privilege of purchasing a whole
township "on the White River, or Wabash," in Indiana territory. They
make this request "that by their compact settlement thereon, they may
be the better able to aid each other in the support of schools and religion. "
Ovid was settled 1790 – 91 and the succeeding years by emigrants from
New Jersey, "Pennsylvania on the New Jersey line," New Englanders,
and eastern New Yorkers. Hotchkin, *Western New York*, 392.

nessee, or the Southern States along the Atlantic coast. The territorial offices had been filled almost without exception by Virginians, but with the coming of statehood new elements entered, and the Southerners were no longer in control. The extremely cold seasons of 1816-17 were responsible for the failure of crops in the East, and many farmers from western New York and northwestern Pennsylvania built large boats upon which they moved their families and household goods down the Ohio River into the southeastern part of Indiana,—into Dearborn, Jennings, Switzerland, and Washington counties. Here they generally formed neighborhood settlements. During the years between 1816 and 1820 Pennsylvanians usually held the rudder politically, aided here and there by a "stray Yankee."[1] These newcomers were not, on the whole, pure New England stock, nor had they moved directly from that section, but they brought the "Yankee" axe, with the crooked helve; they used oxen for rolling logs, and they built their cabins square, not oblong with the chimney in one end, making a fifth corner like the letter "V," as in the Virginia and Kentucky style of frontier architecture. While the Kentuckians built only rude horse-mills, these "Yankees" erected water-mills on the streams. Although the acute economic distress had been the directly impelling motive for their emigration, the remark of one who had been elected a judge in Indiana at this time, and was on a visit to his old home, doubtless voiced the secret aspiration of many an ambi-

---

[1] Rev. Dr. Wood, in Rev. F. C. Holliday's *Indiana Methodism*, 90, 91. Dr. Wood was a circuit-rider and preacher in Indiana in its early days.

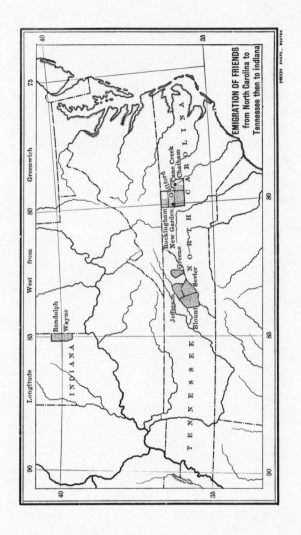

EMIGRATION OF FRIENDS
from North Carolina to
Tennessee then to Indiana

ENGEL ENGRS., BOSTON

tious young Eastern man, when he said: "Do you think I would stay here and be a *common man*, when I can go there and be a *judge?*"[1]

Gradually, beginning after the panic of 1819, the New England emigrants filtered into the towns and counties of Indiana. A family from Brattleboro, Vermont, came in 1820; Calvin Fletcher from Ludlow in the same state, the following year; one of the early settlers of Cass County came in 1826 from his birthplace, New Canaan, Connecticut; one of the first physicians in southeastern Indiana came in 1821 from Massachusetts. One reads sketches of many men of New England birth who came in these early days from Ohio and New York, where they had lived for a few years, and at this period moved on to cheaper land. A more roundabout emigration resulted in opening up Wayne and Randolph counties, which in an early day showed some features of Puritan origin, brought in by Quakers of Nantucket descent, with others who had come of Cape Cod and Pennsylvania stock. They removed either from Guilford County (and the adjoining counties of Rockland, Chatham, and Rockingham) in North Carolina; or the eastern counties of Blount, Sevier, Greene, and Jefferson, in Tennessee. But they all brought strong prejudices against slavery, and maintained them in the midst of neighbors who sympathized with the South.[2]

[1] *Ibid.*, 91.

[2] See map opposite.

E. Tucker, *Hist. of Randolph County, Indiana*, 82, 462; and Levi Coffin, *Reminiscences*, 4, 6, 11. Here are the families of Coffin, Starbuck, and Swain, all of whom were descendants of the Nantucket Quakers who

The great influx of New England settlement came in 1830 and the years succeeding that date. Families came either singly, or in groups of two or three households, most of them between 1830 and 1837, settling the northern tier of counties from Steuben on the eastern border to Lake on the Illinois boundary;[1] going in smaller numbers to the second tier;[2] and only here and

removed to Guilford County, 1770-76. Also J. H. Wheeler, *North Carolina*, ii, 170 ; and A. W. Young, *Wayne County* (Indiana), 29, 30, 98.

[1] See *Hist. of Steuben County*, 423–819. Also *Hist. of DeKalb County*, 540–864 ; *Counties of Lagrange and Noble*, 315–426, 429–477. Almost all the sketches of settlers in both these counties show men of Connecticut or of Vermont birth, with some from Massachusetts, and fewer still from New Hampshire. In the *Hist. of Elkhart County*, 362–364, is given a list of 300 members of the *Pioneers' Association*, who came between 1828 and 1840. They are classified as to nativity as follows : —

Ohio	102
New York	46
Indiana	33
Pennsylvania	32
Virginia	19
Maryland	5
Kentucky	3
Connecticut	3
Vermont	3
New Jersey	2
Tennessee	2
Rhode Island	1
New Hampshire	1
Maine	1
North Carolina	1
South Carolina	1

A large emigration came from Orange County, New York, 1832–40 ; many of these emigrants were of New England stock, as was the author's grandfather, who moved with these emigrants in 1837 and settled at Middlebury in this county. See also *Hist of St. Joseph County*, 375 ff.

[2] *Hist. of Allen County*, 124, 157 ; Goodspeed and Blanchard, *Counties of Whitley and Noble*, 164–309 ; 326–477.

there into the third.[1] To the south, some few drifted
in and around the Quakers of Richmond and Wayne
County;[2] others may be traced in the southeastern corner,[3] and in Evansville.[4] In the central portion of the
state, very few came in the early years;[5] but in Indianapolis there is to-day a "New England Society" made
up of those emigrants who were born in the New
England States.

Certain counties came gradually during these years
to be known as New England counties. These lay in
general along the northern border, dipping south on
the eastern boundary, with scattered families in the centre. La Grange County, in the northeastern part of the
state, will illustrate the point. The leading spirit for
many years in the town of Wolcottville was one George
Wolcott, born in Torrington, Connecticut, who came to
Indiana in 1837. Old settlers whose lives are woven
into the history of the county came from such Massachusetts counties as Worcester, Berkshire, and Suffolk;
from Connecticut counties, — Hartford, Windham, —
and towns like Sherman, Lebanon, and Fairfield; from
Vermont, — Burlington, Brookfield, Huntington, and
Grand Isle. Noble County had a similar heterogeneous
collection of pioneers. La Porte County drew its early

[1] T. B. Helm. (ed.), *Hist. of Cass County*, 493–494, 529, 545–548.

[2] A. W. Young, *Wayne County*, 188–412. There is a sketch of a New
Englander here and there.

[3] *Hist. of Dearborn, Ohio, and Switzerland Counties*, 149–150, 167–173,
560–605, 1185–1237. These settlers came in from 1814 to 1825.

[4] White, *Evansville*, 14, 15, 37, 75, 76, 317–340. Several of these came
in between 1850 and 1860.

[5] *Counties of White and Pulaski*, 223–318. Also J. H. Nowland, *Sketches
of Prominent Citizens [of Indianapolis]*, 152–292.

settlers from Massachusetts towns, — Granville, Boston, Bridgewater, and West Bridgewater, Andover, Nantucket Island, and Hampshire County; from Connecticut, — Colchester, Wethersfield, Granby, and New Haven; from Maine, — Penobscot County, especially; from New Hampshire, — Bradford, Amherst, Goffstown; from Vermont, — Orange and Caledonia counties, the villages of Dorset, Fairfax, and Albany.

There were also New England towns, though such compact settlements were on the whole rare in Indiana. In Steuben County the Vermont settlement at Orland was widely known as a centre of Whig and Free-Soil politicians. Settled in 1834, after John Stocker had gone prospecting for his own and his neighbors' families, and had chosen this county because of the rich burr-oak openings he found, the pioneers from Windham County, Vermont, organized their Baptist church the next year, and before long had laid plans for the " Orland Academy." [1] The " New Hampshire settlement " on Lake Prairie in Lake County was such a compact town which dated from 1855. The next year the families living there established a church and a school, and the town of Lowell perpetuated the traditions thus established in a prairie village. [2]

The biographies of a few typical pioneers will illustrate the transplanting of the New England man to Indiana. Calvin Fletcher of Ludlow, Vermont, state attorney, later state senator, was appointed by the legislature in 1834 to help organize a state bank and to

[1] *Hist. of Steuben County*, 314, 455–492.
[2] Rev. T. H. Ball, *Lake County, Indiana, 1834 to 1872*, 99.

act as sinking-fund commissioner; he was always interested in agricultural societies, was an anti-slavery man " on principle," and for many years a trustee of the Indianapolis schools.[1] James Whitcomb, born in Windsor, Vermont, was taken to Ohio as a boy, and lived there until he moved to Bloomington, Indiana, at the age of twenty-seven. Made governor in 1843, when the state was loaded down with a debt upon which not even the interest had been paid for years, he had at the end of six years adjusted the outstanding obligations so that the state's credit was restored.[2] By his efforts public sentiment in favor of reformatory and benevolent institutions was created. A third illustration is John Comstock of Greenwich, Rhode Island, who was in public life for many years after his arrival in 1836, and was one of those upon whose generosity the " war governor " of Indiana relied to help fill a treasury depleted by a divided state.[3]

An incident from Lake County history shows the New England perseverance in gaining what the people of that section regarded as their rights, organizing and combining to secure and preserve them. The settlers of Lake County, squatters upon unsold lands, were waiting for the passage by Congress of a preëmption law which would insure them their homes. John Robinson, a native of Connecticut, called a meeting at his house on the Fourth of July, 1836, where he was appointed one of

[1] W. W. Woollen, *Biog. and Hist. Sketches of Early Indiana,* 464–466.

[2] *Ibid.,* 81–83. He did this by securing the passage of the Butler Bill, whereby one half the debt was paid through the transfer of the Wabash and Erie Canal, and the other half funded by the issuance of bonds bearing a low rate of interest.

[3] *Hist. of Wabash County,* 286, 287.

a committee to draft a constitution for a "Squatters' Union," and was made one of a board of three arbitrators of claims under this constitution. It was declared that actual settlers ought to have their lands at $1.25 per acre, and not be deprived of them or compelled to pay a higher price by reason of speculation ; that if Congress did not protect the settlers, they would themselves take " *such measures as may be necessary* " to secure one another in their just claims. Therefore a board of arbitrators and a registrar of claims was provided for, each township in the county to have such an arrangement if it so desired. Each signer was to use his influence to get his friends and acquaintances to join the settlement, " under the full assurance that we shall now obtain our rights, and that it is now perfectly as safe to go on improving the public land as though we already had our titles from government." [1]

Upon the whole, Indiana has been influenced more from the South than from New England. Yet the free school system was the work chiefly of a teacher in Wabash College, — Professor Caleb Mills, a graduate of Dartmouth College. In 1846 he prepared his first address to the state legislature, a plea for a public school system for Indiana. The interest which it aroused from the moment a copy was laid upon the desk of every member of the legislature was increased by an address prepared for each session up to 1851. Another paper was placed before the constitutional convention of 1850 by Professor Mills, signed, as the others had been, by

---

[1] Rev. T. H. Ball, *Lake County*, 41–48, 277. Robinson was called "The Squatter King of Lake."

" One of the People." The state legislature had five thousand copies of one of the addresses printed and distributed throughout the state. Finally the system was established, and when it was learned that Professor Mills was " One of the People," " the people he had so well served were quick to honor him by an unsought election to the office of state superintendent of public instruction." [1]

Professor Mills's efforts were not confined to the public schools. He was the first head of Wabash College, which he built up on the lines of Dartmouth College and of Andover Academy, where he had been trained as a boy. His work was done shoulder to shoulder with his classmate from Andover and from Dartmouth, — E. O. Hovey, for forty-four years a trustee of Wabash College. [2]

All through northern Indiana the Congregational Church has its representatives, or the Presbyterian Church to which, as in Ohio and New York, many of those who had been Congregationalists turned because of its larger organization. The first Congregational church in Kokomo was founded in 1863 by the members of a New England family. Plymouth church, in Indianapolis, has always had a large membership of New England descent.

It was to an early settler of Dearborn County, who

---

[1] J. M. Butler, in *Reunion of the New England Society of Indianapolis in 1894,* 38, 39. See, also, Dr. W. A. Rawles, *Centralizing Tendencies in the Administration of Indiana,* Columbia University, " Studies in History, Economics, and Public Law," vol. xvii, no. 1; also Dr. F. T. Carlton, *Economic Influences upon Educational Progress in the United States,* 1820 to 1850, in the " Economics and Political Science Series, Bulletins of the University of Wisconsin," vol. iv, no. 1. For Indiana settlement in 1820, 1830, and 1840, see maps opposite pages 206, 210, and 236.

[2] Rev. J. F. Tuttle, in *Hist. of Montgomery County,* 156.

was born in Mansfield, Connecticut, had lived in Vermont, and came to southeastern Indiana to make his home, that Indiana owes its township system. About 1822 this pioneer secured its adoption as a system local to his own county; but so ingrained had its advantages become in the minds of Dearborn County people, that nearly thirty years later a member of the state legislature from that very county introduced the bill extending the system (modified, to be sure) to all the counties of the state.[1] As one might expect, however, the township is distinctly subordinated to the county, — more so than is the case in states like New York or Ohio, where Puritan influence was stronger than in Indiana.

The settlement of Illinois presents many features in common with that of its neighbor, Indiana. Settlers had worked up into Illinois from the South before 1812, as has been said; in 1818, when the territory became a state, only the southern half had as yet been occupied, and that portion wholly by representatives of Virginia, Kentucky, and the Carolinas, whose influence dominated the territorial stage. Here and there a New England family might be found, as at Collinsville (Madison County), opposite St. Louis, where the three Collins brothers, from Litchfield, Connecticut, established themselves in 1817.[2] They used the same horse-power for a distillery and a sawmill, ran a cooper shop, a blacksmith shop, a wagon shop, and a carpenter shop, besides warehouses both in Collinsville and at St. Louis. They were not wholly engrossed in money-getting, however; they,

---

[1] *Hist. of Dearborn, Ohio, and Switzerland Counties*, 149, 150.
[2] See map opposite.

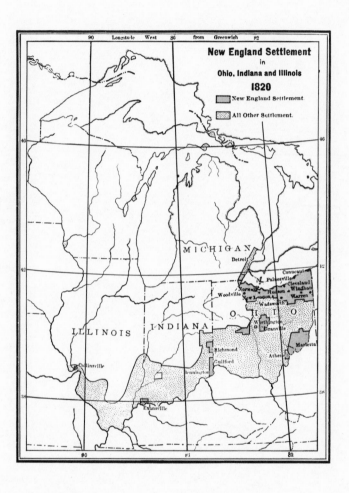

New England Settlement
in
Ohio, Indiana and Illinois
1820

New England Settlement.

All Other Settlement.

with their neighbors, built in 1818 a union meeting-house, which was used for the public school during the week, and for a Sunday school after church service. When the father of these men came in 1824, he made the first substantial subscription for Illinois College.[1] One of the first three settlers in Quincy, Adams County, came about 1823 from Newfane, Vermont, by way of "Canada and the Northern lakes." His reason for emigrating he gives in his diary: "[I was] impelled by curiosity and a desire to see other places than those in the vicinity of my native town."[2]

But such settlers were the exception in the early days of Illinois; Southerners were in the great majority, and in 1818 they shaped the state constitution along the lines of the "Old Dominion" and her neighbors.[3] The first code of laws was a Southern code, mainly from the statute books of Kentucky and Virginia; and every one of the first six governors was a Southern man; for twenty-five years the senators and representatives of the new state were almost without exception men born south of the Ohio.[4] It was later that the fourteen northern counties, the New England stronghold, forced the township system upon the rest of the state.[5] The hostility

[1] J. T. Hair, *Gazetteer of Madison County*, 145, 146.

[2] Asbury, *Reminiscences*, 25, 26.

[3] Dr. Albert Shaw, *Local Government in Illinois*, 9.

[4] H. L. Boies, *Hist. of DeKalb County*, 46 ; Greene, *Government of Illinois*, 36.

[5] E. B. Greene, "Sectional Forces in the History of Illinois," in *Trans. of Ill. Hist. Soc.* for 1903, p. 80. Dr. W. V. Pooley has prepared an admirable study on *The Settlement of Illinois from 1830 to 1850*, vol. i, no. 4 of the "History Series, Bulletins of the University of Wisconsin" (May, 1908). It contains some accurate and suggestive maps.

between the pioneers from the South and their rivals in state-building who came in by way of northern Indiana dated back, however, to the territorial days, when New England was for the most part represented by tricky itinerant clock-peddlers. The Southerners conceived the idea that a genuine " Yankee " was miserly, shrewd to the point of dishonesty, and absolutely lacking in kindliness or hospitality towards his neighbors; they retained this belief long after the peddler had departed and the substantial Puritan farmer had taken up an abode in a state where he meant to spend the rest of his days. The New Englanders, on their side, misunderstood their Southern neighbors, and confused them all with the "poor whites" who had contented themselves with the squatter's log cabin. Many of the Southerners, it is true, were poor; they had been unable to hold slaves in the South by reason of their poverty, and had come into the Northwest Territory not only to better their condition, but also to avoid a system of which they did not disapprove on principle, but had found unpleasant on account of the social distinctions it produced. Others had turned their faces Illinois-ward, even after the passage of the Missouri Compromise; but that measure diverted Southern emigration very markedly to the lands across the Missouri, leaving northern Illinois for the New Yorkers and New Englanders. Most of these later emigrants were wealthy farmers, enterprising merchants, millers, and manufacturers, who built mills, churches, schoolhouses, cities, and made roads and bridges with astonishing public spirit; so that the southern part of the state, though it was many years older in point of

settlement, was noticeably behind in point of wealth
and evidences of public spirit and prosperity.[1] A strong
sectional antagonism sprang up, due to the entire mis-
understanding existing between the northern and the
southern portions of the state. Southerners opposed the
Illinois and Michigan Canal because of the fear that if
completed it would "flood the state with Yankees";[2]
the Northerners resented the attempt to force them to
help pay a heavy state debt which had been recklessly
incurred before their arrival.[3]

This mutual lack of comprehension and consequent
violent sectional antagonism came to a climax in 1840.
In that year a mass-meeting was held at Rockford in
Winnebago County (on the northern boundary), where
one hundred and twenty delegates met, every one of
whom had come from the counties lying north of a line
drawn from the southern bend of Lake Michigan to the
Mississippi River. This region had been added to Illinois
in 1818, largely through the efforts of Nathaniel Pope;
the settlers felt themselves much more closely allied in
their interests with Wisconsin, which contained a popu-

[1] *Hist. of Madison County* (Illinois), 91 ; also ex-Gov. Thos. Ford, *Illinois*, 280, 281. Ford says : " The southerner is perhaps the most hospitable and generous to individuals. He is lavish of his victuals, his liquors,
and other personal favors. But the northern man is the most liberal in
contributing to whatever is for the public benefit. Is a schoolhouse, a
bridge, or a church to be built, a road to be made, a school or minister to
be maintained, or taxes to be paid for the honor or support of government, the northern man is never found wanting." See, also, Shaw, *Local
Government in Illinois*, 11. Also C. A. Church, *Hist. of Rockford*, 160 ff.

[2] Ford, *Illinois*, 281. This was said in a speech by Lieutenant-Governor
Kinney before the state Senate; he said that the Yankees spread everywhere, and that he was looking daily for them to overrun the state.

[3] Church, *Hist. of Rockford*, 161.

lation made up almost entirely of New Yorkers and
New Englanders, as did this northern quarter of Illinois.
Among these delegates of 1840 were several from Vermont, Massachusetts, and Connecticut; a Putney, Vermont, man was made chairman.[1] A set of resolutions
was drawn up, stating that since it was the general belief of the residents of the disputed tract that it ought
to be a part of Wisconsin, therefore a committee should
be appointed to inform the governor of Wisconsin of
the result of the meeting. Other boundary conventions
were held in different parts of the district within the
next eighteen months, and similar resolutions adopted.
In August, 1842, the Commissioners' Court of Winnebago County having submitted the matter to popular
vote, the returns gave 976 for annexation to Wisconsin,
and 6 against it. Yet the movement lost its momen-
tum and the plan came to nothing.[2] Nevertheless, the
episode is most significant of the strong sectional antagonism, and the length to which the Northern pioneers
were willing to go rather than be dominated by an element foreign in aims and interests to their own.

The New Englanders who led this movement for
secession to Wisconsin had practically all come into Illinois since 1830,[3] but the number of emigrants before
that time was only the smallest fraction in comparison
with the host who came during the six or seven years
preceding the panic of 1837, when immigration was
again for a time retarded. The close of the Black Hawk

---

[1] *Hist. of Rockford*, 162.   [2] *Ibid.*, 163, 164.
[3] See maps in chapter ix for 1840 and 1850, and frontispiece for 1860.
See map opposite.

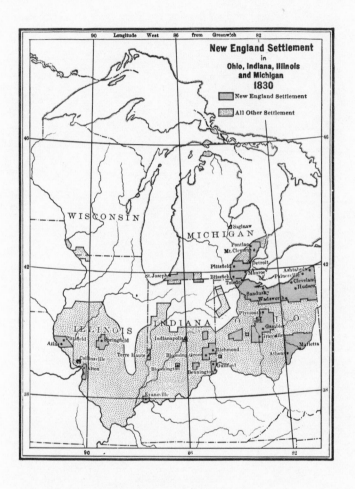

New England Settlement in Ohio, Indiana, Illinois and Michigan 1830

War of 1832 saw a marked increase in the number of settlers to the northern counties, especially, partly because danger from savages no longer confronted the pioneer, and partly because of the increased knowledge of the fertile lands through which the volunteers had passed. Not only did many of the soldiers move here themselves, but they invited their old neighbors and friends to join them.[1] Moreover, writers like Peck were getting out their gazetteers for those who contemplated emigration from the older states, and the prospects for future wealth were most alluring.

In studying the movement of the tide of immigration which poured in from the East after the Black Hawk War, again and again are we impressed with the conservatism of it, — the recurrence of methods which had marked the expansion of Massachusetts or Connecticut two centuries before. Illinois was settled by many New England colonies, such as those with whose type and organization we are already familiar. A company from Gilmanton, New Hampshire, settled Hanover (now called Metamora) in 1835, after the prospecting tour of their townsman, John Page, who had picked out the tract as being peculiarly attractive for farms. Others from Rhode Island, Vermont, and Massachusetts joined the settlement later.[2] A number of settlers from Pittsfield, Massachusetts, joined forces to begin Pittsfield, Illinois, though here the movement was simply a neighborhood affair, and not that of an organized colony.[3] Tremont, in

[1] *Hist. of Stephenson County*, 225. See map opposite page 236.

[2] *Past and Present of Woodford County*, 274–512.

[3] Five brothers and a few other families came in 1820. *Hist. of Pike County*, 650–690.

Tazewell County, was laid out around a public square, the character of the buildings and the whole tone of the village being in 1838 remarkably like that of a New England town.[1] The Wethersfield colony was settled by a company formed of men from Maine to New York, but its impetus came from the pastor of the Wethersfield, Connecticut, Congregational Church. Each $250-share entitled its holder to one hundred and sixty acres of prairie land, twenty acres of timber, and a town lot. A committee of three set out in 1836, after $25,000 had been paid in, and purchased one hundred quarter-sections. The town was laid out with wide streets, one block was set apart for a public square, and one for academy and college purposes. Though only four of the sixty original members of the association ever came to live in the town, it was filled up by New Englanders, a Congregational church was organized in 1839 with fifteen members, and the town of Kewanee perpetuates the New England pioneers.[2]

A church colony from Benson, Vermont, moved as a whole to DuPage County; later, with other New England settlers, they formed a "Squatters' Union" to protect their rights, with separate subordinate organizations in each township.[3] The "Stonington Colony" moved to Stonington, Illinois, in 1837;[4] a Rhode Island company about to migrate in 1832 was deterred by reports of

[1] A. D. Jones, *Illinois and the West*, 72, 73. The village tavern was kept in 1838 by an ex-shipmaster from Duxbury, Mass. *Ibid.*, 71.

[2] *Hist. of Henry County*, 137–145. The streets of the town are named Dwight, Edwards, Tenney, Payson, Hollis, etc.

[3] C. W. Richmond and H. F. Vallette, *DuPage County*, 46–52.

[4] *Portrait and Biographical Record of Christian County*, 336.

Indian massacres, so that only one family actually made the journey.[1] The Mt. Hope colony, however, was a success. The scheme originated in Rhode Island in 1835, and had for its object the opening up of Western lands and the providing of homes for farmers, mechanics, and tradesmen. A constitution and by-laws were drawn up, and a committee of four sent out to locate land for the "Providence Farmers' and Mechanics' Emigrating Society," as the association was called. About fifteen families had already moved to Illinois, when the panic of 1837 broke up the plan. School and church were organized by friends in the East, but the settlement remained small.[2] A Northampton, Massachusetts, colony was a near neighbor of a Norwich, Connecticut, one in La Salle County;[3] while a Hampshire colony, with its church organized in Northampton, Massachusetts, and its own academy, came to Bureau County, and planted a town near one begun by an association from Providence, Rhode Island.[4] A Rhode Island colony settled Delavan, in Tazewell County.[5]

The Maine colony which settled at Rockton, Winnebago County, sent Ira Hersey in 1837 as their representative to visit Illinois and select a good tract of land. He was greatly impressed with the possibilities of the West, and on his return fired his neighbors with an

[1] W. H. Perrin (ed.), *Cass County*, 124.

[2] *Hist. of McLean County*, 579. The land was held in trust till 1854, when a number of men from Bloomington bought what was left.

[3] E. Baldwin, *Hist. of La Salle County*, 374, 375.

[4] H. C. Bradsby (ed.), *Hist. of Bureau County*, 126, 181.

[5] An article signed "New York Observer," in *The New Yorker*, Aug. 31, 1839, page 572.

especial enthusiasm for the beautiful Rock River valley. The colony was formed, and with Mr. Hersey as their leader, they departed. They went from Portland to Boston; then to Providence by rail; by water to New York and Philadelphia; again by rail across Pennsylvania to Pittsburg, where they took passage down the Ohio River. In Cincinnati they purchased provisions and wagons, and continuing their way passed up the Mississippi, and up the Illinois as far as Ottawa, where they bought oxen and cows. Then they finished their journey overland to their new home.[1] In the same year was formed their Congregational church. There were at least twenty-two colonies in Illinois, all of which had their origin in New England or in New York, most of them planted between 1830 and 1840.[2]

One characteristic feature has seemed noteworthy to the writers on this period of Illinois settlement, — the poorest land was chosen for locations. With the con-

---

[1] Carr, *History of Rockton*, 39, 40. See map opposite page 236.

[2] Some colonies which appear as Southern colonies were perhaps New England ones. In the winter of 1905–06 there appeared in the *Boston Transcript* an item asking for certain information hinted at in some old family papers, showing that a New England colony early in the 1800's had emigrated from Charlemont, Massachusetts, to what is now West Virginia, and from there to Edwards County, Illinois; some New Yorkers had been in the colony also. Yet Edwards County is always counted a region settled by Southerners. Another instance of the same sort is in the settlement of Sangamon County; within a few years previous to 1857, sixty or seventy families had removed from Cape May County, New Jersey, to Sangamon County, Illinois. These would be reckoned as New Jersey settlers; Cape May County has, however, always retained much of its New England character. Its first settlers were from New Haven and Long Island, the names in all three places being much alike, and there are Carmans in all. See C. T. Stevens, *Hist. of Cape May County* [New Jersey], 29–59, 280.

servatism inherent in the Anglo-Saxon, the settlers chose land like that to which they had been accustomed at home. The prairies, with their boundless sweep, were unknown factors; hence the pioneers doubted the practicability of cultivating them to advantage. The first log cabins were built close to woods and streams, the prairies being used simply as ranges for cattle and sheep, and he was a visionary and a foolish enthusiast who dared to state that the prairies would ere long be settled as thickly as the timbered stretches.[1] But as land became scarcer, the newcomers were forced to buy prairie-land, and found ready to their hand the richest soil of all.

Although the fourteen northern counties, with their attractive combination of wooded river-banks and rolling prairie, were settled solidly by emigrants from the states east of the Hudson River or from New York itself, yet many other counties had numerous representatives of New England within their borders. Nearly every county above Springfield drew a large proportion of settlers from the East, while to the south there were very few, though a stray Connecticut or Massachusetts pioneer might be found here and there.[2] In Henry County alone there were five New England colonies: Andover,

[1] H. L. Boies, *Hist. of DeKalb County*, 35.

[2] One of the founders of Cairo was born in Hartford, Connecticut; he had lived in Kaskaskia from 1832 until 1843, when he removed to Cairo. See W. H. Perrin (ed.), *Hist. of Alexander, Union, and Pulaski Counties*, 33. Pittsfield, Pike County, Illinois, is named for the old Massachusetts home of its first settlers. See *Hist. of Pike County*, 650. The statement made above is based upon a detailed study of the early emigrants in all these counties, as contained in about thirty county histories; the results are set forth in the maps of Illinois and the rest of the old Northwest Territory, for 1830, 1840, 1850, and 1860.

Wethersfield, Geneseo, Morristown, and La Grange, all of which had educational projects in mind.[1]

With the map of New England settlement in Illinois in mind, it is not difficult to trace the location of Congregational churches. Yet not until the decade 1830–40, when immigration was filling up the northern counties most rapidly, when five hundred towns were laid out in two years, did Congregationalism secure any other foothold than that of a precarious missionary enterprise.[2] Illinois College, itself a child of Yale,[3] was a

[1] The first three were also strongly imbued with a missionary spirit. *Hist. of Henry County*, 117. S. DeW. Drown, in his *Record and Hist. View of Peoria*, 117, gives the place of nativity of the voters of that city in 1845. Of 642 listed, 107 were from New England, 111 from New York. The distribution in New England is as follows : —

Massachusetts	52
New Hampshire	23
Vermont	15
Connecticut	12
Maine	3
Rhode Island	2

Chicago was from the beginning a favorite goal for New Englanders, and its largest banking and mercantile houses are the work of Connecticut and Massachusetts men like Marshall Field. The first president of the great First National Bank was born in Norfolk, Connecticut, but had spent his boyhood in New York. The early directors came from the following towns : Hanson, Danvers, and Groton, Massachusetts ; Sharon, Connecticut ; Winchester, Gilsum, and Newport, New Hampshire ; Rutland and Swanton Falls, Vermont ; Machias, Maine. See H. C. Morris, *First National Bank of Chicago*, 133–168. The first three pastors of the First Presbyterian Church of Chicago came from Hadley, Massachusetts ; Lebanon, Connecticut ; and Bridgeport, Connecticut. Many professional men — lawyers and doctors — were from New England. A. T. Andreas, *Hist. of Cook County*, 243–290.

[2] J. M. Peck, *Gazetteer of Illinois*, 109 ; J. Moses, *Illinois Historical and Statistical*, ii, 1705.

[3] Peck, *Gazetteer of Illinois*, 83, 84.

leader in the movement to establish churches, of which four were founded in 1833, five in 1834, one in 1835, ten in 1836, and by 1840 forty-eight had made more or less feeble beginnings. There were recorded in 1840 sixty ministers, and 1500 church members; in 1870, when the churches numbered 244, the membership was 17,689.[1]

With the coming of the Eastern pioneers, there came a change in the character of the ruling powers in the state; whereas in 1818 the Southerners had been in control and had maintained their supremacy for a quarter of a century thereafter, nevertheless gradually Northern men became dominant in the legislature, and Puritan traditions began to manifest themselves here and there upon the statute-book. The Southerners did not yield without many skirmishes to save their supremacy. In the constitutional convention of 1847 the struggle culminated, but it ceased almost entirely after the amended constitution was adopted the next year; for there the question of local government was adjusted by a compromise. The contention had been over the acceptance of the county system prevalent in the central and southern parts of the state, or the township system which the northern counties had adopted. By the new constitution, each county was to decide its own form of local government by popular vote; the northern counties adopted the township system, the southern counties retained their old organization. Within the next ten years, however, a large number of the central counties followed the example of their neighbors on the north, probably

[1] Moses, *Ill. Hist. and Stat.*, ii, 1075.

owing largely to the greatly increased immigration into that part of the state from New York and New England.[1]

Until the Civil War, Illinois continued to receive a large quota of immigrants from the East. The lines of development had been largely marked out by 1840; here and there, however, Puritan tradition changed their course, as it had already in the case of the township system. For example, a little later came the triumph of the struggle for free schools, the bill to introduce this system being fathered by a Massachusetts man who had lived in Kentucky and Mississippi, but had brought his educational ideas unchanged through his pioneering, to Illinois.[2] At Evanston, the "Biblical Institute" was modeled in 1855 after the theological seminary at Newbury, Vermont; and the Bowdoinham, Maine, pioneer who laid out the town was instrumental in founding Northwestern University.[3] Southern Illinois is to-day very like Kentucky; northern Illinois is to-day a new home of Congregationalism, public schools, and the township system, transplanted to the West by descend-

---

[1] Dr. Albert Shaw, *Local Government in Illinois*, 11.

[2] *Hist. of Shelby and Moultrie Counties*, 159.

[3] F. E. Willard, *Classical Town* (Evanston), 25–44. Rockford College for Women was begun as a seminary in 1851 by men and women of New England stock. See Church, *Hist. of Rockford*, 107, 288–290. The first endowment gift to Shurtleff College, Alton, was from Benjamin Shurtleff, of Boston. See Jones, *Illinois and the West*, 119. The Female Seminary at Monticello was begun by a native of Chatham, Massachusetts. See Hair, *Gazetteer of Madison County*, 151. Almira College, Greenville, was founded by two men educated at New Hampton, New Hampshire, and Brown University, Providence, Rhode Island. See *Hist. of Bond and Montgomery Counties*, 109, 110.

ants of the Puritans. The two sections of the state, each contributing its quota to the welfare of the whole, have produced a new commonwealth which is neither Southern nor Puritan ; — it is Illinois, a part of the great " Middle West."

BIBLIOGRAPHICAL NOTES

As in the earlier maps, the maps illustrating this chapter are prepared from a great amount of detail gathered from many sources not enumerated in the footnotes, nor cited in these notes. Fifty-six county and local histories were used for the Illinois maps, besides the ones specifically cited. The material for this chapter and the next was collected almost exclusively in the library of the State Historical Society of Wisconsin.

For Indiana, the county histories prepared by unknown persons to be sold by subscription are often poor, and badly put together ; but they contain biographies of many inhabitants of the locality, and from the statistics so obtained one may draw safe conclusions. Rev. T. H. Ball, *Lake County, Indiana*, 1834 to 1872 (Chicago, 1873), stands in a class by itself, for it is excellent. Thomas B. Helm's *History of Cass County, Indiana* (Chicago, 1878), and Goodspeed and Blanchard's *Counties of Porter and Lake* (Chicago, 1882), as well as their *Counties of Whitley and Noble* (Chicago, 1882) are fairly good, as are H. W. Beckwith's *History of Fountain County* (*History of Montgomery County* is bound in the same volume), and his *History of Vigo and Parke Counties*. In Levi Coffin's *Reminiscences* (Cincinnati, 1876) is given much suggestive material on the Quaker settlements in Wayne and Randolph counties, and their emigration from North Carolina. J. H. Wheeler in his *Historical Sketches of North Carolina*, 1584 to 1851 (2 vols. in 1, Philadelphia, 1851), gives similar information. Rev. Dr. F. C. Holliday's *Indiana Methodism* (Cincinnati, 1873) is suggestive and valuable. John H. B. Nowland has a volume of *Sketches of Prominent Citizens of 1876*, on Indianapolis people. W. W. Woollen prepared the *Biographical and Historical Sketches of Early Indiana* (Indianapolis, 1883), and with D. W. Howe and J. P. Dunn edited the *Executive Journal of Indiana Territory*, 1800–16, which is in the *Indiana Historical Society Publications*, vol. iii. These form the best sources for the history of Indiana before it passed out of the territorial stage. Almost all of these last-named works on Indiana history were from the Howe Collection in the Public Library of Indianapolis.

For Illinois, there are some excellent county histories, — A. T. Andreas, *History of Cook County* (Chicago, 1884) ; H. L. Boies, *History of DeKalb County* (Chicago, 1868) ; C. A. Church, *History of Rockford and Winnebago County* (Rockford, 1900) ; James T. Hair (compiler), *Gazetteer of Madison County* (Alton, 1866). Thomas Ford, at one time governor of Illinois, wrote the best account of his state from an intimate knowledge of it, — *A History of Illinois*, 1818–1847 (Chicago and New York, 1854). Professor E. B. Greene's *The Government of Illinois* (in Handbooks of Amer. Govt. Series, New York, 1904) is very suggestive on the influences which went to the making of Illinois ; while Dr. Albert Shaw, in his *Local Government in Illinois* (J. H. U. Studies in History and Political Science) has done an admirable piece of work under a famous teacher. John Moses, *Illinois: Historical and Statistical* (2 vols., Chicago, 1892); J. M. Peck, *Gazetteer of Illinois* (Jacksonville, 1834) ; A. D. Jones, *Illinois and the West* (Boston and Philadelphia, 1838) ; S. DeW. Drown, *Record and Historical View of Peoria* (Peoria, 1850) ; — all these have done good work in gathering information relative to Illinois in its early days. A good example of the value which a history of a local institution has, is afforded by H. C. Morris's *History of the First National Bank of Chicago* (Chicago, 1902). Miss F. E. Willard has given valuable information in *A Classic Town*. (Evanston, Illinois. Published in Chicago, 1891.)

Newspapers of the decades 1820–60, such as *The New Yorker*, have letters and notices sometimes which mention Western emigration.

The admirable studies in the University of Wisconsin and the Columbia University Series have been referred to in the footnotes on pages 205 and 207.

CHAPTER IX

THE NEW ENGLANDERS AS STATE BUILDERS:

MICHIGAN AND WISCONSIN, 1820-1860

THE preceding chapters have shown phases of the westward movement of population out from the Hudson River, as well as north of the Ohio, during the first half-century after 1800. The rapid growth of western New York, the filling in of Pennsylvania, the early settlements in Ohio have been traced, one after the other; the growing density of population in Indiana, then in Illinois, has been shown. One other region was being peopled during the second quarter of the century, along the same lines, — the territory now called Michigan and Wisconsin.

Until some years after the close of the War of 1812, Michigan offered little attraction to the emigrant bound for the West. Ohio lands were still cheap and plentiful, and nearer to the markets which the East and the South afforded; western New York was still very tempting, with its fertile lands not yet too dear for a farmer's purse, and there was therefore no need to pierce the wilderness which lay to the north and west of the upper counties of Ohio.[1] Moreover, Michigan was scarcely known at all, save as a rendezvous for Indians; the lands had not yet been brought into the market, and

[1] See map for 1810, facing page 182 ; and for 1820, facing page 206.

the man who determined to make a home in such a region must run the risk of being a dispossessed " squatter," reaping no reward for years of pioneering, with its attendant dangers, toil, and hardships. Tecumseh and his Indian warriors had terrorized the settlers of Indiana and Ohio until after 1815; even then the agents who were sent out to select tracts where the government proposed to locate the bounty-lands for the soldiers of the late war brought back very unfavorable reports of the prospects which Michigan offered. Lastly, there was an entire absence of roads, and Indian trails leading off into deep woods afforded the only passage to the interior. According to the census of 1800, Michigan had 3206 inhabitants, excluding Indians; in 1805 its white population was still confined to the settlements of Detroit, Frenchtown, Mackinaw, and the vicinity of the Detroit River. Five years later, the census gave an increase of only 1500; Detroit was a village with 1650 inhabitants; [1] there was not a single farm or village in any direction five miles from the territorial boundaries. The map for 1820 shows no further extension of the frontier line, though the population of the district about Detroit had grown more dense. [2] But the next decade saw the completion of the Erie Canal and the rise of steamboat navigation to the West; to these factors may be traced the beginning of growth for both Michigan and Wisconsin. Furthermore, the same two factors determined to a large extent the character and the future institutions of those states, since by way of the

[1] J. V. Campbell, *Polit. Hist. of Mich.*, 234.
[2] See map facing page 206.

canal and the steamboat New Englanders and transplanted New Englanders from New York made their way to these portions of "the West." Into the building of these two commonwealths have thus been wrought the traditions and ideals of Puritan origin.

A word as to the earliest laws in this part of the country will be significant. When Michigan was first erected into a territory it included Wisconsin within its bounds; in 1805 one fourth of the territorial laws were taken from the Virginia statute-books, with the remainder from Ohio, Massachusetts, and New York in about equal proportions.[1] In 1815, however, an act reincorporating Detroit provided that the electors might in town-meeting levy taxes for such purposes as they saw fit.[2] The year that lands were put on sale (1818), an act provided that for certain offenses the culprit should be whipped at the whipping-post, — a punishment which was taken from the laws of Vermont.[3] These laws show successive stages in the settlement of the territory; by 1818 a few New Englanders were straggling in, and their influence was beginning to make itself felt in the statute books, as it was to do later in the institutions of the new state.

The character of the Michigan settlers was very largely

---

[1] E. W. Bemis, *Local Government in Michigan and the Northwest* (in "J. H. Univ. Studies," v. i, no. 5), p. 10. The Ohio laws were partly Virginian and Pennsylvanian, at this period. Professor Salmon has called the author's attention to the fact that Judge Woodward of Detroit, whose influence was great at this time, was a profound admirer of Jefferson.

[2] This privilege was also granted to Prairie du Chien, Wisconsin, in 1821. *Ibid.*, 10.

[3] *History of St. Clair County*, 207. After being reënacted once, the law was abolished in 1831.

determined by the fact that most of them came to stay. They did not expect to leave the clearing in the forest as soon as half a dozen neighbors surrounded them; here they intended to plant permanent homes for themselves, and here they meant to rear their children.[1] The sober perseverance of New England, the enterprise of New York, the steadiness of Pennsylvania, — all these were called into requisition by the difficulties of pioneering in Michigan, where almost every mile of ground had to be cleared of trees before large farms could be cultivated.[2] Few wealthy men came at first; the population was made up of hardy, honest, small farmers, very tenacious of their rights, but willing to concede to others the same privileges each demanded for himself.[3] As a consequence there grew up a very independent state, but one which is more flexible in its character than those of New England, by virtue of the compromises necessary where men come from different parts of the country to meet in a wilderness where a commonwealth must be welded by the union of all the diverse elements within its boundaries.

In 1824 there were but nine villages besides Detroit in the whole territory ;[4] a few pioneers had pierced their

[1] Judge Albert Miller, "Pioneer Sketches," in *Mich. Pion. Soc. Coll.*, vii, 251.

[2] The first cabinet-maker in Grand Rapids, now the greatest centre for the manufacture of furniture in the United States, came from Keene, N. H. The lumbering interests of Michigan have been of importance since its early history.

[3] J. H. Lanman, *Hist. of Michigan*, 295–297.

[4] A. D. P. Van Buren, "Pioneer Annals," in *Mich. Pion. Soc. Coll.*, v, 248. These were Port Lawrence, Monroe, Frenchtown, Pontiac, Brownstown, Truax's (near Detroit), Mt. Clemens, Palmer, and Saginaw. See map opposite page 206.

way into the southwestern corner through an absolutely
unbroken wilderness, some on foot, others on ponies,
fording streams, following Indian trails, crossing
swamps, and dropping down at night to sleep in the
woods.[1] That year, however, saw the Erie Canal completed, and together the New Englanders and New
Yorkers took steamboat passage from Buffalo for Detroit.
The Ohio River afforded a highway for emigrants to the
southern portions of Ohio, Indiana, and Illinois, but the
way to northern Illinois and Indiana, and to Michigan
and Wisconsin, was overland, — a long and tedious
journey. The Erie Canal made possible the settlement
of these states by people from the North; the whole
character of the region north of the Ohio might have
been very different had not that great highway, with
steamboat navigation, opened up to the pioneer from
New England and New York the possibilities of the
Northwest.

At Detroit the possible routes to the West divided;
— the first comers followed the "Chicago road," which
was laid out and built in 1825 by the government as
a military measure, and ran from Detroit through
southern Michigan, around the end of the lake to Fort
Dearborn, Illinois.[2] Those who followed this thoroughfare peopled the southern tier of counties, dotting the
prairies with hamlets and farms. The stream which came
after 1834 went out over the territorial road directly

---

[1] D. A. Winslow, "Early History of Berrien County," in *Mich. Pion.
Soc. Coll.*, i, 122.

[2] A. B. Copley, "Early Settlement of Southwestern Michigan," in
Mich. Pion. Soc. Coll., v, 151. See map for 1830, facing page 210.

west, and settled the second tier of counties, until they reached the southwestern corner of the state, where they found themselves preceded by hardy frontiersmen from Kentucky, Tennessee, the southern parts of Ohio, Indiana, and Illinois, who had followed in the footsteps of Indian fighters like Wayne. This advance guard had already selected the choicest land in the counties northeast of Berrien, and later comers passed north to find fertile lands as yet unoccupied. By 1835, at least seventeen more towns had been settled, besides many farms not near any village.[1] From that time, the settlement of Michigan went on with astonishing rapidity. The fever for purchasing lands which preceded the panic of 1837 affected Michigan as it did the states to the south and west; the crisis of 1837–39 checked the movement for a short time; then the tide of immigration poured in even more strongly than before. This tide after 1825 always carried the New Englanders with it, and New Yorkers as well.

For this study, the New England immigration is of peculiar interest. Upon the publication of John Farmer's map of Michigan, 1825–30, New Englanders found therein the accurate information concerning that territory which their caution demanded; by 1837 "it seemed as if all New England were coming" to the state.[2] The fever for emigration pervaded the whole region from Rhode Island to Vermont, and every one seemed to have adopted for his own the popular song,

---

[1] A. D. P. Van Buren, "Pioneer Annals," in *Mich. Pion. Soc. Coll.*, v, 249. See maps opposite pages 236 and 246.

[2] Silas Farmer, *Detroit*, 335.

"Michigania." [1] Vermont sent most emigrants; — 12,588 of Michigan's citizens in 1880 were born in the Green Mountain State. Massachusetts had by the same report 9591; Connecticut, 6333; Maine, 5079; New Hampshire, 3300, and Rhode Island, 974. In the earliest days most of the Bay State representatives moved to Detroit and Kalamazoo, while Kent County was most attractive to Vermonters. But the whole state is filled with representatives of the New England region, mingling with their near neighbors of the same stock from New York.

A glance at Berrien County will show the character of the New England settlements. From 1831 to 1842 pioneers came from Norwich, Stamford, and New Milford, Connecticut; Leominster, Chicopee, and Harwich, Massachusetts; Weybridge, Shoreham, Westminster, Addison, East Poultney, and Windsor County, Vermont; Nelson, New Hampshire; and from Maine. [2] One pioneer will serve to typify hundreds. John Perrin, his wife, five sons, and four daughters, were the first settlers of Jefferson township, Hillsdale County. In 1835 they left their home in Woodstock, Connecticut, took a vessel from Norwich to Albany, and made their journey through New York over the Erie Canal. At Buffalo they boarded a steamer bound for Detroit, which they reached three weeks from the day they bade good-by to their old home. Leaving the rest of the family behind,

---

[1] The first verse runs thus : —

> "Come, all ye Yankee farmers who wish to change your lot,
> Who 've spunk enough to travel beyond your native spot,
> And leave behind the village where Pa and Ma do stay,
> Come follow me, and settle in Michigania, —
> Yea, yea, yea, in Michigania." — *Detroit.*

[2] *Hist. of Berrien and Van Buren Counties,* 144–310.

the father and the two eldest sons started out from
Detroit to locate a farm; they passed the Bear Creek
valley, traveling on till they found a spring gushing
from a rock on the hilly slopes of Jefferson township.
All the surroundings were so like the old Connecticut
home, that there the pioneer cabin was built,—the first
house in the township.[1] Again and again did the settlers seek out the wooded lands which bore a striking
resemblance to the tree-covered hills to which they
were accustomed in the East.

Nor did the pioneers come always by single families.
In many an instance neighborhoods were settled by
small colonies, who came in sufficient numbers to give
to their new homes the character of the old; and once
wholesome social surroundings were established, others
were attracted, who had come to the West to better
their condition. Such a colony was that which settled in
Sylvan township, Washtenaw County; ten or twelve
families came from Addison County, Vermont, between
1832 and 1834, to form what has always been called
the "Vermont Settlement."[2] Here their Congregational
church was organized in 1835. Another example is the
Monroe colony, which was begun in 1816 by two brothers from Royalston, Massachusetts, whose neighbors
in the succeeding years were from various Connecticut
towns, from Scituate in Rhode Island, from New Hampshire, and Vermont. It was known in 1834 as a New
England colony;[3] "it was composed of men of such

[1] C. Johnson, *Hillsdale County*, 272.

[2] *Hist. of Washtenaw County*, 753, 764.

[3] T. E. Wing (ed.), *Hist. of Monroe County*, 158–590, for lives of
pioneers.

intelligence and strength of character that in the early days of the State it was known as 'the independent state of Monroe.' " [1]

The Vermontville colony deserves a longer description.[2] Here an organized company of emigrants from the Green Mountain State, " with Michigan, a church and a school in their minds," purchased land of the government under a written compact, drawn up at East Poultney, upon the advice and under the direction of their minister, Rev. Sylvester Cochrane, who alone of all the band had ever seen the land upon which it was proposed to settle. With the threefold purpose of promoting the spread of the Gospel in the wilderness, of advancing their own prosperity, and of carrying their moral and intellectual ideals to the frontier, they drew up a constitution and by-laws, and dispatched a committee to prepare the way for the arrival of the colony. The committee had no easy task, for in 1836 the fever for speculation in Michigan lands had sent the price of the unoccupied tracts to a point far beyond their worth, and it was difficult to find a place where each of the thirty investors whose money the committee carried might have a quarter-section for his farm and a ten-acre lot for his village home as well situated as those of any of his neighbors. After several weeks of careful prospecting, the site for the town was finally chosen at what is now Vermontville, Eaton County; and the purchase made at the land-office in Kalamazoo. Trees were felled, and a village laid out around a public square;

[1] *Ibid.*, 158.

[2] E. W. Barber, "The Vermontville Colony," in *Mich. Pion. Soc. Coll.*, xxviii, 2, 197–265.

then the colonists began to arrive. By wagon, canal, lake, and rude Michigan forest-roads, they made their way from East Poultney to their Vermontville home. Their Congregational church, with Rev. Sylvester Cochrane as pastor, was organized at the very beginning; for the first few years the minister was paid in work on his land, in money or in produce, as the parishioners could best afford. The school was held for a year in the log cabin of one family; then a log schoolhouse was erected, and the children were taught for seven months in the year. A few years later an academy on the Vermont plan was organized to carry on the education of those who had finished the work in the little log schoolhouse. In politics the colonists at Vermontville were divided, curiously enough; those who came from Rutland and Addison counties were Whigs, while their neighbors from Bennington County were "rock-rooted Democrats." But all had the democratic idea, all held to the equality of man in all his rights, political and social, and when in 1854 the Republican party was organized, Vermontville became practically united in its ranks in a warfare against the extension of slavery.

Marietta, Ohio, played no mean part in helping to shape Michigan's future character. Itself a New England colony, Marietta sent the first settler to Detroit after the British evacuation of that post in 1796, — Solomon Sibley, who became a judge of the Supreme Court. General Lewis Cass, born in Exeter, New Hampshire, served an apprenticeship at pioneering for fourteen years in Marietta before he became the second governor of Michigan Territory in 1815, — a post he filled till 1831.

During those sixteen years he negotiated twenty-one Indian treaties, thereby making Michigan a safe home for hundreds of families which were soon to give to the state its distinctively New England character. General Cass left the governor's chair to be Secretary of War; then after a time United States Senator from Michigan; in 1848 a candidate for the presidency; and lastly, Buchanan's Secretary of State; — such was the part played in the national councils by the most eminent of Michigan's statesmen.[1] William Woodbridge, the Secretary of the Territory after 1815, though born in Norwich, Connecticut, was a Marietta lawyer who had studied in the same office with Cass; he became governor of the state in 1839.[2] Isaac Crary, the territorial delegate and the first representative Michigan sent to Congress, was born in Preston, Connecticut.[3]

Such were the men who helped lay the foundations of Michigan's development in the territorial days; but New England influence did not end with statehood. A list of the first fourteen men who occupied the governor's chair after Michigan's admission to the Union will illustrate the prominence of New England and New York pioneers in politics,[4] — six from New England, six

---

[1] *Representative Men of Michigan*, 35, 36. Also J. V. Campbell, *Outlines of the Polit. Hist. of Mich.*, 217.

[2] *Representative Men of Michigan*, 156.

[3] *Ibid.*, "Third Congressional District," 28.

[4] First   governor . .   native of Virginia.

Second   "   . . . .   "   of Norwich, Ct., but had lived in Ohio.

Third   "   . . . .   "   of Amherst, N. H., but had lived in Vt.

Fourth   "   . (2 terms) "   of Limerick, Me.

Fifth   "   . . . .   "   of Hamilton, N. Y.

Sixth   "   . . . .   "   of Massachusetts.

from New York, one from Virginia, and one from Pennsylvania.

From the character of the population it is easy to predict that the attention of Michigan pioneers would be centred at the first opportunity upon the question of schools. S. F. Drury, born in Spencer, Massachusetts, who had become much interested in common school education in his old home, originated and organized in the state of his adoption a teachers' institute, which grew into the State Normal School of Otsego.[1] He worked for the charter of Olivet College in 1859, and several years later helped to found Drury College in Illinois. Michigan normal schools owe a debt of gratitude to Rev. John D. Pierce, a graduate of Brown University, who had come to Michigan as a Presbyterian missionary, and was the first superintendent of public instruction after Michigan became a state; Mr. Pierce suggested the idea of a system of normal schools in 1836.[2] But Michigan's chief pride is her university, the

Seventh governor . . native of Greencastle, Penn.
Eighth   "   . . . . "   of Hoosick, N. Y.
Ninth   "   . . . . "   of Camillus, N. Y.
Tenth   "   . . . . "   of Springport, N. Y.
Eleventh   "   . . . . "   of Caroline, N. Y.
Twelfth   "   . . . . "   of Dartmouth, Mass.
Thirteenth "   . . . . "   of Coventry, R. I.
Fourteenth "   . . . . "   of Medina, N. Y.
              (This to 1877)

In *Portrait and Biographical Record of Genesee, Lapeer, and Tuscola Counties*, 105–157.

[1] J. B. Porter, "Memoir of S. F. Drury," in *Mich. Pion. Soc. Coll.*, vii, 382, 383.

[2] A. C. McLaughlin, *Higher Education in Michigan*, 99, 100. (In Bureau of Education, Circular no. 4, 1891.)

head of the public school system of the state, and the model of almost all state universities since founded. Isaac Crary, of whom mention has been made, was chairman of the committee on education in the Michigan constitutional convention, and to him may be attributed, more than to any one else, the system as it is to-day. He had made a study of Cousin's famous report on the Prussian system of education, and German influence was especially strong, when it was carried out along practical lines by men with strong predilections for popular education.[1] Mr. Crary had been educated at Bacon Academy, Colchester, Connecticut, and at Washington (now Trinity) College, Hartford. President Angell, under whose administration the university has taken a place in the front rank of American colleges, is a native of Scituate, Rhode Island, and a graduate of Brown University.[2]

Olivet College represents New England, and Puritan Congregationalism in Ohio. Founded in 1844, it was the child of Oberlin; to its planting Oberlin graduates contributed more than any other persons. The original plan was for both a college and a Christian colony, the latter to found and foster the former; but the scheme

[1] Professor Lucy M. Salmon has a valuable article on Judge Woodward's plan for a university in the days when Michigan was still a territory, "Education in Michigan during the Territorial Period," in *Mich. Pion. Soc. Coll.*, vii, 36–38.

See, also, Professor Salmon's article, "Types of State Education," in the *New England Magazine*, January, 1897, pp. 601, 607.

[2] A. C. McLaughlin, *Higher Education in Michigan*, 34, 35, 73. The university was not coeducational until 1870. It would be interesting to know how great a part economy has played in making Western institutions so largely coeducational.

did not work out wholly in practice. The Congregational church of Olivet was, however, organized the year after the college was founded, and the two have always been intimately connected.[1]

Hand in hand with the school goes the church, following Puritan tradition. At first Congregationalism in Michigan was "largely merged in Presbyterianism" by the "Plan of Union" with which we were familiar in New York, and many of the churches so constituted in the beginning have continued to be Presbyterian down to the present.[2] In 1835 six Congregational churches had been organized, most of which never made any compromise with the "accommodation system"; within five years the formation of an association of their own denomination gave them the advantage of organization which they had lacked before. By 1855 there were 106 Congregational churches in Michigan under their own associations, with 4987 members; in 1880, 226, with a roll of 17,064 names. Congregationalism has been from the beginning strong in Michigan; it would have been stronger probably, but for the change it had already undergone in New York and Ohio through the "Plan of Union" system, — a compromise to frontier conditions which emigrants from those states transplanted to their Michigan homes.

Nor is the third traditional institution wanting; Michigan was the first Western state to adopt the town-

[1] S. W. Durant, *Hist. of Ingham and Eaton Counties*, 530, 532. Also George W. Keyes, "Sketch of the First Congregational Church," *ibid.*, 535.

[2] Rev. D. P. Hurd, "Congregationalism in Michigan," in *Mich. Pion. Soc. Coll.*, vii, 103–116.

meeting, though her example has been followed by
Wisconsin, Illinois, and Minnesota. Ohio, Indiana, and
Illinois all show a compromise system analogous to that
of New York and Pennsylvania; the Michigan system
is most like that of Massachusetts. On the first Monday
in April of each year the meeting is held, and may be
attended by every male citizen of the state who is over
twenty-one years of age. Here the supervisor presides,
and is one of three inspectors of election, the others
being the justice of the peace whose office soonest
expires, and the clerk of the township. All who attend
the meeting may participate in the conduct of it. After
officers have been chosen, the electors discuss town business. They listen to complaints, — as of cattle running
at large; they regulate such matters as licensing dogs,
keeping and selling gunpowder, maintaining hospitals,
and so on. The various officers of the township also
make their reports at this time. The difference between
the Michigan town-meeting and that in New England
is that in Michigan incorporated villages which exist
within the township may either in village-meeting or
through their trustees provide for the administration of
their own local affairs, as in the regulation of the fire
department, police, and streets, — and therefore do not
vote in town-meeting. Where Massachusetts has three
selectmen, Michigan has one supervisor, whose duties
are not administrative as in Massachusetts, but rather
executive and clerical. Most distinctive is the Michigan
township board, which is made up of the supervisor,
township clerk, and two justices of the peace, and which
exercises many of the powers of the Massachusetts select-

men. "Michigan borrowed the organization [of this body] from the county board of New York, and its powers from Massachusetts." [1]

But one state remains for our study, — Wisconsin. Save for a few French settlers scattered here and there, a remnant which had followed in the footsteps of Jesuit priests and Canadian fur-traders, Wisconsin was until 1826 a veritable wilderness. In that year there came to the southwestern corner of the territory, following up the Mississippi River, some venturesome Southerners from Kentucky, Tennessee, and Missouri, attracted to the region by the rich lead mines found there. It was in this way that Galena came to be for many years a far more important market and trading point than was Milwaukee, and was well-known when Chicago was nothing more than a fort. Lead mining was a great industry on one side of the territory, when agriculture was just beginning on the other. Finally, the two streams of emigrants met about midway, but even to-day southeastern Wisconsin has characteristics which quite distinguish it from the other portions of the state. [2]

The Black Hawk War was a very potent factor in directing the attention of the East to the great tracts of land north of Illinois which were not only unoccupied, but were only slightly explored. The newspapers published glowing accounts of the rich country of northern Illinois and its neighbor on Lake Michigan; soldiers carried back tales to their friends; and speedily thou-

[1] E. W. Bemis, *Local Government in Michigan and the Northwest*, 14–17. For settlement in 1840, see map opposite.

[2] Tenney and Atwood, *Memorial Record of the Fathers of Wisconsin*, 14.

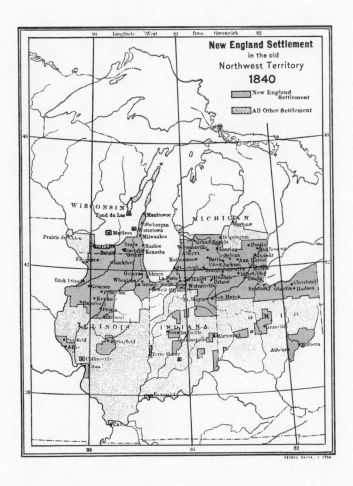

sands of "intelligent, hardy, and enterprising" people
from New York and New England swarmed in. Settlements were begun along the lake shore in 1834. The
land in Green County was brought into the market in
1835; within five years that section had many inhabitants, most of whom came from Illinois, Indiana, Ohio,
Pennsylvania, or Virginia, Illinois contributing the
most. Hardly any came from New England, but some
who were the children of New England parents came
from New York.[1] Prairie du Chien, an old French town,
had in 1837 nearly one hundred French families, but
only ten American ones, and four unmarried American
men.[2] Among these Americans was an itinerant Meth-
odist preacher from Connecticut, a wanderer from
Machias, Maine, who had lived a year in Michigan, and
one man from Vermont.[3] Before 1841 settlements had
been made in the fertile Rock River valley, and in the
country between these farms and the shore of Lake
Michigan. The panic of 1837 brought many families
who sought to retrieve their fortunes in the West; these
came in, many of them, by way of the Wisconsin River
valley; lastly settlers came up the Mississippi River, and
moved along its eastern tributaries. By 1850, even the
northwestern corner of the state was receiving its small
share of immigrants.[4]

The institutions of Wisconsin would naturally, so one
might suppose, have been shaped by the workers on its

---

[1] H. M. Bingham, *Hist. of Green County*, 15.
[2] W. H. C. Folsom, *Fifty Years in the Northwest*, 19.
[3] *Ibid.*, 26, 28.
[4] W. C. Whitford, "Early Education in Wisconsin," in *Coll. of Wis.
Hist. Soc.*, v, 335. See maps opposite pages 236 and 246.

two frontiers, — by Kentuckians and their coadjutors in the lead-mining regions, as well as by the emigrants who had come in around Racine and Milwaukee by way of the Erie Canal and the Great Lakes. At first this was true, and two systems of local government grew up in Wisconsin during the territorial stage; — in the earlier settled counties in the southwestern corner the county system came in with the Southern emigrants; while the eastern districts, filled up by New Yorkers and New Englanders, adopted the township form of organization. These two systems existed side by side, as it were, throughout the territorial stage, until the state constitution was formed in 1846–47. But they did not exist in peace; in 1841, when emigrants from the East had become sufficiently numerous to protest, their influence was strong enough to secure a change from the county commissioner plan which had been in force up to that time, and a law was passed by which the people of each county might determine whether for them local government should be based on the Southern plan or on that of New England. When Wisconsin was admitted as a state in 1848, only five counties were retaining the county system, and these were the southeastern counties of the lead-mining district, where Southerners were still in the majority.[1]

In the end the New York system of local government — itself a compromise with leanings toward the New England form — triumphed, and was embodied in the state constitution. The reason for its adoption is not

[1] D. E. Spencer, "Local Government in Wisconsin," *Coll. of Wis. Hist. Soc.*, xi, 505–507.

difficult to ascertain when one has examined the *personnel* of those bodies which determined the lines along which Wisconsin's development as a state should run. There were two constitutional conventions held in Wisconsin, the first in 1846, whose work was rejected, the second in 1847. In the 1846 convention of one hundred and thirty-four delegates, twenty-nine were known to be New England men, ten more had New England parents, and " of the forty-two natives of New York . . . many names . . . suggest Puritan origin." [1] The convention of 1847 contained sixty-nine delegates, of whom twenty-four were from New England, and five more of New England origin. Thirty-two men were in both bodies and held positions of prominence; of these fourteen were of New England birth or stock.[2] Under such conditions the outcome as to local government could not be doubtful. A law was framed by which each county was to have a board of three supervisors, one from each district into which the county was to be divided. These were given charge of the general concerns of the county, while the town government was left in-

[1] E. B. Usher, " Puritan Influence in Wisconsin," *in Proc. of Wis. Hist. Soc.* for 1898, p. 119.

[2] *Ibid.* One of these was born in East Haddam, Connecticut, and came to Wisconsin from the Western Reserve. He was a Whig, and governor of the state in 1861. Others were from New Hampshire, Rhode Island, Vermont, and Massachusetts. In the convention of 1846 there were eight men of Connecticut birth, eighteen of Vermont, one of New Hampshire, one of Rhode Island, one of Maine. Tenney and Atwood, *Fathers of Wisconsin*, 20. Four men were from New Jersey.

In the convention of 1847, nine men were of Connecticut birth, six of Massachusetts, five of Vermont, three of New Hampshire, one of Maine. *Ibid.*, 21.

tact. To-day Wisconsin has three supervisors who correspond in their duties to the New England selectmen.[1]

Racine County is a typical New England region in Wisconsin, for it was from an early day a favorite with settlers from the East. Its original pioneer of 1835 was born in Chatham, Massachusetts; within a year after his arrival hundreds of actual settlers had begun log cabins near his own. Several of the newcomers were from Derby, Connecticut; within sixteen years others had come from every New England state, except Rhode Island, though some had sojourned for a time in New York and had been swept on toward the Mississippi by the outgoing tide of emigration. One of the earliest arrivals had been born in Burlington, Vermont; he had lived in New York and Pennsylvania, then in Illinois, and in 1835 took up his permanent abode in Racine, having doubtless had enough of pioneering.[2]

To show how like the settlement of New York, Ohio, and Michigan is the beginning of Wisconsin, it is only necessary to tell the story of the founding of Beloit.[3] Here, as in most other Wisconsin towns, the pioneers

[1] Bemis, "Local Government in Michigan and the Northwest," in *Johns Hopkins University Studies*, i, no. 5, p. 17.

[2] *Hist. of Racine and Kenosha Counties*, 567. In Racine County mingled arrivals from Bennington, Tunbridge, and Brattleboro, Vermont ; from Sunderland, Royalston, Westford, Sandisfield, Greenwich, Williamstown, Ashfield, Berkshire County, and Monson, Massachusetts ; Londonderry and Deerfield, New Hampshire ; Cheshire, Bristol, and Colebrook, Connecticut ; Boothbay and Dexter, Maine. See *ibid.*, 567–629. This is but one of dozens of counties which give the same mixture from all over New England ; the examples might be multiplied indefinitely.

[3] H. M. Whitney, "The settlement of Beloit," in *Proc. of Wis. Hist. Soc.* for 1898, 129–136. The following paragraphs follow his little sketch very closely.

came with the intention of staying. They were not the restless sort who came to settle temporarily, expecting to sell later at a higher price, and move on to Minnesota or to Dakota, there to repeat the toil and privation, the hardship and frequent disappointment of the earliest pioneer in the wilderness. Such emigrants had passed by the site of Beloit, and turned their eyes to other fields.

Twelve men in the village of Colebrook, New Hampshire, banded together in October, 1836, to form the "New England Emigrating Company," with one Dr. Horace White as their agent. Determined to move to the West, they sent Dr. White ahead to select for the company a new home in Wisconsin. The level fields, the water power of Turtle Creek, the "unlimited gravel" of the country about Beloit fixed the site of the intended village and farms, and here Dr. White made the purchase for his company. By the middle of the next summer the colonists were on the ground, and were beginning to build homes and cultivate fields. Besides the Colebrook settlers, six families came from Bedford, New Hampshire, doubtless because they had heard of the purpose of Dr. White's company from their fellow townswoman, Mrs. White.

Professor Whitney, in his sketch of Beloit, brings out the practical, hard-headed business sense of these pioneers; he tells how they looked about for a location which would prosper with the rest of the region; he says they knew "the moral value of having gravel under their feet," and they realized the necessity of getting good land. They saw, too, the advantage of having a quarry and good oak trees on their tract. They had come from New Hampshire to better their condition, to give perchance to their children advantages which would have been beyond their purse had they stayed upon the stubborn soil of New Hampshire. Moreover, the whole Rock River valley has "a New England look," and that made them feel at home immediately.

They planted their village in 1838, and laid out wide streets which to-day remind the traveler instantly of a town in the heart of New England; "College Street" was the name they gave one of the choicest, for they intended from the first to have a college as soon as they could. They were of the stock which sees the school go hand in hand with the church, and far from the one college in New Hampshire, they determined to plant another at their very doors. Beloit College is a memorial of the lofty ideals of these Colebrook emigrants. In its development the college has followed more closely the lines of organization and administration of Yale than those of Dartmouth; its presidents and many of its professors have been from the Connecticut institution. But it is a Congregational and a New England product, as is Dartmouth, and a lasting symbol of the vision of its founders, who dreamed from the first that a Christian college should find its place in their frontier home, to perpetuate the Puritan tradition and the Puritan ideal.

The colonists had brought a deacon in their company, and as soon as they arrived they began to hold services in a kitchen of one of the farmhouses, all the congregation arriving in ox-wagons on Sunday morning. When they were ready to build a church, they bought the shingles in Racine on credit, hauling them overland with an ox-team; "and they honestly paid for the shingles in the spring."[1] When the Congregationalists of Madison began to build a church themselves, the Beloit pioneers, as yet hardly out of the log-cabin stage of their history, gave $50 to help their neighbors. The great tenacity of purpose of these colonists, their lofty ideals of religion, education, and state-building, — these have left an impress upon Wisconsin which none can mistake.

New England settlement is ever the same, whether it is found on the Mohawk, or on the banks of the Wisconsin. Here on the frontier, — "wherever . . . a . . . number of Eastern emigrants settled together in the state they started at once a school."[2] There were in 1836 eight little private schools in the territory, with 215 pupils, exclusive of the schools in Milwaukee, Kenosha, and Sheboygan. After 1837 Wisconsin took her school code almost bodily from Michigan; it is to-day a very close reproduction of the Michigan system, with a few additions from New York.[3] The public school system, with the state university at the top, and with the normal schools for the training of teachers for the lower schools, — all this is like Michigan.[4]

---

[1] "The church they built was the most stately of the three Congregational churches existing in Wisconsin in 1844, — so stately, indeed, that it got into two editions of the American Encyclopedia." — H. M. Whitney, "The Settlement of Beloit," in *Proc. of Wis. Hist. Soc.* for 1898, 134.

[2] W. C. Whitford, "Early History of Education in Wisconsin," in *Coll. of Wis. Hist. Soc.*, v, 335.

[3] *Ibid.*, 337–344.

[4] The normal schools are largely the work of a Connecticut man who came to Wisconsin from New York. Usher, *Puritan Influence*, 121.

Wherever a large proportion of New England emigrants is found, there one is certain to come upon Congregational churches. Indeed, in going over the Western States, one can almost locate New England people by the presence of Congregational churches. Wisconsin proves the rule; a few typical churches will tell the story of many. When the congregation of Troy, in Walworth County, was gathered in 1839, it was made up of six persons from North Hadley and two from Roxbury, Massachusetts.[1] The First Congregational Church of Janesville had fifteen charter members, eleven of whom came from New England; another had moved from Athens, Pennsylvania, but came of Plainfield, Connecticut, stock.[2] The Madison church had eight pastors in the half-century following its organization in 1840; of these, seven were born in New England.[3] The Emerald Grove congregation had fourteen charter members, six of whom were born in Vermont;[4] while the Prairie church with eighteen members numbered five from Vermont and two from Connecticut.[5] Of the four deacons in the Bloomington church, one was born in Stonington, Connecticut; three were from Vermont, — Hart-

[1] Manuscript report of the formation of the Congregational Church of Troy, among the *Dwinnell Papers* in the Library of the Wisconsin Historical Society.

[2] S. P. Wilder, "Hist. of the Congregational Church," in *Fiftieth Anniversary of the First Cong. Church of Janesville*, 43. Also *ibid.*, "Our Charter Members," 47–51.

[3] F. J. Lamb, "Former Pastors," in *Fiftieth Anniversary of the First Cong. Church of Madison*, 93 ff.

[4] Rev. R. L. Cheney, "Charter Membership," in the *Fiftieth Anniversary of the Emerald Grove Church*, 30.

[5] Rev. R. L. Cheney, "Charter Members," in *Prairie Church*, 17.

ford, Derby, and Jericho. The Beloit church would, of course, be almost wholly a New England product: of its twenty-four members, seven were from Colebrook, and three from Groton, New Hampshire ; two from Hartland and three from Milton, Vermont; two from Maine; one each from Enfield, Connecticut, and Providence, Rhode Island.[1] The Presbyterian churches also show a large New England and New York membership, as is to be expected, and are quite as strong and as numerous as the Congregational organizations.

Into the building of a state go always the characters of those men who are most prominent in its history, — as governors, judges, legislators, or men of business. A glance at some whose names are bound up with the story of the institutions, political and commercial, which they have builded, will serve to illustrate what has gone before as to the influence exerted by New England upon this Western state.

Of the eighteen governors of Wisconsin four were born in Connecticut, one in Massachusetts; another was of Connecticut parentage, and one of Massachusetts stock, while yet another came of Puritan ancestry.[2] Two Vermont men have been judges of the Supreme Court of the state, four more have been circuit judges, as have three Maine emigrants and one from Massachusetts. There have been eleven United States senators, — four from Vermont, and one from Maine, while two came of New England stock. The proneness of the Ver-

---

[1] Rev. L. D. Mears, "Hist. Address," in *Services at the Fiftieth Anniversary of the First Congregational Church, Beloit, Wis.*, pp. 27, 28.

[2] Usher, *Puritan Influence in Wisconsin*, 121, 122.

monter to go into politics is illustrated by the fact that
every man of prominence connected with the state organization of the Republican party in 1880 in Wisconsin was a Vermonter, from Senator Spooner down. Six
state superintendents of schools have been either New
England men or the children of such parents. New
Englanders built the Chicago, Milwaukee, and St. Paul
Railroad, as they did three others in the state.[1] From
the beginning of Wisconsin's history as a state, its institutions "have been dominated by Americans of the
Puritan seed."[2]

Into the making of Wisconsin, then, has gone much
of New England practice and tradition, part of it
brought directly from the old states on the coast, more
of it from western New York, but all of it a Puritan
heritage, tempered by frontier and wilderness conditions.
The schools, the churches, the local institutions of the
state all show their origin, whether they were copied
directly from Massachusetts or Connecticut, or had been
altered in New York or Michigan on their way to shape
another commonwealth planned on the same lines. The
great immigrations of foreigners have not changed
the fundamental institutions of the state, though they
have given a different character to its population. There
never can be erased the sturdy independence, the democratic spirit, the deep moral purpose of the pioneers

[1] Usher, *Puritan Influence in Wisconsin*, 123–126. Two are great systems, — the Wisconsin Central, the Omaha system ; while a third is the
Green Bay R. R. The president of the Milwaukee and Mississippi R. R.
was a native of Vermont, the manager of the C., M. & St. P. R. R. was
a New Hampshire boy.

Ibid., 127. See map opposite, and frontispiece.

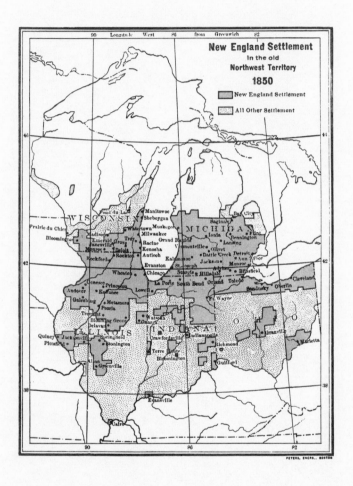

New England Settlement
in the old
Northwest Territory
1850

New England Settlement
All Other Settlement

who made Wisconsin in its early years a modified New England.

One feels in passing through the Michigan and Wisconsin towns the kinship of the two states to each other, to northern Illinois, to northern Ohio, and to western New York; that kinship has come, it is believed, through their common heritage of ideals and ideas, drawn from the same source, — the home of the Puritans. Settled by the same stock, built by the same sort of pioneers, their resemblance to each other is no accident, no haphazard similarity. They represent a New England whose history is shaped and moulded on the lines of the old. New England history is incomplete when it takes up the story of but six states; it will be finished only when it tells the tale of a greater New England extended to the Mississippi.[1]

[1] Nor does it stop with the Mississippi. During the later years of this study, from about 1840 to 1865, people from New England were moving in a steady stream (and an increasingly large one) to Minnesota, Iowa, Kansas, Oregon, and Washington. Worthington, Minnesota, was settled by a colony somewhat like those we have examined; Lawrence, Kansas, is a New England town, as is Grinnell, Iowa. Far out in the Willamette Valley is Whitman College, Congregational to the core. Only with a study of emigration to the Pacific Coast can the story of "greater New England" be complete.

BIBLIOGRAPHICAL NOTES

For Michigan, the great source of information is the *Pioneer Collections,*
issued by the Pioneer Society of Michigan (34 vols., Lansing, 1877–1906).
The series is admirably edited, and contains all sorts of information, —
biographical, historical, and statistical. To supplement the biographical
material found in these collections, there is a large volume of a popular
character in a series called "American Biographies," — *Representative
Men of Michigan* (Cincinnati, 1878). The sketches given here afford a
means of identifying men of New England stock.

There are four general histories of Michigan : James V. Campbell has
given the political phase especial prominence in the *Outlines of the Political History of Michigan* (Detroit, 1876) ; there are many anecdotes and
local sketches in Silas Farmer's *History of Detroit and Michigan* (Detroit,
1884) ; a good brief history is in the American Commonwealth Series, by
Judge T. M. Cooley, entitled *Michigan* ; and lastly, the work of J. H.
Lanman, *History of Michigan* (New York, 1839) is good as far as it goes.

Some of the better county histories are as follows : Samuel W. Durant,
History of Ingham and Eaton Counties (Philadelphia, 1880) ; Crisfield
Johnson, *History of Hillsdale County* (Philadelphia, 1879); T. E. Wing,
editor, *History of Monroe County* (New York, 1890) ; and those for whom
no one assumes the sponsorship, — *History of Berrien and Van Buren
Counties, History of St. Clair County,* and *History of Washtenaw County.*

Professor A. C. McLaughlin prepared the *History of Higher Education
in Michigan,* Circular no. 4 in a series for the Bureau of Education at
Washington dealing with the subject in various states. Edward W. M.
Bemis prepared a study on *Local Government in Michigan and the Northwest,* in the Johns Hopkins University "Studies in History and Political
Science," March, 1883. It is not so thorough as Dr. Shaw's study in the
same series on Illinois.

For Wisconsin, there is a series corresponding to the *Michigan Pioneer
Society Collections,* issued by the State Historical Society of Wisconsin,
and called the *Collections of the Wisconsin State Historical Society* (18 vols.,
Madison, 1855–1908). The editing here is admirable. There are also
Proceedings of the Society, in 12 vols., Madison, 1875–1908, and *Reports*
(1875–1908, 101 vols.), containing many short articles of value. H. A.
Tenney and David Atwood have done signal service in preparing the
Memorial Record of the Fathers of Wisconsin.

In county histories, many were used for the maps which cannot be cited here ; but Miss H. M. Bingham's *History of Green County* (Milwaukee, 1877) and C. W. Butterfield's edition of a *History of Racine and Kenosha Counties* (Chicago, 1879) proved especially helpful. W. H. C. Folsom's *Fifty Years in the Northwest* (St. Paul, 1888) gives the experiences of an early settler.

There are several histories of individual churches which are of value : Rev. R. L. Cheney in "The Charter Members," bound in a memorial of the *Fiftieth Anniversary of the Old Blake's Prairie Church ;* F. J. Lamb, "Former Pastors of the Church," in the *Fiftieth Anniversary of the First Congregational Church of Madison;* Rev. L. D. Mears, "Historical Address" in *Services at the Fiftieth Anniversary of the First Congregational Church of Beloit ;* and S. P. Wilder, "History," in the *Fiftieth Anniversary of the First Congregational Church of Janesville* — all these are suggestive.

These are but a few books and pamphlets of the vast collection of material for Western history stored in the library of the State Historical Society of Wisconsin at Madison.

Finally, reference ought to be made to the volumes prepared by the directors of the United States Census for 1870 (which contain statistics of 1790 to 1870 inclusive), 1880, 1890, and 1900, where figures and maps are to be found. The *Blue Books* of various states give information as to prominent men in politics and public life.

CHAPTER X

TWO CENTURIES AND A HALF OF NEW ENGLAND
PIONEERING

1620–1865

THE westward march of the Puritan and his descendants has now been traced for two hundred and fifty years, — not always completely, sometimes merely in broad outline; but an attempt has been made to show where New England men and women have gone to plant towns, to build states, to help weld the American nation.[1] Nor has the purely formal side of the actual movement of population alone been studied; the presence of a number of New England people in New Jersey or in Wisconsin would of itself mean nothing. Wherever Puritan blood has gone, Puritan traditions have been carried, — that is the essential thing to note. Therefore, the influence these transplanted Englishmen have exerted, the institutions they have wrought, the character ingrained by inheritance and altered by environment which differentiates them from any other element in the United States, — all these are material for the student who notes the growth of the American nation from its small beginnings to its stature to-day.

As the frontier has moved to the West, so the Puritan has marched, his log cabin marking for two centuries

[1] See frontispiece, for New England settlement east of the Mississippi River to 1860.

the edge of civilization. At first his villages were but fishing or farming hamlets, scattered along the Atlantic coast; by degrees, actuated by a desire to better his material condition through enlarged farms or more extended fur-trade with the Indians, or by unrest which social, religious, or political restraint produced, the settler moved inland with his family and his neighbors. Certain conditions bound him down in his choice of a new home: he must build his cabin near a river, for the water-courses supplied the only means of transportation for himself and his goods; he must seek out the best lands available, and these were, so far as New England was concerned, the intervale lands along the rivers; lastly, he must (in so far as he could) keep out of the way of hostile Indians. Hence the first settlements were stretched in a reasonably compact manner along the coast, and up the larger water-courses.

Familiarity with frontier conditions bred daring and unrest; the men and the women who had been pioneers once were not afraid to brave the wilderness again, and consequently dissatisfaction with the iron rule of Massachusetts Bay might send one hundred families to the Connecticut River, or a church quarrel might cause thirty more to remove to Cape Cod. It was this fearlessness (combined, to be sure, with other motives) which made it possible for emigrants to betake themselves to Newark and other New Jersey towns as well as to those upon Long Island.

From 1660 down to the years just preceding the Revolution, expansion radiated from the centres established in the forty years preceding the Restoration.

Inland from the coast, following up the rivers, keeping close together at times when the French and Indians threatened every isolated settlement, new farms were laid out and new towns planted. When all the best land had been taken, later comers had to be content with poorer tracts, till all was occupied. Now and then the frontier line was thrust back by war, but it advanced beyond its former limit when peace was restored, and the movement after the peace of Utrecht was upon the whole a steady advance. It was the poorer quality of the land that kept central Massachusetts a wilderness long after the Connecticut valley was well peopled; it was the insecurity attendant upon a disputed title that made the prospective settler pass by the lower counties of Vermont and build his log cabin farther north. For the New England pioneer was a hard-headed man of business; if he moved to better his condition, he did not mean to be balked in his purpose by poor judgment at the beginning. By 1770 all the best land had been occupied in the three Southern colonies, the lower parts of Maine and New Hampshire were filled with towns, and the frontier line was being pushed back from southern Vermont; while Long Island and New Jersey, as well as several counties on either side of the Hudson River in New York, had received the overflow from New England.

The impending struggle between the mother country and the colonies did not trouble the pioneer; his wanderings were checked only by actual hostilities. Between 1760 and 1775 three plans for emigration were formulated, and two were carried out. The first was the great

movement to the Wyoming country in northwestern
Pennsylvania, — a scheme which drew hundreds of settlers from Connecticut to the new town of Westmoreland. The second was the removal of many Nantucket
Quakers to Guilford County, North Carolina, — an
instance of a search for good land and congenial religious surroundings.[1] The third was the ill-fated plan
for the Phineas Lyman colony near Natchez, in which
at least four hundred Connecticut families were interested, for that number removed to the Mississippi country; with the opening of the war, many returned to
their old homes, while others sought new ones in different parts of the South. Certainly the New Englander
was by this time a seasoned frontiersman, whom no
wilderness could daunt.

With the close of the Revolution, the flood of emigration, pent up during the war, rushed forth, this time
to central and western New York, to northern and
western Pennsylvania, and to southern Ohio, as well as
to the three northern New England States. Now new
factors altered the situation, for the lands to the west
were unlike those of the coast states, and the product
of a year's labor seemed little short of marvelous to
those who had wrung but a pittance from the stony
soil of New England. Not only did young men move,
but older ones as well, lured on by the tales of returning travelers, by the fascinating prospect of wealth in
the West, and often also by the innate unrest of the
Anglo-Saxon. Hardy emigrants swarmed from every

[1] Many Pennsylvania Quakers were moving down the Piedmont plateau
to the uplands of North Carolina at this time.

New England state to the westward, the less venturesome ones moving to the North, — to Vermont, Maine,
and New Hampshire.

In Ohio the soldier found a new home upon the government bounty lands, and Revolutionary officers, as
well as men of the line, established homes at Marietta.
To the north lay the " Western Reserve," and thither
flocked thousands of settlers to build a new Connecticut
upon the shores of Lake Erie. Farther out, the "squatter" built his home, waiting for the land to be brought
into the market, that he might purchase a quarter-section
of the new government tracts which the states had each
ceded for the welfare of all. The possession by the
general government of a seemingly inexhaustible supply
of cheap and fertile land to the west gave an impetus
to emigration unparalleled in American history up to
that time.

From 1781 until 1812 the movement of population
from New England continued in these channels. After
the second war with Great Britain, the sons and daughters of the Puritans went farther West, into the northern parts of Indiana and Illinois. Indiana was never a
favorite stopping-place for the New Englanders, for the
Southern element was strong here, and the Virginian
or Kentuckian was apt to confuse the shrewd, unscru-
pulous "Yankee" peddler of cheap clocks with the
substantial Connecticut farmer, and to treat the two
alike. This same hostility between the New England
toilers of a frontier line working down from the North
and the Southern farmers building up from the South
is found in Illinois; it grew until the fourteen northern

counties were eager to secede to Wisconsin that they
might affiliate with their own kind. From 1816 until
1840 the movement of emigrants into Indiana took place,
that into Illinois from about 1825 until 1850.

In the latter part of this period, from about 1830
until 1837, the New Englanders were clearing for themselves new homes north of Ohio, Indiana, and Illinois,
in Michigan and Wisconsin. Working into the interior
from the southeast corner of each of these states, for a
few years the growth of population in all of what had
been the Northwest Territory went on at once; after
1840 Michigan and Wisconsin received most of the newcomers. Farther to the west, across the Mississippi, New
England was contributing hundreds of families to Iowa
and Minnesota, while a few were already making their
way across the Rocky Mountains to lay the foundations
of Washington and Oregon.

Such has been the actual movement of settlement during these two centuries. What has been the character
of the emigration? The emigrants have betaken themselves to new homes in three ways: by single families,
by groups of two or more households, and by whole
colonies. When families have gone singly, — and this
was rarely the method for the first half-century, and
has never been the most popular one, — their influence
has been exerted only by an especially strong personal-
ity here and there; the rest have been lost in some little
town on the Wabash or the Fox. Where two or three
households have gone together to build cabins in the
same neighborhood, there New England tradition has
been preserved, and the influence of Puritan institutions

has made itself felt; state-building in the West has been the work of these little bands toiling with their neighbors from other parts of the United States. But when a whole church or a colony has moved out to plant a new town, there the character of the settlement has remained longest unchanged, and its citizens have constructed what is to all intents and purposes a veritable New England town, — church, school, and often a college, — far from Massachusetts or Connecticut, in the heart of New York or New Jersey, or in an oak clearing of Michigan or Wisconsin. There are many of these towns scattered over the states north of the Ohio and its tributaries; some of them, like Kirkland, Granville, Oberlin, Vermontville, Rockford, and Beloit have been mentioned, but many more have a more obscure story not written as yet. In a number of these towns the old tendency to proceed in an orderly and law-abiding fashion has led to the drawing up of a compact or a constitution closely resembling those under which the founders of Plymouth, Springfield, and many other towns agreed to live until some regularly constituted government should be set over them. Anglo-Saxon conservatism has shown itself very strongly in the survival of the written compact.

When these families or colonies made up their minds to move, they did not set out with any vague notion of their destination; they knew exactly where they were going, for the way had been traveled before their departure, and usually the site for their future homes already chosen. Certain states and parts of states have had a fascination for the Connecticut man, still others for the pioneer from Massachusetts, and yet another for the Vermont emigrant.[1] Connecticut settlers have moved in largest numbers to Long Island, New Jersey, and southern New York east of the Hudson; they have followed the Housatonic into western Massachusetts, the Connecticut into New Hampshire and Vermont; turning their faces westward, they have moved by hundreds into northwestern Pennsylvania and into central and western New York; by thousands they have emigrated to their own Western Reserve and to Michigan. Far from remaining in the "land of steady habits," the former inhabitants of Connecticut towns are found from one end of the United States to the other.[2]

[1] No reason can be assigned for this, so far as the writer knows, save the desire to live in the neighborhood of other pioneers from the same region in the East. No particular kind of soil seems to attract the Vermonter any more than the Massachusetts man ; no sort of business seems to draw one here and another there. Stories told by an emigrant who has gone back to visit the old home on the coast have led again and again to removals to the region described by the wanderer. The tendency to settle together is there, — just why, it is impossible to say.

[2] B. C. Steiner, in his *History of Guilford, Connecticut,* has made an interesting and valuable study of the movement of emigrants from that one town. Beginning with the first removals to Branford in 1644, he traces settlers in 1663–64 to Killingworth, to Saybrook, and to Newark, New Jersey ; in 1700, to Durham ; in the next quarter-century, to Middlefield and Westfield ; about 1750, to Litchfield, Goshen, Salisbury, and Canaan. Between 1760 and the end of the Revolution, he has found the movement taking a turn northward, to settle Richmond and Stockbridge in western Massachusetts, to begin Guilford, Vermont, and to fill up Chittenden County in the same state. After the Revolution, others went to Claremont and Charlestown, New Hampshire, and to Greenville, New York. Early in the nineteenth century, some settled at Paris, Westmoreland, and Verona in New York, in the Connecticut Western Reserve, in other parts of Ohio, and, about 1830, at Fairfield and other Illinois towns. This close study simply bears out the deductions made above for the

Massachusetts has sent pioneers to Maine, New Hampshire, Vermont, Ohio, Illinois, Michigan and Wisconsin; almost none to Pennsylvania and Indiana.[1] Rhode

whole state. See B. C. Steiner, *History of Guilford*, 139. E. D. Larned's *Hist. of Windham County*, ii, 586, 587, gives Wyoming, Vermont, New Hampshire, western Massachusetts, New York, Ohio, and the territories westward as the destinations of emigrants from that county, adding to the list a few who have gone to Maryland, North Carolina, and New Orleans. Bowen's *Woodstock*, p. 58, gives the destination of former inhabitants of Woodstock as Vermont, New Hampshire, New York, Pennsylvania, and Ohio ; and adds that " nowadays, nearly every state has representatives of this town." F. Atwater (*Hist. of Plymouth, Conn.*, 437) gives descendants from that town who live in Tecumseh, Nebraska, and in McGregor, Iowa.

[1] A celebration held in Granville, Massachusetts, in 1845, gave an opportunity for the preparation of statistics as to the residence of emigrants from Granville, living in that year: 286 emigrants were distributed as follows : —

Ohio (in 27 towns, mostly in northern Ohio)	67
New York (in 27 towns, in all parts of the state)	67
Massachusetts (in 11 towns, mostly in the western part)	57
Connecticut (in 12 towns, mostly in the northwestern part)	36
Illinois (in 7 towns, in the northern part)	11
Wisconsin (in 4 towns)	6
Michigan (in 4 towns)	5
Indiana (in 2 towns)	4
Vermont	4
Pennsylvania	3
Rhode Island	3
Louisiana	3
Iowa	3
New Jersey	3
Florida	2
Alabama	2
Missouri	2
New Hampshire	1
District of Columbia	1
South America	1

See *Granville Jubilee*, 127–135.

Weymouth has sent representatives just as indicated in the text

Island is represented in all the states, but not by great numbers anywhere.[1] Maine settlers have moved least of all, probably because there have always been vacant lands in their own state, at low prices, and within easy distance.[2] New Hampshire has sent most of her emigrants to New York, but many have gone to Ohio and to Illinois also.[3] Vermont people, mostly descendants from Connecticut stock, have shown the same migratory spirit as their ancestors, and have been the great "movers"; in New York they are more numerous than in any other state, but they are represented in goodly numbers in Ohio, Illinois, Michigan, and Wisconsin.[4] The great exodus from New York into Ohio, Indiana, Michigan, and Wisconsin, is probably largely the movement of New England stock, in the second or third generation.

What factors have operated to send inhabitants to the frontier? Over and over again the search for cheap and fertile land has been most potent, for until after the Revolution the chief business of all the colonial inhabitants save those in the coast towns was connected in some way with agriculture. When the best land in New England had been taken, it became necessary to

above. See Gilbert Nash, "Weymouth," in *Hist. of Norfolk Co.*, 566. Roxbury is said to have been the mother of fifteen towns in the United States. See Bowen, *Woodstock*, 11.

[1] See *Census Reports* for 1850 and 1860, in Appendix B. Note the small number for New Jersey, Indiana, and Wisconsin.

[2] *Ibid.* Note the small number for Indiana and Michigan.

[3] *Ibid.*

[4] *Ibid.* Note that Vermont stands third in number of settlers that New England contributed to New York, Pennsylvania, and Ohio ; first in Indiana, Illinois, Michigan, and Wisconsin. See, also, settlement of Vermonters in Wisconsin by counties, in Appendix C.

remove to some more productive region, or else to change one's occupation, — a thing not so easy of accomplishment a hundred years ago as it is to-day. Letters sent back by a Hugh White, telling of the marvelous yield of his farm in central New York, proved irresistible to his former Connecticut neighbors, and out to Whitesboro and its vicinity they moved, that they, too, might profit by the extraordinary prodigality of nature. The prairies of Illinois and Wisconsin were far preferable to a stony, hilly patch of ground in the " Granite State," when once their attractions had been set forth in gazetteer and guide-book.[1] To obtain a farm of a goodly size, — that has been the object of the majority of emigrants from the beginning.

Inseparably connected with the search for land there has often been discontent with existing conditions, — social, economic, religious, and political. When a church quarrel arose, what need was there to yield or to compromise, when the disgruntled minority could have its will in another region not far away? There was no necessity for yielding to the will of a majority with which one did not agree when wide stretches of unoccupied land were inviting settlers who could do as they pleased. With this assurance, excessive independence and assertive individuality needed no curb, for there was room for all ideas, political and social. The contented, the prosperous, the conservative, — these

---

[1] The number of these guide-books and gazetteers, such as Peck's, which were issued from 1830 to 1850 is astonishing, and their influence in attracting settlers to the West must have been great. Every detail of expense by canal, steamboat, and stage is there, with minute descriptions of infant settlements in need of farmers and merchants.

remained in the old town; the discontented, the poor, the radical, — all such elements moved to the frontier.

Whether the discontent was for social, political, or religious conditions, the same idea underlay it all; and that idea was that greater advantages might be gained for one's self and for one's children in the new home than in the old. Ambitious in a land where they saw their work grow under their hands, it was but natural that the goal for the pioneers should be the gaining of wealth which should place their children at least one round farther up on the social ladder than their fathers had been. Yet even in their ambition, the frontiersmen from New England have not been unmindful of the moral and religious side of life, for that has always been most firmly ingrained and most thoroughly characteristic of the Puritan and his descendants. Therefore, the emigrants carried with them their school, their church, and their town-meeting; certain that their own institutions were best, backed by their conviction of their own keenness of judgment, aided by the conservatism which clings to what it knows by experience is good, they insisted upon the adoption of their traditional institutions in the newer states of the West. In the adoption, though, the church, the school, and the town-meeting must needs undergo change; the church must become more liberal, it must take on the Presbyterian form if that would insure its growth; it must be divorced from politics, since one reason for the removal to the frontier had often been the union of church and state upon the coast. Far from escaping from the majority rule, the pioneer had become subject to it anew; but it was now his majority, and he could afford to yield to gain his ends. The school had to change also. Separation of the sexes had been the rule in New England; coeducation became the habit of the West. Partly due to lack of funds, partly perhaps owing to the intense feeling of equality not only between man and man, but between man and woman, the coeducational plan became the custom for the Western States. It was not always adopted willingly, for conservatism and tradition in such matters die hard; but in the end a shrewd business sense dictated the policy, and it won.[1]

Such are some phases of the influence of the older civilization upon the new; but there has been also a reaction whereby the older civilization has in its turn been altered by the new which it had helped to shape. The frontier demanded recognition; and it had its way. Beginning with insignificant quarrels between settlers and non-resident proprietors, where the former demanded the advantages of roads and bridges which they had enjoyed in the older towns and were now too poor to

---

[1] In 1842 the question of the separation of the sexes in the public schools arose in Rochester, New York. It was argued that the old plan of having boys and girls go to separate schools interfered with grading and classifying pupils, and required an unnecessary number of instructors. On the other hand, the prejudice against "mixed schools" was strong among the New England element which made up the majority of Rochester inhabitants. In 1849–50 the old district system was abolished, and all educational matters were, by the new city charter, left to the common council. An ordinance was passed requiring that all pupils be seated, classified, and taught without regard to sex. Quite a number of pupils were withdrawn from school, but after a year or two discussion ceased, and the ordinance was generally accepted. See Ellis, "Hist. of Rochester Public Schools," in *Pub. of Roch. Hist. Soc.*, i, 74, 75. Neither the University of Wisconsin nor that of Michigan was made coeducational without a struggle.

provide for themselves, the divergence of views grew wider. In the matter of roads and bridges, it seemed to the pioneer that every property owner should help in paying for public works, and that the whole expense should not be borne by the resident farmer. He complained first to the proprietors, then to the legislature; and he frequently won his case.[1]

Going beyond the confines of a single town, the whole frontier sometimes rose in what it considered righteous indignation against a conservative and arrogant coast population. The story of the adoption of the Massachusetts constitution will illustrate such a contest.[2] In 1778–79 the county of Berkshire, which had been settled mostly from Connecticut towns, was in almost open rebellion against the state of Massachusetts, on the matter of admitting the authority of the General Court and the judicial courts as well. The question had arisen over the adoption of a constitution, and "for other reasons to be enumerated," it was argued that the laws of the state ought not to operate in that town.[3] Richmond

---

[1] See the case of Westminster settlers *vs.* proprietors, given by Heywood, "Westminster," in *Hist. of Worcester Co.*, ii, 1148. Also complaint of the inhabitants of Deering, New Hampshire, against proprietors who refused to help build a meeting-house and pay for a lot for the minister. See Hammond, *Town Papers*, xi, 495. Also, the case of Dorchester, in *ibid.*, xi, 501. Also the case brought before the legislature for settlement of a dispute between proprietors and settlers in Bartlett. See *ibid.*, xi, 161, 162.

[2] The material for this paragraph has been obtained from a manuscript thesis, "The Struggle for the Constitution in Massachusetts," by Dr. F. E. Haynes, in the Harvard College Library, pp. 165–183.

[3] *Great Barrington Town Records*, Nov. 16, 1778, cited by Dr. Haynes, 166. The method of representation was considered defective, and the western towns, tenacious of the rights they believed were theirs, protested thus in typical frontier fashion.

protested in no uncertain way against laws established on what was considered an uncertain basis.[1] Lenox voted that there was in Massachusetts no constitution which controlled the inhabitants of that town, and petitioned the General Court to be allowed to be set off to be a part of a neighboring state.[2] The northern towns of the county were the most hostile to the General Court; coercion would probably have been fatal to any future harmony for the new state, and would perhaps have meant dismemberment.[3] From 1774 to 1780 the civil authority was really helpless as far as Berkshire County was concerned, the real power being exercised by each town without regard to its neighbors. In 1778 the courts were closed, while Richmond turned over the punishment of criminals to the selectmen.[4] Only in 1780, when a constitution had been formed by a convention elected for that express purpose, and therefore drawn up by the people themselves, were the demands of the Berkshire radicals on the one hand and the Essex conservatives on the other harmonized, and the new constitution adopted.[5]

But another portion of the Massachusetts frontier protested against " Essex conservatism " in the years following the adoption of this very constitution. In

[1] *Richmond Town Records*, Nov. 12 and 16, 1778. Cited *ibid.*, 168. Dr. Haynes says the vote of Nov. 12 was 31 to 21, of Nov. 16, 24 to 13.

[2] *Lenox Town Records*, Feb. 8, 1779. Cited *ibid.*, 169, 171.

[3] *Ibid.*, 171, 172.

[4] *Ibid.*, 176–183.

[5] *Ibid.*, 264–266. Dr. Haynes says, " Anglo-Saxon tradition, Berkshire democracy, and Essex conservatism gave us the venerable constitution of 1780."

1785 discussion in Maine over its establishment as an independent state was the chief theme of political discourse. Not only was the discussion between Maine as the frontier and Massachusetts as the conservative coast, but there was division within the borders of Maine itself between office-holders and the people at large. The first newspaper in Maine — the "Falmouth Gazette"— was established to further the proposed separation, the first number appearing on New Year's Day, 1785. A list of grievances drawn up by a committee of the convention assembled for discussion contain some typical frontier complaints: " The interests of these three counties [York, Cumberland, and Lincoln] are different from those of Massachusetts, and therefore, they can never be fully understood by her, nor will they for the same reason ever be duly attended to and promoted. . . ."

" The seat of the government is at a distance, the General Court large, and its business multifarious and perplexing; so that the petitioners and suitors in their journies, as well as in delays, have to suffer many and great inconveniences, expenses, and discouragements. . . ."

" The present regulations of trade operate unequally and unjustly toward these Counties; for they tend to depress the price of lumber. . . ."

" A great part of the inhabitants of these Counties are deprived of representation in the popular branch of the Legislature, where all the money-bills originate. . . ."

The document ends with complaints of unjust excise

and impost taxes. Here, then, is quite as typical a complaint as the ones of which it is distinctly reminiscent,
— those documents of the whole colonial frontier directed against the conservative British Parliament.[1]

Another instance may be cited to illustrate a somewhat different side of the friction between frontier and
coast.[2] In 1786 fifty towns of Hampshire County, Massachusetts, drew up a list of grievances, among which
was one complaining of the mode of representation then
in operation ; another, " that all the civil officers of government " were not elected annually by the representatives of the people assembled in General Court; a third,
that the present mode of taxation operated unequally between polls and estates, and between the landed and the
mercantile interests; a fourth, that the General Court
sat at Boston.[3] The first outbreak of sharp rebellion in
1786 occurred at Northampton, in western Massachusetts,[4] but the rising was not confined by any means to
that portion of the state.[5] In New Hampshire the more
conservative settled parts were opposed to paper money ;
whereas the more radical rural population demanded it.[6]
Vermont went through a similar experience ;[7] — in fact

[1] This trouble in Maine is given quite fully in Williamson's *History of
Maine*, ii, 521–527 (edition of 1832).

[2] The material for this paragraph is taken from a manuscript thesis in
Harvard College Library, by Dr. J. P. Warren, on *Shay's Rebellion*.

[3] *Massachusetts Centinel*, Sept. 9, 1786, cited by Dr. Warren, 81, 82.
There are thirteen grievances enumerated ; those not mentioned above
deal with complaints concerning the operations of courts and lawyers, etc.

[4] *Ibid.*, 89.

[5] *Ibid.*, 108.

[6] *Ibid.*, App. iii, 128–135.

[7] *Ibid.*, 137, 138.

the frontier, which has always had naïve ideas on finance in general, demanded paper money as the panacea for all economic ills. The exception is Rhode Island, whose conservative class was too small to win the day for a sound currency as the mercantile interests of Massachusetts did, in spite of the opposition which had crystallized in "Shay's Rebellion."

After the election of Thomas Jefferson to the presidency, the reaction in New England against clerical control manifested itself in no uncertain manner. The dissenting sects, religious and political, who had resented the "machine" management of state government by the Congregational Church and its members for a long time, now caused an upheaval; and it was easily ascertained that these opponents of the old order of things were from the outlying, democratic districts, — northwestern Connecticut, western Massachusetts, western New Hampshire, and Vermont. From their brethren and neighbors who had removed to New York or to Ohio, they had learned that manhood suffrage and the divorce of state affairs from clerical control were no dream, but might be made a reality. It took time to accomplish their purpose; but in the end the frontier won, and the extension of the franchise followed, together with the fall of the Congregational Church as a political power. The decline of the Federalist party, the Dartmouth College case, many of the events of the first twenty years of the nineteenth century, show the reaction in New England caused by the demands of the new and the old frontier.

In 1820 Clay and Calhoun, the former a radical Kentuckian of pioneer stock, used the frontier standard of democracy as a measure of John Quincy Adams's fitness for the presidency. Though Adams was neither a Congregationalist nor a Federalist, he represented some of the ideas for which Congregationalism and Federalism had stood, and astute politicians saw that he could not appeal to the democratic elements of his native New England, to say nothing of the failure certain to come if his name were broached as that of a possible president for the whole nation. The administration of Adams was a failure because of the lack of sympathy between him and the people of the whole country save a remnant of the more conservative New Englanders.[1] He went out of office because of the triumph of the frontier, represented in Andrew Jackson. The same elements which, speaking by the voice of Henry Clay, had forced the War of 1812 upon reluctant conservatives like Madison had grown to such strength and raised such a following even in the older states that the presidency was now in their hands. It is an old story, — the history of Jackson's administration, when he broke with all tradition, social, political, and financial, and followed the policy which seemed to him best, in spite of the opposition which at some time in his term he met with in every quarter. He had no sympathy with the intense loyalty of the Southerner to his state, for he was a product of the frontier, of a state whose history did not begin until the Revolution was imminent. He came from a region

---

[1] The movement for internal improvements to be made by the federal government belongs to this period. It was to a large extent induced by frontier demands, especially from those parts of the country which were as yet too poor to make expenditures out of their own pockets.

where all the elements mingled, as they have always done upon the edge of the wilderness; the homogeneous character of an Eastern commonwealth had no place in a state to whose building the sons of many states had contributed. The frontier man, a complex of many men, yet differentiated from them all, — such was Andrew Jackson.

Passing over the panic of 1837, which was caused by speculation in Western lands combined with frontier banking, the rise of the Free-Soil party shows a slightly different phase of the question. The first organized movement for the formation of such a party came from an anti-slavery society which had been formed in Burlington, Racine County, Wisconsin, in 1840. That region had been settled by New England or New York men, in whom the political sense was keenly developed. Generations of town-meetings had produced an especial capacity for transacting public business; most of these Wisconsin men had served their apprenticeship in such local gatherings. To such politicians the policy of the abolitionists was incomprehensible, the vagueness of their platform unattractive, and the narrowness of their plan of action "positively distasteful." [1] Two newspapers were secured for the Free-Soil side, and the campaign began, — a frontier movement at its very beginning.

It was the rapid settlement of the West which turned the eyes of the Southerners toward Texas, with its wide areas for cotton culture. The rapid development of the

[1] For the history of the Free-Soil party in Wisconsin, see Professor Theodore Clarke Smith, in *Proc. Wisconsin Hist. Soc.* (1895), pp. 101–107. The phrase used above is his. For interesting observations on the effect of the town-meeting in developing politicians, see Dwight, *Travels*, i, 249–252.

lower South, with its peculiar system of immense plantations developed out of English economic demands in the
decade 1830–40, had made expansion to the West a
necessity. The Mexican War was essentially a war of ag-
gression begun at the behest of a frontier which seemed
to be cut off from further extension.[1]

When, in 1854, the Republican party was formed, it
was in answer to the demands of the frontier that slavery
should not be thrust upon pioneers building new states.
Stephen A. Douglas, a Vermonter by birth, had no
chance for the presidency in the face of Lincoln's can-
didacy under the Republican party's standard. The election of Abraham Lincoln was brought about by the
union of many factions and many creeds under the leadership of a frontier man to carry out a frontier policy.
Transplanted New Englanders joined with emigrants
from many other states, and carried a representative of
pioneer stock in a pioneer state to the chief magistracy
of the nation. When the war had broken out, when the
Southerners had withdrawn from the Congress of the
United States, one of the first acts of the national legislature was to pass the Homestead Act, the great triumph
of the Northern pioneer, the crystallization in statute of
the frontiersman's protest against bringing into the
West the large plantations run by slaves.[2]

[1] See William Garrott Brown, *The Lower South in American History.*
Also Professor F. J. Turner, "The South, 1820–1830," in the *American
Historical Review*, April, 1906, especially 565–573. James Russell Lowell's
Biglow Papers are invaluable as an expression of contemporary opinion
on the Mexican War.

[2] Payson J. Treat, manuscript thesis on the influence of New England
on the public land system.

Besides the active influence that emigration from New England had exerted, there is a negative side to be noted as well. The rise of steamboat navigation and of the railroad developed the West in an extraordinarily short time. Travel became easy, markets for surplus products came almost to the farmer's door, and pioneering lost many of its hardships. To the steamboat and the railroad may be traced the marvelous growth of Michigan and Wisconsin especially. But this drain of population had an effect upon New England; the increase of population fell off in the decade ending with 1840, to 14 per cent; it had been 17 per cent between 1820 and 1830.[1] The agricultural sections were affected especially, for the emigrants to the West had been mostly farmers. In at least five of the New England States the agricultural population, between 1830 and 1840, either remained stationary, or actually decreased. Maine had an extensive farming territory, and there the increase was nearly equal to the annual increase in the United States. Between 1830 and 1840 two counties out of the eight in Connecticut decreased in population, and one increased by only thirty-five inhabitants. Washington County, Rhode Island, lost 1087 persons; almost the whole increase of the entire state was in Providence and the surrounding county. In New Hampshire, Cheshire County lost 587; the increase was confined almost entirely to the cities of Manchester, Nashua, and Dover. Six of the thirteen counties of Vermont decreased.

With the decrease in population went a change in occupation. The intensive cultivation required in New

[1] See Chickering, *Statistical View of Massachusetts Population*, 71, 72.

England could not compete with the extensive system of the prairie states, and New England, worsted in competition with the West, was forced to change from agriculture to manufacturing.[1] With this change, the character of the population was altered. The small farmer, the ambitious mechanic, had emigrated; their places were taken by immigrants from foreign countries who could be used as factory hands, as well as to supply the demand for manual labor for which emigration was largely responsible. By the call of the frontier, the character of New England was changed.

When one notes how many of the cities and towns of New England are to-day controlled politically by those who have neither Puritan traditions, Puritan background of ancestry, nor Puritan ideals, one feels dismayed, for it would seem that the old order had passed away save in memory and in history.[2] But it is not an unintelligent and sentimental optimism alone which asserts that New England is still a living force, and Puritan traditions and ideals still working models. Such an assertion is proved to be undeniable fact when the sons and daughters of New England have been sought out in the West. The history of New England is not confined to six states; it is contained in a greater and broader New England wherever the children of the Puritans are found.

[1] The invention of the McCormick reaper in 1834 gave a tremendous impetus to the system of extensive farming in the West, and had great influence in developing the competition in agriculture whereby the East was worsted.

[2] See Hugh McCulloch, quoted along this same line, by E. P. Powell, in "New England in Michigan," *New England Magazine*, xiii, 427.

APPENDICES

APPENDIX A

THE methods used in making the maps for this study may need explanation. For the New England ones, the date of settlement of every town has been ascertained as nearly as possible, and each one has then been plotted in its proper place in the period covered by the map. When the date of settlement is unknown, the date of incorporation has been taken; but that was necessary in comparatively few cases. After all the towns settled in a given period were drawn on the map, the outer line of all has been taken as the frontier line at the last date chosen, and the whole area within that line has been colored as the settled area of the period. Of course each period includes all previous frontier lines, with the towns added between the new dates taken, except where Indians have destroyed towns and the settlers have not rebuilt them; in that case they are omitted.

The maps outside of New England are done in a different manner, and are of two kinds : the first kind of maps indicates the counties and towns where New Englanders actually settled, their presence having been ascertained from many sources. In these no account is taken of any other sort of settlement save that directly from New England. In the second kind of maps, the census maps in the *Statistical Atlas* of 1890 have been made the basis of the work, since they show the whole area settled at the end of each decade. Upon these has been overlaid the New England settlement of the maps before 1790 as well as afterward.

The bibliography of this study includes only the books actually referred to in the text; the maps represent research through an enormous mass of material afforded by the facilities of the libraries of Harvard College, the Wisconsin State

Historical Society, the University of Wisconsin, Leland Stanford Junior University, and the city of Indianapolis. There have been called into requisition colonial records; proceedings and collections of historical societies; state, county, and town histories; genealogies and family histories; church records; papers of missionaries and missionary societies; tax lists and lists of ratable polls; city directories; college catalogues; manuscript letters and papers; lists of marriages, deaths, and births : — any sort of material that could throw light upon the settlement, history, annals, or population of a town. The maps are intended to illustrate the text by showing the actual area of settled land, with the frontier line, at any given time.

APPENDIX B

NATIVITY OF POPULATION

Census of 1850. (Includes only natives of New York and the New England States.)

	Conn.	Mass.	Vermont	New Hamp.	Maine	Rhode Island	New York
New York	66101	55773	52599	14519	4509	13129	
Penn.	9266	7330	4532	1775	1157	1946	58835
New Jersey	2105	1494	280	301	287	264	20561
Ohio	22855	18763	14320	4821	3314	1959	83979
Indiana	2485	2678	3183	886	976	438	67180
Illinois	6889	9230	11381	4288	3693	1051	24310
Michigan	6751	8167	11113	2744	1117	1031	133756
Wisconsin	4125	6285	10157	2520	3252	690	68595

NATIVITY OF POPULATION

Census of 1860. (Includes only natives of New York and the New England States.)

	New York	Vermont	Conn.	Mass.	New Hamp.	Maine	Rhode Island
New York		46990	53141	50004	12497	5794	9555
Ohio	75550	11652	16741	16313	4111	3011	1558
Indiana	30855	3539	2505	3443	1072	1293	455
Illinois	121508	18253	11192	19053	7868	7475	2252
Michigan	191128	13779	7636	9873	3482	2214	1122
Wisconsin	120637	19184	7203	12115	5907	8467	1462

From all the New England States.

Ohio	53386
Indiana	12307
Illinois	66093
Michigan	38106
Wisconsin	54338

APPENDIX C

SETTLEMENT OF VERMONTERS IN WISCONSIN BY COUNTIES

	1870		1870		1870
Adama . . .	168	Green . . .	391	Polk . . .	30
Ashland		Green Lake .	353	Portage . .	192
Barron . . .	8	Iowa . . .	72	Racine . . .	357
Bayfield . .	2	Jackson . .	140	Richland . .	258
Brown . . .	211	Jefferson . .	632	Rock . . .	171
Buffalo . . .	194	Juneau . .	298	Sauk . . .	609
Burnett		Kenosha . .	235	Shawano . .	23
Calumet . .	130	Kewaunee . .	27	Sheboygan. .	272
Chippewa . .	143	La Crosse . .	333	St. Croix . .	231
Clark . . .	80	La Fayette .	150	Trempaleau .	177
Columbia . .	680	Manitowoc .	136	Vernon . . .	218
Crawford . .	137	Marathon . .	46	Walworth . .	736
Dane . . .	1061	Marquette . .	216	Washington .	58
Dodge . . .	764	Milwaukee .	478	Waukesha . .	440
Dorr . . .	21	Monroe . .	458	Waupaca . .	378
Douglas . .	4	Oconto . . .	90	Waushara . .	354
Dunn . . .	146	Outagamie . .	222	Winnebago .	940
Eau Claire .	208	Ozaukee . .	2	Wood . . .	46
Fond du Lac .	995	Pekin . . .	135		
Grant . . .	317	Pierce . . .	228		

INDEX

INDEX

Abingdon, Massachusetts, 84 n.
Academies, Connecticut, Lebanon, 132 n.; New London, 132 n.; Michigan, 230; New Hampshire, Amherst, 132; Atkinson, 132; Concord, 132; New Ipswich, 132.
"Accommodation system" of Congregational churches, 163, 187, 188, 234.
Adams, John Quincy, 268.
Adams, Massachusetts, 110, 158.
Adams County, Illinois, 207.
Addington, Isaac, 73 n.
Addison, Vermont, 142, 227.
Addison County, Vermont, 228.
Agricultural societies, 185.
Aix-la-Chapelle, peace of, 102, 108.
Albany, New York, 157, 227.
Albany, Vermont, 202.
Alden, Timothy, 152.
Alford, Massachusetts, 80.
Alleghany College, Pennsylvania, 152.
Alleghany Mountains, The, 9, 131.
Allegheny County, Pennsylvania, 151.
Allen, Ethan, 128.
Almira College, Greenville, Illinois, 218 n.
Alstead, New Hampshire, 144.
Alton, Illinois, 218 n.
Amesbury, Massachusetts, 31, 49.
Amherst, Massachusetts, 79.
Amherst, New Hampshire, 89, 202, 231 n.
Amherst, Ohio, 185 n.
Andover, Illinois, 215, 216.
Andover, Maine, 141.
Andover, Massachusetts, 113, 114, 141, 202.
Andover, Ohio, 185 n.
Andover, Vermont, 129 n.

Angell, President James F., 233.
Annapolis, Nova Scotia, 88.
"Anne," The, 13.
Appalachian Mountains, The, 118, 171.
Arlington, Vermont, 116.
Arnold, Jonathan, 144.
Aroostook County, Maine, 145.
Ashburnham, Massachusetts, 83 n., 98.
Ashfield, Massachusetts, 240 n.
Ashford, Massachusetts, 90.
Ashley River, The, 68.
Ashtabula County, Ohio, 179.
Athens, Pennsylvania, 244.
Athol, Massachusetts, 109 n.
Atkinson, Maine, 141.
Atkinson, New Hampshire, 89.
Attleborough, Massachusetts, 168 n.
Atwater, Joshua, 196.
Auburn, Maine, 141.
Auburn Theological Seminary, New York, 161.
Auction-sales of townships, 93, 110.
Augusta, Maine, 114.
Augusta, New York, 158.
Austinsburgh, Ohio, 179.
Ayer, Massachusetts, 58 n.

Bacon Academy, Colchester, Connecticut, 233.
Baldwin, Maine, 114.
Banking in New England, 105.
Baptists, 164. See also Baptist Church.
Baptist Church, 6, 164, 202.
Barkhamstead, Connecticut, 92, 93, 109, 111.
Barnard, Vermont, 117 n.
Barn-raisings, 7.
Barnstable, Massachusetts, 28, 49, 54, 65, 84 n., 109, 167 n., 168 n.
Barre, Massachusetts, 143.